"Sacraments have theological, spiritual, practical, and societal premises and implications. Timothy R. Gabrielli provides a meticulous investigation of late nineteenth- and twentieth-century 'streams' of mystical body theology that illuminate these dimensions. Rather than the oft-used 'model,' his more flexible term 'streams' readily incorporates his rich analytical foundations and appropriations of mystical body theology, thereby observing similarities and differences among theologians. Gabrielli's analysis of Virgil Michel's mystical body theology with nuances from Louis-Marie Chauvet provides a platform to revisit the social and theological implications of sacraments given new realities of a 'global body.' Gabrielli's work also might be used in continued dialogue with the historical practice of that theology in the United States."

> —Angelyn Dries, OSF
> Professor Emerita
> Saint Louis University

"Contributing significantly to our understanding of twentieth-century theology, Gabrielli identifies three streams of mystical body theology: German, Roman, and French. Locating both Virgil Michel and Louis-Marie Chauvet in the French socio-liturgical stream, he brings together pre– and post–Vatican II theologies in a trans-Atlantic perspective that opens out beyond ecclesiology to include Christology, liturgy, social ethics, and fundamental theology, and he offers promise for a renewed mystical body theology. A stunning piece of historical theology and a fruitful frame for future developments!"

> —William L. Portier
> Mary Ann Spearin Chair of Catholic Theology
> University of Dayton

"This is a book for anyone interested in the connection between liturgy and social concerns that was prevalent in the United States liturgical movement under the leadership of Virgil Michel. Gabrielli traces its roots to the French stream of mystical body theology and makes a persuasive proposal for the reappearance of this stream in the theology of Louis-Marie Chauvet."

> —Margaret Mary Kelleher, OSU
> Professor Emerita
> School of Theology and Religious Studies
> The Catholic University of America

"The mystical Body of Christ played a profound role—for good and ill—in twentieth-century Catholic ecclesiology, liturgical theology, and social engagement. Gabrielli makes a major contribution by carefully delineating the major streams of mystical body theology and charting their conflicts and influences. Engaging figures as diverse as Émile Mersch, Sebastian Tromp, Virgil Michel, Dorothy Day, Henri de Lubac, and Louis-Marie Chauvet, this book brings more than a century of theological inquiry to bear on questions we continue to face in the present."

—Vincent J. Miller
Gudorf Chair in Catholic Theology and Culture
University of Dayton

"Through admirably sophisticated research and lucid prose Timothy Gabrielli delivers a compelling (if not page-turning) analysis of the modern history of mystical body theologies to demonstrate the dead ends the concept reached when narrowly restricted to ecclesiastical and even nationalistic agendas, as well as a new realization of its pastoral-theological potential in the fundamental theology of Louis-Marie Chauvet. The climactic chapter on Chauvet provides fresh contextualization and insight into a body of work that continues to revitalize the interconnections between word, sacrament, and ethics as the very life of the church."

—Bruce T. Morrill, SJ
Edward A. Malloy Chair of Catholic Studies
Vanderbilt University

One in Christ

Virgil Michel, Louis-Marie Chauvet,
and Mystical Body Theology

Timothy R. Gabrielli

To Kaitlin,
Thanks for all of
your hard work!!

LP/A

**LITURGICAL PRESS
ACADEMIC**

Collegeville, Minnesota
www.litpress.org

1   2   3   4   5   6   7   8   9

Library of Congress Cataloging-in-Publication Data

Names: Gabrielli, Timothy R., 1982– author.
Title: One in Christ : Virgil Michel, Louis-Marie Chauvet, and mystical body
    theology / Timothy R. Gabrielli.
Description: 1 [edition]. | Collegeville, Minnesota : Liturgical Press, 2017.
    | "Liturgical Press Academic." | Includes bibliographical references.
Identifiers: LCCN 2017009668 (print) | LCCN 2017030064 (ebook) | ISBN
    9780814683989 (ebooks) | ISBN 9780814683972
Subjects: LCSH: Jesus Christ—Mystical body. | Catholic Church—Doctrines. |
    Michel, Virgil George, 1890–1938. | Chauvet, Louis-Marie, 1942–
Classification: LCC BV600.5 (ebook) | LCC BV600.5 .G33 2017 (print) | DDC
    262/.77—dc23
LC record available at https://lccn.loc.gov/2017009668

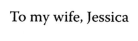

To my wife, Jessica

Contents

Acknowledgments

I t is a magnificent experience indeed to write about the mystical body of Christ while being graced by so many profound expressions of it. This work is indebted to so many people without whom it surely would not have come to completion. First and foremost, I am grateful to Bill Portier. His encouragement and care throughout the research and writing were unmatched.

The genesis of this research is indebted to several important people who helped me to conceive of it, its possibility, and its importance: Tim Brunk's mention of Virgil Michel, in his important work on Chauvet, got my wheels turning about the wider reasons that one might mention them in the same breath; Sandra Yocum's insistence that there is more to mystical body talk among American Catholics than meets the eye; and Vince Miller's interest in the ways that mystical body theology might apply to our contemporary context as well as his concern with the ways that Chauvet's project could be fruitfully developed. I am not sure that I have done any of their insights justice in my treatment of the twentieth-century development of mystical body theology; nevertheless, their encouragement and interest fired my own.

The University of Dayton generously supported this research in four Graduate Student Summer Fellowships in 2009, 2010, 2011, and 2012. With one of those fellowships, I traveled to the Michel Papers at Saint John's Abbey Archives, where Br. David Klingeman generously aided my cause. Br. Bernard Montgomery at Conception Abbey Archives sent me several of Michel's letters from the Cummins Papers. Tim Brunk sent me obscure Chauvet article after obscure Chauvet article with helpful bibliographical notes, and then read the entire manuscript, offering helpful comments. Glenn Ambrose shared his paper on Chauvet and Lacan with me, as well as several other leads on the 1980s French philosophical context. My old friend, Al Liberatore, offered a remarkably thorough, astute, and careful reading of the manuscript.

Adam Sheridan shared conversations about Chenu and the mystical body over lots of good food and offered several helpful insights. Derek Hatch encouraged me at every turn. Michael Cox—with his library carrel down the hall from mine—made long hours of research a bit less lonesome. Katherine Schmidt shared some of her research on the de Lubac/de Certeau connection and, with her husband, Jordan Goldmeier, her home on my trips back to Dayton. Ethan Smith shared insights and research on Alan Segal's Paul. Michael Lombardo offered numerous comments, research leads, moral support, and some specific recommendations for the introduction.

The hard-working bunch of creative minds at Meadowlark Restaurant in Dayton gave me needed respite from writing, grounded conversations, and camaraderie in honest work. My brother, Karan Singh, repeatedly pointed to the significance (and insignificance) of this work and dared me to think grand thoughts, often while buying me comfort food.

My colleagues at Seton Hill have humbled me in their generosity. They encouraged me throughout the writing, gave me as much space as possible to complete it, and heartily celebrated with me at the end. I am particularly grateful for the Seton Hill Faculty Fellowship course release I received in 2016 to bring the project to completion. Student worker Katie Smith spent a good bit of time cheerfully cross-checking footnotes to bibliographical entries.

Hans, Colleen, Lauren, Tara, and the rest of the expert staff at Liturgical Press were wonderful to work with in bringing this book to print. Sylvia Coates brought care and great expertise in composing the index.

I am so grateful for the support and love of my father and my sister. Their patience with me, and that of my in-laws, when I holed away during holidays and family visits made it easier to do so. My children, Sofia, Lidia, and Leo, are rays of light when I return home from a long day.

I owe my most profound gratitude to my wife, Jessica. Her humble, steadfast witness to Christ's agape has inspired me and pulled me through the darkest moments.

Timothy R. Gabrielli
Feast of St. Elizabeth Ann Seton, 2017

Introduction

Among the members of this Body . . . there must be solidarity of interests and reciprocal communication of life. One member must therefore help the other; no one may remain inactive and as each receives he also must give. Now, as every Christian receives the supernatural life which circulates in the veins of the Mystic Body of Christ—that abundant life that Christ Himself said He came to bring on earth—so he must transfuse it into others who either do not possess it, or who possess it too scarcely and only in appearance.

— Virgil Michel, OSB [1]

The Spirit is precisely the agent that makes possible the expression of the crucified Word by removing it to another space than that of the concept: the space of the conversion of attitudes, the space of the *body*. Hence, the primary mediation of God's revelation in Christianity is . . . that of the body and living. . . . Where human beings give flesh to their confession of the Risen One by following him on the way of the cross for the liberation of their brothers and sisters (and thus for their own as well), there the body of Christ comes forth. Of this body, the Church is the eschatological promise in and for the world.

— Louis-Marie Chauvet [2]

[1] Virgil Michel, OSB, "With Our Readers," *Orate Fratres* 8 (May 1934): 327–28.
[2] Louis-Marie Chauvet, *Symbol and Sacrament: A Sacramental Reinterpretation of Christian Existence*, trans. Patrick Madigan and Madeleine Beaumont (Collegeville,

At the end of his history of the liturgical movement in the United States, Keith Pecklers laments, as have many others since, the contemporary disconnect between liturgy and social consciousness. Pecklers suggests that perhaps a recovery of the theology of the mystical body of Christ would reignite this connection that Virgil Michel and others so passionately articulated.[3] Suffice it to say that there has not been a raging theological response to Pecklers's clarion call from two decades ago. There could be a variety of reasons for this silence, ranging from disinterest to lack of confidence in the purchase of a theological category to do what Pecklers describes. Yet, it seems that a general perception that the theology had run its course, was superseded, and flamed out as a useful theological category plays at least some role in the muted response. This book aims to throw some light on both the diversity of mystical body theologies in the early twentieth century and the heritage of mystical body theology in the later decades of that century.

My own interest in mystical body theology began with earlier research on the sacrament of confirmation.[4] Michel was a key figure in the early twentieth-century history of confirmation at the intersection of Catholic Action and the Liturgical Movement. Michel was always discussing the mystical body of Christ. It struck me that the phrase does not have the same currency today as it did then. Teaching Dorothy Day's *The Long Loneliness*, I noticed that Michel's contemporary referred to the mystical body of Christ in likewise interesting ways. Theologically speaking, one of the main arguments of *Confirmation* is that a theology of confirmation that conceives of and celebrates the sacrament as the time when young Catholics choose Catholicism for themselves is misguided. The overemphasis of choice in the US context supports the opposite effect (disengagement from public Catholic life) from what is intended (deeper engagement). In this light, the almost explicitly nonvoluntarist characteristics of mystical body theology—as a reality we find ourselves

---

MN: Liturgical Press, 1995), 528–29. The French original is *Symbole et sacrement: Une relecture sacramentelle de l'existence chrétienne* (Paris: Cerf, 1987).

[3] Keith Pecklers, *The Unread Vision: The Liturgical Movement in the United States of America, 1926–1955* (Collegeville, MN: Liturgical Press, 1998), 287.

[4] Timothy R. Gabrielli, *Confirmation: How a Sacrament of God's Grace Became All about Us* (Collegeville, MN: Liturgical Press, 2013).

caught up in and gripped by, rather than something we dissect, explain, and choose—struck me as both fascinating and worthy of exploration in our contemporary context.

Meanwhile, Louis-Marie Chauvet's complex, layered account of Christian identity and deep theological engagement with bodiliness or "corporality" stood out to me as relevant to many of the same questions, especially as I continued to meet Catholics who either reject the tradition based on an overly narrow interpretation of it or, on the other side of the coin, assert a very narrow subset of the tradition as truly Catholic.

A decade ago, Timothy Brunk analyzed an array of attempts, preceding Chauvet, to conceptually bring together liturgy and ethics. Michel stands among those Brunk analyzes as a lone preconciliar voice. He recognizes Michel as a pioneer in making the link between liturgy and ethics the primary concern of his work but finds Chauvet's work superior because he attends, anthropologically, to how ritual *qua* ritual informs the lives of believers outside of liturgy.[5] Brunk's excellent work provokes consideration of this other commonality between Michel and Chauvet: their relentless emphasis on the importance of the body.

The Legacy of the Mystical Body of Christ

Nevertheless, it is clear that any turn to mystical body theology is fraught with difficulty. There is widespread scholarly disagreement about the nature of a theology that permeated Catholic thought in the early twentieth century. For some, it was too abstract; for others, too rigid. For some, it was socially poignant; for others, a sociopolitical failure. For some, it was an ecumenical boon; for others, a triumphal truncheon. For many, it is an ecclesiological image or model; for a few, not a theology at all, but a way of living in the world. Rather than disciplinary preference or ideological leaning, the research here demonstrates that many of these divergent impressions of mystical body theology owe their conclusions to the concerns of a particular stream or streams of the theology in the early twentieth century.

---

[5] Timothy Brunk, *Liturgy and Life: The Unity of Sacraments and Ethics in the Theology of Louis-Marie Chauvet* (New York: Peter Lang, 2007), 37–39.

This book argues that Michel and Chauvet share more than a common emphasis on the social implications of the liturgy of the church; they both inhabit the long, winding French stream of mystical body of Christ theology. As we shall see, this thesis has ramifications not only for understanding mystical body theology in the twentieth century—a necessary prelude to any attempt at a recovery à la Pecklers—but also *places* Chauvet, a contemporary figure whose thought often has been examined only at the conceptual level. If Chauvet is indeed an heir to the French stream, engaging his thought—consciously situated in that stream—is a path toward a critical recovery of mystical body theology in our own context.

Obviously, then, the book's central argument rests on the claim that mystical body of Christ theology in the early twentieth century is variegated into distinct streams. Different impressions of mystical body theology's heritage can be explained by delineating these streams and their implications. For example, the critique of mystical body theology as triumphalist and centralizing applies mainly to what I will call the "Roman stream" as well as aspects of the "German-Romantic stream." The ecumenical potential of mystical body theology, on the other hand, is indebted to aspects of that same German-Romantic stream but developed extensively in the "French Social-Liturgical stream." Obviously there is plenty of cross flow among these streams as thinkers and writers standing in one take insights from those standing in others. Yet, one can discern certain key distinctions among them.

As a relatively early body theology—indeed an extended reflection on the Christian tradition's earliest theological engagement with bodies in Paul's First Letter to the Corinthians (see 11:17–13:13)—perhaps it should not be surprising to us that the theology of the mystical body of Christ was always a bit nebulous, more suggestive than determinative. This is in line with how Yves Congar describes the paradigm shift in theology leading up to, and embraced by, the Second Vatican Council:

> A *fixed* theology is one in which everything has been defined in a way which leaves no aspect unfixed. . . . This theology, therefore, is composed of the totality of theses which have been successively established or fixed affirmations deposited, as it were, in standard formulae which are put, like objects or things,

before the mind. . . . But "doctrine" cannot be separate from the mind professing it, it cannot be cut off from history and the world. . . . Admittedly, the positions of the Church must be expressed without being betrayed. This should be done in such a fashion as not to shock and repel others. . . . Saying that [doctrine] is perfectible, that it is possible to see and formulate truth better, thanks to "resourcing," that it is possible to dialogue with others, is not betraying truth or relativising it. What is true is definitively true. . . . In the end, the difference between the two attitudes is the difference between a purely conceptual approach and an approach of real things.

The Council has followed the way of reality.[6]

Likewise, mystical body theology naturally eschews attempts at rationalistic calculus while at the same time opening the doors to less appealing, and sometimes downright appalling, applications: supporting Nazi race theory, for example. A major thinker in the French stream, Émile Mersch, says that mystical body theology "necessarily retains a certain vagueness."[7] Less sympathetically, Edward Hahnenberg alludes to the same characteristic.[8] This is not to say that more clear and distinct approaches to theology in the early twentieth century, generated by neoscholastic thinkers, did not themselves support what in retrospect are clearly misguided political positions. They did. Reginald Garrigou-Lagrange's support for *Action Française* and eventually the Vichy regime, for example, has been well documented.[9] Yet, the vitality of mystical body theology opened a path for a nonrationalistic response to the world of the late nineteenth and early twentieth centuries, a response that by its nature required an anchor.

---

[6] Yves Congar, "Theology in the Council," *The American Ecclesiastical Review* 155, no. 4 (October 1966): 218–19.

[7] Émile Mersch, *The Whole Christ: The Historical Development of the Doctrine of the Mystical Body in Scripture and Tradition*, trans. John R. Kelly (Milwaukee: Bruce, 1938), 452.

[8] Edward Hahnenberg, "The Mystical Body of Christ and Communion Ecclesiology: Historical Parallels," *Irish Theological Quarterly* 70, no. 1 (March 2005): 13.

[9] See, for example, Joseph Komonchak, "Theology and Culture at Mid-Century: The Case of Henri de Lubac," *Theological Studies* 51, no. 4 (1990): 601.

The Shape of the Book

Thus, the different streams of mystical body theology in the early twentieth century can be distinguished by how they anchor or ground the slippery theological image of the mystical body of Christ. Chapter 1 lays out the characteristics of the three major streams of mystical body theology by examining some key contributions to those streams. Differing estimations of the theology's legacy are at least partially explained by these different "streams." Several reasons emerge for highlighting the French stream, in particular.

Chapter 2 follows the French stream across the ocean as Michel develops it in an American context. Michel was sent to Europe to study neoscholastic philosophy; however, he found many European neoscholastics uninteresting and disengaged with pressing social problems. Much more exciting on his study tour were the various Benedictine centers of the burgeoning liturgical movement. Chief among these was Mont César in Belgium, the abbey of Lambert Beauduin, a professor at Sant'Anselmo and important early representative of the French stream. When Michel returned to the United States to begin its arm of the liturgical movement, he brought Beauduin's unique link between the liturgy and social questions with him. Further, he developed the mystical body of Christ as a fundamental theological norm to hold together the many arms of his stateside labors. For Michel, the mystical body of Christ was solidarity formed in the liturgy and rooted in Christ.

At the time when Michel returned to the United States in 1925, mystical body theology was not a regular facet of American Catholic discourse. Joseph McSorley had published what is likely the first English-language article on the topic in 1905, but it did not take off. [10] By the 1930s and early 1940s, mystical body of Christ, was ubiquitous on both sides of the Atlantic. By the 1960s, however, the phrase had faded from its central place in Catholic theology. Later twentieth- and twenty-first-century works of ecclesiology treat mystical body of Christ, or simply body of Christ, as one image among others for the church. Something had changed. Chapter 3 investigates the sources and causes of this shift, arguing that the theology began fading before the Second Vatican Council. The ties between the

---

[10] Joseph McSorley, "The Mystical Body of Christ," *Catholic World* 131 (1905): 307–14.

German-Romantic stream and Nazi race rhetoric damaged the theology following the Second World War. And Catholic historical-critical biblical scholarship, picking up after 1943, questioned the assumed Pauline heritage of the image. Keeping in mind the distinct streams of mystical body theology that had developed earlier in the century provides a helpful hermeneutic to understand more clearly the various reasons for its eclipse.

Though it faded after mid-century, the mystical body theology of the French stream endured under the surface. Chapter 4 introduces another way of looking at the effects of the early twentieth-century mystical body recovery. It uncovers a genealogical connection between the work of Chauvet and the French stream of mystical body theology. Establishing this connection enables us to see in Chauvet's work an example of the postconciliar provenance of mystical body theology, not immediately recognizable as such. In situating Chauvet's work, this chapter also examines Henri de Lubac's seminal work *Corpus Mysticum*, which has been at the center of conversations about—and criticisms of—the theology of the mystical body of Christ.

Turning to Chauvet's "sacramental rereading of Christian existence," chapter 5 develops the previous chapter's contextualization work, uncovering the emphases of the French stream manifest in Chauvet's treatment of de Lubac and in his work more broadly. Chauvet's emphasis on the body or *corporeité* can be seen as a development of the thinking of the French stream before him in dialogue with some of the dominant voices in French philosophy in the seventies and eighties.

A Note on Terminology

"Stream" has a variety of senses and evokes a variety of images. In one sense, it means something that comes relentlessly, as in a stream of praise, a stream of cars, or a stream of electrons. In another, ideas that come, one upon the other in no reflective order, as in a stream of consciousness or, more reflectively, as in a stream of thought. If we think of bloodstream or bit stream, continuous circulation comes to mind. The fluent quality in all of these uses of the term is tied to its Indo-Germanic root *srou*, meaning to flow.

Avery Dulles's *Models of the Church* is the classic work on models in theology. Dulles gives us six models in the revised edition, each with particular theologian representatives. Anyone familiar with the work knows that Dulles is very clear that various models of the church amalgamate in particular theologians or at least that theologians can "straddle two or more models."[11] Though, perhaps for clarity's sake, he refrains from discussing particular theologians as representative of more than one particular model. Nevertheless, with the image of a model, those who stand at the intersection of them are understood as working with distinct paradigms. This is helpful as a heuristic, but does not always do historical justice to the flow of theology.

A stream is different from a model in a variety of ways. Models are independent, so they can overlap (or be straddled). They are conceptual, often idealized, types based often on a common terminology. They are irreducibly distinct and aim at solutions to problems.[12] Thus, a model is better the more potential it holds for deductions adequate to a task.

Streams flow. Water streams connect to other bodies of water. They are, by their nature, messy. One stream moves in a common direction but is at times diverted around rocks and trees. Eddies form. Sticks and other debris are gathered into the flow, which nevertheless continues in a direction together. Streams cross; they interpenetrate. Currents change. The character of the water upstream can be rather different from that downstream, but it is still recognizable (at least from a helicopter) as the same stream. It is this variety of implications that I wish to evoke with "stream" instead of "model."

Solidarity and Mediation

At a transitional point of *Models of the Church*, Dulles writes:

> We have noted a certain tension between the institutional and the mystical visions of the Church. The institutional model seems to deny salvation to anyone who is not a member of the organization, whereas the communion model leaves it problematical why anyone should be required to join the institution at all. In order to bring together the external and internal aspects into some

---

[11] Avery Dulles, *Models of the Church*, exp. ed. (New York: Doubleday, 1987), 205. See also 11–12.

[12] Ibid., 21.

intelligible synthesis, many twentieth-century Catholic theologians have appealed to the concept of the Church as sacrament.[13]

Thus begins chapter 4, "The Church as Sacrament," which follows
"The Church as Mystical Communion." To some extent, the emphases
of various streams of mystical body theology can be mapped onto the
tension identified here by Dulles. That is, some versions of it emphasized
firm borders: either one is in the body or out of it. And some versions
emphasized the more amorphous character of the mystical body of Christ.
This is one of the reasons why the sacramental character of the Christian life is of momentous importance for understanding the lineage of
mystical body theology. Yet, the heritage of mystical body theology is
not reducible to these ecclesiological questions because it is not merely
an ecclesiological category.

For a variety of reasons, not the least of which is Pope Pius XII's claim
that "the Mystical Body of Christ" is the most "noble," most "sublime," and
most "divine" way to describe the church,[14] mystical body theology often
has been considered under the lens of ecclesiology. Dulles mentions it
under the "mystical communion" model. Because of his analysis, especially
the framework he lays out above in which the sacrament model is the
both/and of the institutional and mystical communion models, Dulles's
excellent work has had the downside of leading us to see more readily
the distinctions between mystical body theology and reflections on the
sacramental character of life in Christ (as Michel would put it), rather
than their convergences. This has some historical warrant, as the theology
of the church as sacrament came into tension with the ecclesiology of
the mystical body at Vatican II.[15] Nevertheless, exploration of the French
stream demonstrates a certain friendliness of these two notions—a rich
understanding of mediation paired with a sense of communion or, better,
solidarity. Solidarity because, in the French stream most commonly, the

---

[13] Ibid., 63.

[14] Pope Pius XII, *Mystici Corporis Christi*: On the Mystical Body of Christ (29
June 1943), no. 13. Unless otherwise noted all magisterial documents are accessed
from the Vatican's website.

[15] These issues are explored by Dennis M. Doyle in "Otto Semmelroth, SJ, and the
Ecclesiology of the 'Church as Sacrament' at Vatican II," in *The Legacy of Vatican II*,
ed. Massimo Faggioli and Andrea Vicini (Mahwah, NJ: Paulist Press, 2015), 203–25.

unity of the body is grounded in the church, but opens up to a broader collaboration with, and bondedness to, other people.[16] In the long French stream, there is a consistent emphasis on the mediating power of the liturgy and sacraments of the church as well as the extension of that sense of mediation to the wider Christian life.

[16] On collaboration as the proper act of solidarity, along with an exhortation that "interdependence must be transformed into solidarity," see Pope John Paul II, *Sollicitudo Rei Socialis*: On the Twentieth Anniversary of *Populorum Progressio* (30 December 1987), no. 39.

CHAPTER I

Resurgent Body

Mystical Body of Christ Theologies
in Interbellum Europe

On 29 June 1943 Pope Pius XII promulgated the encyclical *Mystici Corporis Christi*, which gave official sanction to the theology of the mystical body of Christ that had been bubbling on the continent for decades. It was not the first time a pope had formally referred to the mystical body of Christ, but it was the first time that the theme had been treated extensively in a curial document. The encyclical brings together the burgeoning mystical body movement with a more juridical understanding of the church as *societas perfecta*.[1] As one might expect of a curial document, a comprehensive look at *Mystici* reveals several tensions.

---

[1] The clearest example of Pius's endeavor to connect mystical body and perfect society approaches is in his explanation of the modifier "mystical": "We come to that part of Our explanation in which We desire to make clear why the Body of Christ, which is the Church, should be called mystical. This name, which is used by many early writers, has the sanction of numerous Pontifical documents. There are several reasons why it should be used; for by it we may distinguish the Body of the Church, *which is a Society whose Head and Ruler is Christ*, from His physical Body, which, born of the Virgin Mother of God, now sits at the right hand of the Father and is hidden under the Eucharistic veils; and, that which is of greater importance in view of modern errors, this name enables us to distinguish it from any other body, whether in the physical or the moral order" (Pope Pius XII, *Mystici Corporis*, no. 60; emphasis mine). Commentators often emphasize the encyclical's identification of the mystical body of Christ and the Roman Catholic Church. For some examples, see Bernard P. Prusak, *The Church Unfinished: Ecclesiology Through the Centuries* (Mahwah, NJ: Paulist Press, 2004), 279; Michael J. Himes, "The Development of Ecclesiology: Modernity to the

1

The first tension involves the relationship between participation in the mystical body of Christ and concrete, bodily action. At the outset, the pope insists that the reality of the mystical body of Christ calls Christians to reflect, despite the horrors of World War II, on what unites them. Even soldiers on opposite sides can take solace in being bonded in the mystical body. These initial reflections tend toward abstraction.[2] They suggest that an awareness of participation in the mystical body of Christ confers a vague feeling of unity regardless of what we happen to be doing with our bodies. When the pope reflects on why the church is called a body, however, he emphasizes its *visibility*. In this respect, Pius joins his predecessor Leo XIII in a clear rebuttal of the Reformation emphasis on an invisible church.[3] The end of the encyclical, however, predicates the visibility of the mystical body on concrete, bodily actions. The pontiff exhorts "all good men" to respond "in supernatural charity" to "bodies racked with pain" and thus "the inexhaustible fruitfulness of the Mystical Body of Jesus Christ [will] shine resplendently throughout the whole world."[4] The implication here is that the mystical body is broken by the sufferings of particular people throughout the world and only fortified by love in action.

The second tension concerns membership in the mystical body of Christ, specifically the extent to which we can discern its outer bound-

---

Twentieth Century," in *The Gift of the Church: A Textbook on Ecclesiology in Honor of Patrick Granfield, O.S.B.*, ed. Peter C. Phan (Collegeville, MN: Liturgical Press, 2004), 64; Massimo Faggioli, *True Reform: Liturgy and Ecclesiology in* Sacrosanctum Concilium (Collegeville, MN: Liturgical Press, 2012), 59–60; Kenan Osborne, *A Theology of the Church for the Third Millennium: A Franciscan Approach* (Leiden: Brill, 2009), 87–88; Thomas Rausch, *Towards a Truly Catholic Church: An Ecclesiology for the Third Millennium* (Collegeville, MN: Liturgical Press, 2005), 29–30; Richard R. Gaillardetz, *The Church in the Making:* Lumen Gentium, Christus Dominus, Orientalium Ecclesiarum, Rediscovering Vatican II (Mahwah, NJ: Paulist Press, 2006), 43. Richard P. McBrien offers a more extensive, and nuanced, treatment of the encyclical in *The Church: The Evolution of Catholicism* (New York: Harper Collins, 2008), 121–26.

[2] *Mystici Corporis*, nos. 4–5. William T. Cavanaugh illustrates the ethereal quality of these words aptly in his essay, "Dorothy Day and the Mystical Body of Christ in the Second World War," in *Dorothy Day and the Catholic Worker Movement: Centenary Essays*, ed. William J. Thorn, Phillip M. Runkel, and Susan Mountin, Marquette Studies in Theology 32 (Milwaukee: Marquette University, 2001), 457–58.

[3] *Mystici Corporis*, no. 14. He refers to Pope Leo XIII, *Satis Cognitum*: On the Unity of the Church (29 June 1896), "the Church is visible because she is a body."

[4] *Mystici Corporis*, no. 97.

aries. Toward the beginning of the letter Pope Pius describes the Roman Catholic Church as the mystical body of Christ.[5] Yet, toward its end, Pius mentions those who are separated by schism, who "represent the person of Jesus Christ on earth"[6]—a frank admission that non-Catholic Christians represent Christ. In the following section, Pius says that those who are not members of the visible church nevertheless "have a certain relationship with the Mystical Body of the Redeemer."[7] At first, Pius seems to draw hard boundaries, but then, toward the end of the encyclical, those boundaries are revealed to be more porous. Tempering the claims of the beginning of the encyclical with these assertions at the end further illustrates why it is not entirely accurate to claim in terms of the encyclical that the mystical body of Christ is coextensive with the Catholic Church. This openness to the possibility of salvation for those outside the visible bounds of the Roman Catholic Church gave a boost to Catholic participation in ecumenical questions, which, according to one commentator, "became more and more pressing" in the years following *Mystici*.[8]

---

[5] *Mystici Corporis*, no. 13. "If we would define and describe this true Church of Jesus Christ—which is the One, Holy, Catholic, Apostolic and Roman Church—we shall find nothing more noble, more sublime, or more divine than the expression 'the Mystical Body of Christ'—an expression which springs from and is, as it were, the fair flowering of the repeated teaching of the Sacred Scriptures and the Holy Fathers." After "Roman Church," Pius cites chapter 1 of Vatican I's Divine Constitution on the Catholic Faith, *Dei Filius* (24 April 1870). Thus, he effectively adds "Roman" to his list of the traditional four marks of the church. It is important to note here that the encyclical describes the church as the mystical body of Christ and does not define the mystical body of Christ as the church. It is this distinction that seems to have opened up the possibility for the Second Vatican Council to declare in that the Church of Christ "subsists in the Catholic Church," after asserting that "the society structured with hierarchical organs and the Mystical Body of Christ, are not to be considered as two realities." "Roman" is notably absent from this formulation in *Lumen Gentium*, as well as from the list of the marks of the church in the same section. Second Vatican Council, *Lumen Gentium*: Dogmatic Constitution on the Church (21 November 1964), no. 8.

[6] *Mystici Corporis*, no. 102.

[7] *Mystici Corporis*, no. 103. In Latin, *ad mysticum Redemptoris Corpus ordinentur*, that is, "they are ordered to the mystical body of the Redeemer."

[8] J. Eileen Scully, "The Theology of the Mystical Body of Christ in French Language Theology 1930-1950: A Review and Assessment," *Irish Theological Quarterly* 58, no. 1 (March 1992): 62. Along with the more open notes sounded by the encyclical, there were other parts that struck a potentially more restrictive tone. For example in

It was not only Christian unity that the encyclical was commonly seen as furthering but, especially in the United States, racial unity. For example, from Ruth Fox: "The stupendous Encyclical Letter of His Holiness on the 'Mystical Body of Christ' left me weak and ever so happy. For now none who will read it, will be able to justify any kind of prejudice against the Negroes." And from Catherine de Hueck Doherty: "If one tenet of the Church may be called all-inclusive, it is this doctrine of the Mystical Body. And in its perfected application it has no common ground with racial discrimination of any sort." [9] Beyond the encyclical, the theme of racial reconciliation and the Catholic critique of racism would continue to be a key locus of mystical body theological reflection deep into the twentieth century.

The contrast between two contemporary commentators on the encyclical, William Cavanaugh and Robert Krieg, serves as a poignant example of its internal incongruities. Cavanaugh is sharply critical of *Mystici*, which, he claims, places "the church . . . above merely human institutions like states and civil societies." [10] In *Mystici*, Pius claims that the horrors of World War II "naturally lift souls above the passing things of earth to those in heaven that abide forever," [11] and Cavanaugh concludes that "the Pope's words would be slight comfort to the Christian on the battlefield who finds that a fellow member of the mystical body of Christ is trying to blow his legs off." [12] Krieg, on the other hand, lauds the very same passages in *Mystici* of which Cavanaugh is so critical. Informed by his deep study of World War II German Catholicism, Krieg appreciates *Mystici*'s clarification that mystical body theology "highlights the church's universality" and so leaves "no conceptual room for theologians to link the church

---

no. 22: "Actually only those are to be included as members of the Church who have been baptized and profess the true faith, and who have not been so unfortunate as to separate themselves from the unity of the Body, or been excluded by legitimate authority for grave faults committed."

[9] Ruth Fox, "Catholicism and Racism," *Interracial Review* 17 (February 1944): 25; Catherine de Hueck Doherty, "The Baroness Jots It Down," *Harlem Friendship House News* (April 1944): 6. Both quoted in John T. McGreevy, *Parish Boundaries: The Catholic Encounter with Race in the Twentieth-Century Urban North* (Chicago: University of Chicago Press, 1998), 52.

[10] William T. Cavanaugh, *Torture and Eucharist: Theology, Politics, and the Body of Christ*, Challenges in Contemporary Theology (Malden, MA: Blackwell, 1998), 210.

[11] *Mystici Corporis*, no. 4.

[12] Cavanaugh, *Torture and Eucharist*, 212.

and nationalistic talk about ethnicity and race."[13] Cavanaugh worries that mystical body theology in general has a tendency to abstract ecclesiology into a disembodied, spiritualized realm, and Krieg worries that mystical body theology has a tendency to root itself too deeply in particular, even nationalistic, rhetoric, à la Nazism. Cavanaugh reads *Mystici* as indicative of the danger he sees, and Krieg reads the encyclical as a corrective to the one he sees.

The ambiguities of the encyclical are representative not only of the nature of Roman documents but also of the plurality of mystical body theologies in early twentieth-century Europe. Some commentators have given a silent nod to these tensions by acknowledging that the encyclical was influenced both by Mersch—the Belgian theologian of the mystical body—and Roman-trained Dutch theologian Sebastian Tromp, though all agree that it was ghostwritten by the latter.[14] That both Jesuits lived and worked on different parts of the continent and were influenced by different developments in Catholic theology is significant for understanding the variegation in mystical body of Christ theology at the time. What has been called a "virtual explosion"[15] of mystical body theology in the 1920s and 1930s was not monolithic. While some have at least obliquely acknowledged this fact in writing about the mystical body of Christ, few have made it thematic to their conclusions about it, which have been, in general, rather sweeping.[16]

---

[13] Robert A. Krieg, *Catholic Theologians in Nazi Germany* (New York: Continuum, 2004), 169, though Krieg does find the encyclical lacking in its restrictive, highly "institutional" ecclesiology.

[14] Yves Congar, *L'Église: De Saint Augustin à l'époque moderne* (Paris: Cerf, 1970), 469–72. That Tromp was the dominant hand in its composition does not mean that he was responsible for its entirety. Pius XII had a famous independent streak as well as a confidence in his own abilities to complete a given task. It is, therefore, likely that Pius's concerns were wider than Tromp's and that those concerns are responsible for the encyclical's tensions. See also Alexandra von Teuffenbach, *Aus Liebe und Treue zur Kirche: Eine etwas andere Geschichte des Zweiten Vatikanums* (Berlin: Morus, 2004), 40.

[15] Scully, "The Theology," 58.

[16] Those who draw conclusions about mystical body of Christ theology are, of course, numerous. Some of the clearest examples of my point are Anselm K. Min, who asserts that mystical body theology failed in the political realm. See his "The Church as the Flesh of Christ Crucified: Toward an Incarnational Theology of the

There were several schools of thought that emphasized different aspects of the theology, with varied results. The purpose of this chapter is to identify those schools, or "streams" as I prefer to call them, and some of their major differences in order to establish the unique emphases of the French stream, which are important for the following chapters. To delineate the differences is not to suggest that these streams of mystical body theology held nothing in common. Across the mystical body movement, there was a nearly universal emphasis both on the centrality of Christ and on unity—people bound to Christ and to one another. Likewise, admitting a certain family resemblance among those paddling in each stream does not discount differences that exist among them.[17]

Church in the Age of Globalization," in *Religion, Economics and Culture in Conflict and Conversation*, ed. Maureen O'Connell and Laurie Cassidy, 2010 College Theology Society Annual Volume (Maryknoll, NY: Orbis Books, 2011), 91–107. Cavanaugh distinguishes dominant mystical body theology from Henri de Lubac's project and then asserts the abstracting qualities of the former in his *Torture and Eucharist*. For Cavanaugh, Dorothy Day's espousal of mystical body theology is the exception that proves the rule in "Dorothy Day and the Mystical Body of Christ in the Second World War," 457–64; also, Nathan Mitchell, "Liturgy and Ecclesiology," in *Handbook for Liturgical Studies*, ed. Anscar J. Chupungco (Collegeville, MN: Liturgical Press, 1998), 113–14. Those who offer distinctions among mystical body theologies are fewer. For example, see Hahnenberg, "The Mystical Body of Christ and Communion Ecclesiology: Historical Parallels," esp. 10–11, where he contrasts Tromp and Karl Pelz, placing Émile Mersch in the middle, and Bernard J. Cooke, "Body and Mystical Body: The Church as *Communio*," in *Bodies of Worship*, ed. Bruce T. Morrill (Collegeville, MN: Liturgical Press, 1999), 45. Cooke distinguishes Tromp from Mersch and Congar.

[17] Romano Guardini, discussed below, offers an interesting case that does not fit neatly into a particular stream. With respect to the French stream, for example, Congar critiqued Mersch in the 1930s for coming close to making Christ the sole proper subject of theology. See Fergus Kerr, "Congar and Thomism," in *Yves Congar: Theologian of the Church*, ed. Gabriel Flynn (Leuven: Peeters, 2005), 75–76. Congar's critique—suggesting that Mersch does not make fine enough distinctions in his theological analysis and, therefore, does not follow St. Thomas in situating all of theology under God—fits into Kerr's project of arguing that Congar is more of a Thomist than his later interpreters often suggest. As a commendable contrast to Mersch, Congar cites the work of mystical body theology critic Mannes Koster. Kerr raises the possibility that Congar himself was undergoing a shift in theological sensibility at the time, from more scholastic to more *ressourcement*/Romantic.

Those emphases played out differently in the three streams of mystical body theology: the Roman, the German-Romantic, and the French socio-liturgical. As their names indicate, these streams were less demarcated by the lines of religious institutes and more identifiable by linguistic and geographical bounds. Benedictine Fr. Beauduin's sensibilities, for example, were more in line with Jesuit Fr. Mersch's than with those of the Benedictines at Maria Laach in Germany. The streams can be distinguished by, among other factors, where they tend to ground, locate, or anchor, the slippery mystical body theology. For the Roman theologians, the mystical body of Christ was grounded in the structures and offices of the Roman Catholic Church. For a cadre of German-Romantic theologians, especially leading up to and during the Second World War, the mystical body was grounded in the national body, the German *Volk*. For the French socio-liturgical theologians, the mystical body was anchored in the liturgy and sacraments of the church. Over and against the Roman stream, and to a lesser extent the German, in the French socio-liturgical stream, mystical body theology was not only an ecclesiological image or descriptor but rather pervaded theology such that it can be described as a fundamental theological norm.

Unearthing the distinctions between these streams of mystical body theology helps to explain not only the ambiguities of *Mystici Corporis* but also why the two encyclicals of Pope Pius that followed it, *Mediator Dei* (1947) and *Humani Generis* (1950), emphasized alternatively different aspects of the mystical body of Christ.[18] In terms more specific to the wider goals of this book, this analysis contextualizes Michel's appropriation of mystical body theology, which he derives predominately from Beauduin of the French stream. Finally, these distinctions help to sort—as we shall see in chapter 3—the various reasons why mystical body theology recedes just after mid-century.

---

[18] Pope Pius XII, *Mediator Dei*: On the Sacred Liturgy (20 November 1947); idem, *Humani Generis*: Concerning Some False Opinions Threatening to Undermine the Foundations of Catholic Doctrine (12 August 1950). In *Mediator Dei*, the mystical body has more porous boundaries. *Humani Generis*, by contrast, offers a more restrictive interpretation of *Mystici Corporis*, "the Mystical Body of Christ and the Roman Catholic Church are one and the same thing" (no. 27). Though there are some sections of *Mediator Dei* that emphasize the more hierarchically ordered aspects of the liturgy, there are significant sections that broaden participation in the mystical body and, in turn, in the priesthood of Christ. See esp. nos. 88 and 106.

"Mystical Body of Christ"

The phrase "mystical body of Christ" is, on its face, a curious amalgamation. "The very name puts us on our guard," warns British Jesuit Alban Goodier. "The two words [mystical and body] almost contain a contradiction."[19] At the common-sense level, mystical connotes a flight of fancy or fantasy. Its theological use descends from the Greek *mysterion* (μυστήριον), a union—more or less sacramental—with God and, by implication, with other people that transcends the immediate concrete. While the phrase "mystical body of Christ" never appears in Scripture itself, μυστήριον (*sacramentum* in the Vulgate) describes God's revelation reaching its apex in Christ in several Pauline epistles: Romans 16:25-27; Ephesians 3:4-6; 6:18-20; and Colossians 1:24-27; 4:2-4. In Pauline usage μυστήριον enables communion with God in a profoundly new way, the way of divine filiation. Further, Christ is the "image of the invisible God" (Col 3:10). Therefore, because of Christ—the great Mediator—the deprivation of the senses inherent to μυστήριον is reduced significantly.[20] The linguistic root of μυστήριον is the Greek word from which we get "mystical" in the sense of "mystical experience" (μυειν; literally, "closed," in the sense of eyes and lips). There are quite a few theories about the impact of the term "mystical" applied to the body of Christ. *Mystici Corporis* indicates that the term distinguishes the church from the historical body of Christ, the latter of which, in the encyclical, is more closely associated with the Eucharist, as well as from any other body, physical or societal.[21]

---

[19] Alban Goodier, "The Mystical Body," *The Month* 159 (1932): 297.

[20] Chapter 3 explores some questions surrounding the Pauline understanding of the Body of Christ. Commenting on *Mystici Corporis*, Michael Connolly has written, "The relation of the Church to Christ, in virtue of which she is called the Body of Christ, is something more than the mere, extrinsic, juridical relation by which, for instance, the King is called head of the body politic. To call attention to this 'something more,' as well as to distinguish Christ's Church from His physical Body, hypostatically united to the Word of God (59, 60), Christian usage has added the adjective 'mystical,' calling the Church the 'Mystical Body of Christ.' The Pope's Encyclical is chiefly concerned with bringing out the implications of this term 'Mystical Body of Christ.' He wishes to underline the inner, spiritual, super natural life of the Church—its greatest glory and title to our esteem (61)." See Michael Connolly, "The Glory of Mother Church," *The Irish Monthly* 72, no. 857 (1944): 463.

[21] *Mystici Corporis*, no. 60.

Holding a distinction uncommon in the 1930s between Pauline phrase-ology and the doctrine, Gerald Ellard, associate editor of *Orate Fratres*, writes, "Body of Christ is Scriptural; the word *Mystical* has been added by theologians to designate the mysterious unity of the whole." [22] More than thirty years later, Dulles echoes Ellard's perspective, noting that mystical indicates a deeper, more profound union than a mere sociological one. [23] There is consensus that this union grants broader, even universal, significance to the more immediate, concrete community. [24] Paul Hanly Furfey emphasized that mystical indicated a nevertheless real union with those who are not in visible or physical proximity. [25] In this vein, Mersch pushes more toward the sense of mystical theology or mystical experi-ence when he says the term "signifies something which in plenitude and reality surpasses the things of nature and the positive concepts that our reason can elaborate." [26] That is to say, for Mersch, mystical is roughly equivalent to supernatural. Nevertheless, it is not a qualifier that in itself brings immediate clarity. For instance, Friedrich Schleiermacher warns

[22] Gerald Ellard, *The Mystical Body and the American Bishops* (St. Louis: The Queen's Work, 1939), 14. Ellard's reflections in this regard were notably pneumato-logical: "the mysterious (or mystic) unifying bond between Christians and the Holy Ghost and between individual members of The Mystical Body is sanctifying grace, which is accompanied by the actual indwelling of the Holy Ghost" (33). Ellard cites Martin Cyril D'Arcy, who claims that mystical body theology answers secular forms of unity across space (e.g., Communism) (35).

[23] Dulles, *Models of the Church*, 51, 57.

[24] Sandra Yocum emphasizes this aspect of the doctrine in her study of the gradu-ates of St. Mary's pioneering graduate program in theology for women. She writes of "the Mystical Body of Christ, the theological framework which highlighted the universal significance of all local activities. This theological-biblical image, which reached its peak of popularity in the decade preceding the council, provided a location for this sense of the inter penetration of the local and universal. The biblical image, of course, comes from the Pauline corpus. The additional qualification, 'mystical,' subtly but significantly shifts the phrase to emphasize Catholicism as transcending temporal and spacial categories." In "'A Catholic Way of Doing Every Important Thing': U.S. Catholic Women and Theological Study in the Mid-Twentieth Century," *U.S. Catholic Historian* 13, no. 2 (1995): 62–63.

[25] Paul Hanly Furfey, *Fire on the Earth* (New York: Macmillan Co., 1936), 43.

[26] Mersch, *The Whole Christ*, 9.

that mystical is "an expression which is better avoided, as much in its good as in its bad sense, because of its lack of precision."[27]

"Body" is much more located, drawing us into our fleshiness—though not limited to it—and, perhaps, those to whom we stand in immediate concrete relation. The two senses are made clear when we think of two English synonyms for body, corpse and corps, both descendants of *corpus*, the Latin term for body.[28] Then there is the prepositional phrase, drawing all of this together with the Redeemer and rooted in the words of institution and the practice of the Eucharist. Many saw the phrase as predicated on, and continuous with, the hypostatic union, which was a particular emphasis of the nineteenth-century Tübingen School, especially Johann Adam Möhler, who facilitated a recovery of mystical body theology.[29]

The meaning of the image also depends on where the breath is taken when it is uttered. There is either "the mystical body . . . of Christ," distinguishing *this* mystical body from every other mystical body. Or rather "the mystical . . . body of Christ," distinguishing the *mystical* body of Christ from every other body of Christ, or at least every other form of the body of Christ. Thus, before even entering into the specific contextual differences of its application and development, the phrase itself evokes a variety of interpretations. Variance is, it seems, endemic in its very formulation.[30]

As such, the image of the mystical body of Christ and its theological purchase is precarious. In christological terms, there are both Arian and Docetic temptations. Each temptation flattens out the sacramental or mediatory sense of the modifier "mystical." The Arian tendency shears off the vertical impact of "mystical" and therefore means to indicate a

[27] Quoted in Michael Himes, *Ongoing Incarnation: Johann Adam Möhler and the Beginnings of Modern Ecclesiology* (New York: Crossroad, 1997), 111.

[28] The *Oxford English Dictionary*, 3rd ed., s.v. "Body," suggests Germanic origin for the English word, but admits that complete etymology is unknown. Nevertheless it concludes that the sense development of the word "body" in English has been influenced by the meaning of *corpus*.

[29] Himes's *Ongoing Incarnation* provides an excellent overview of Möhler's project, especially its emphasis on the church as the continuation, throughout history, of the hypostatic union.

[30] These ambiguities extend, as far as I can tell, to the other relevant languages: *Corps mystique du Christ* (French), *Mystici corporis Christi* (Latin), and *mystischen Leib Christi* (German).

merely sociological or moral union, effected by any type of deeply held or felt common characteristic or cause. There is this "body of believers," that "body of soldiers," or another "body of politicians." The mystical body of Christ is then simply the body of Christians. All that remains is a corporate sense. The opposite error, the ungrounded or Docetic one, is a tendency to erase any necessary *res medians* between humans and Christ. That error—or at least one version of it—is mentioned explicitly in *Mystici Corporis* and functions as the encyclical's counterpoint. In response to, or in anticipation of, this potential error, theologians tend to ground, locate, or anchor mystical body theology on some firmer conceptual or practical ground.

The Deeper Context of *Mystici Corporis Christi*

On 18 January 1943, five months before the promulgation of *Mystici*, Archbishop Conrad Gröber of Fribourg wrote a letter to his German confrères in which he addressed some Docetic tendencies of mystical body theology.[31] "I am concerned by the sublime supernaturalism and the new mystical attitude that is spreading in our theology," he wrote. "It can degenerate into a mysticism in which the borders of creation vanish."[32] Gröber was particularly critical of Karl Pelz's *Der Christ als Christus* in this regard.[33] Pelz was a parish priest in Berlin who, in that text of 1939, argued that, according to the doctrine of the mystical body of Christ, Christians *are* Christ. Pelz's was something of a theology of Christification (or deification) on steroids, a kind of Christic pantheism. Quoting texts from the Fathers, he asserted that by Christ's sacrifice, the hypostatic

---

[31] The letter appears in Theodor Maas-Ewerd, *Die Krise der liturgischen Bewegung in Deutschland und Österreich: Zu den Auseinandersetzungen um die "liturgische Frage" in den Jahren 1939 bis 1944* (Regensburg: Pustet, 1981), 540–569.

[32] Ibid., 548. See Lorenzo Capelletti, "Sixty Years after *Mystici Corporis*: The Distinction between Creator and Creature," *Thirty Days in the Church and in the World* 21, no. 6 (2003): 46. I have followed Capelletti's translation.

[33] Karl Pelz, *Der Christ als Christus: Der Weg meines Forschens* (Berlin: Pelz, 1939, printed from manuscript). From the foreword, "*Das Studium unserer Einverleibung in Christus, das mit der Feststellung endigte, dass wir Christen tatsächlich Christus geworden sind*" (7). The modifier *tatsächlich*, or "actually," distinguishes Pelz's theology from a traditional theology of deification.

union has been extended to all, effectively eradicating the sacramental mediation of the church.[34] Gröber feared the implications of this "sublime supernaturalism": "The future will tell where we will be led—in preaching, in catechesis and in the Christian life—by the devaluation of the historical Christ, with his stupendous closeness to mankind, his exemplary glory and his liberating reality, in favor of a more sublime Christ located entirely beyond space and time."[35]

While Gröber explicitly mentioned Pelz, World War II is not an unimportant context for reading the archbishop's letter. By 1943, Gröber had abandoned his early conciliation approach to National Socialism and involved himself in efforts help Jews escape from Germany.[36] He was also the only prelate to write a public defense of Max Metzger, the Catholic founder of the ecumenical *Una Sancta* movement who was executed in 1944 for his public opposition to the Reich.[37] When Gröber voiced concern about the vanishing boundaries between creator and creature, and particularly for the youth in Germany who were increasingly becoming "perfect unbelievers,"[38] he was likely concerned about some efforts to use mystical body theology in Germany to prop up Nazism. Gröber's long letter also explicitly wondered about the perils of inaction, asking, "Can we German bishops remain silent, can Rome remain silent?"[39] He got his answer from Rome five months later in the form of *Mystici Corporis*.

The encyclical was addressed to ordinaries throughout the world but was primarily, though not solely, a response to the rather unique situation in Germany.[40] Jerome-Michael Vereb explains Pius's alarm at Hitler's attempt to nationalize the Protestant Church in Germany as well as the

---

[34] On Pelz, see Dulles, *Models of the Church*, 44-47.

[35] Gröber in Maas-Ewerd, *Die Krise*, 552. Capelletti, "Sixty Years," 47.

[36] Krieg, *Catholic Theologians in Nazi Germany*, 141-44.

[37] See Jerome-Michael Vereb, *"Because He Was a German!" Cardinal Bea and the Origins of Roman Catholic Engagement in the Ecumenical Movement* (Grand Rapids, MI: Eerdmans, 2006), 97-106.

[38] Gröber in Mass-Ewerd, *Die Krise*, 549. Capelletti, "Sixty Years," 46.

[39] Mass-Ewerd, *Die Krise*, 569.

[40] Pius XII also was concerned with the French context in the 1940s, especially as regards the lack of a Catholic pastoral presence among French working-class Catholics, the worker-priest experiment that sought to address it, and the theology that supported the movement.

pope's deep concern for the suffering of German Catholics during the war. Vereb concludes that "fear was certainly a factor when in 1943 he issued a papal encyclical about ecclesiology titled *Mystici Corporis.*"[41] Dulles also thinks that Pope Pius had Pelz in mind when he wrote of the "false mysticism," which attempts "to eliminate the immovable frontier that separates creatures from their Creator" and, in so doing, "falsifies the Sacred Scriptures."[42] Pelz's book had been placed on the Index in 1940. Kevin McNamara also reads the encyclical as primarily a response to the tumultuous German situation.[43] While there was a growing ecumenical sensibility among German theologians discussing the mystical body, there was also a tendency—and this is key—to separate the unitive aspects of mystical body theology from its sacramental aspects. Pelz represents the extreme of this tendency. In 1940, Dominican Mannes Koster argued that

[41] Vereb, "*Because He Was a German!*," 131. See also Susan Wood, *Spiritual Exegesis and the Church in the Theology of Henri de Lubac* (Grand Rapids, MI: Eerdmans, 1998), 65–73. Wood says that *Mystici Corporis* firmly grounded mystical body theology in the structures of the Church because of extensive fear of the opposite tendency, which separated the "invisible communion of grace from the visible Church" (73).

[42] *Mystici Corporis*, no. 9. Avery Dulles, "A Half Century of Ecclesiology," *Theological Studies* 50 (1989): 422. Thomas Merton dedicates a chapter to "false mysticism" in his *The Ascent to Truth: A Study of St. John of the Cross* (New York: Harcourt and Brace, 1951), 44–54, explicitly connecting a type of false mysticism to Nazi ideology. He writes: "We are living in a time when false mysticism is a much greater danger than rationalism. It has now become much easier to play on men's emotions with a political terminology that sounds religious than with one that sounds scientific. This is all the more true in an age in which the religious instincts of millions of men have never received their proper fulfillment. A nation that is starved with the need to worship something will turn to the first false god that is presented to it. Hitler showed the world what could be done with an *ersatz* mysticism of 'Race' and 'Blood' " (44). Mersch had warned of false mysticism before the encyclical in *The Whole Christ*, 7. Mersch seems to understand the term to mean sentimentalism, spiritual ambition, or "aspirations to extraordinary, ecstatic, sometimes morbid states." He cites all of these misunderstandings of mystical body theology. The deeper genealogy of false mysticism needs further exploration. With respect to "immovable frontier," the Latin is *immobiles limites*. *Limites* derives from *limes*, meaning path. For the Roman military, it was used to indicate a boundary line or reinforced frontier, but it was also used to mean distinction; this latter nuance is a more helpful shade of meaning here.

[43] Kevin McNamara, "The Ecclesiological Movement in Germany in the Twentieth Century," *Irish Ecclesiastical Record* 102 (November 1964): 351.

mystical body theology was only a metaphorical description of the instrumentalist institution and should be dismissed as irrelevant to our age.[44] Koster was interested, nevertheless, in maintaining the German-Romantic organic view of the church. The image "people of God" served that purpose best, he thought. The mystical body movement, he asserted, moved too quickly and hastily from the cold view of *societas perfecta* to a warm communitarian vision and, in so doing, failed to distinguish properly between ecclesiology, the theology of grace, and Christology. According to Koster, mystical body theology not only was devoid of important distinctions (a natural critique from a Dominican thinker) but also did not establish robust theological support for communal salvation.[45]

While many have cited *Mystici* as joining mystical body theology to a more juridical "perfect society" vision of the church, the context into which the encyclical was thrust explains *why* that was the case. Pius's concern in the encyclical is to save mystical body theology—and its numerous theological, pastoral, and spiritual fruits—while grounding it to resist the Docetic Pelzian tendency. He does this by planting it firmly in the Roman Catholic Church and, ultimately, its papacy. In the neoscholastic mind of

---

[44] Donald J. Dietrich, "Catholic Theology and the Challenge of Nazism," in *Antisemitism, Christian Ambivalence and the Holocaust*, Papers from a Workshop at the Center for Advanced Holocaust Studies of the United States Holocaust Memorial Museum in Washington, DC, Summer 2004, ed. Kevin P. Spicer (Bloomington: Indiana University Press, 2007), 88. The work in question is Mannes Dominikus Koster, *Ekklesiologie im Werden* (Paderborn, DE: Verlag der Bonfacius-Druckerie, 1940). On Koster, see Piotr Napiwodzki, "Eine Ekklesiologie im Werden: Mannes Dominikus Koster und sein Beitrag zum theologischen Verständnis der Kirch" (PhD diss., University of Fribourg, 2005). Koster, whose work would influence later ecclesiology, argued that the phrase "people of God," highlighting the church as the new chosen people, drove more to the heart of Pauline theology and described the church as it really was.

[45] In the words of Napiwodzki, *Problematisch ist vor allem die ekklesiologische Verwendung des Bildes, das grundsätzlich zur Beschreibung der Gnadenökonomie angewandt wird* ["The main problem is the ecclesiological use of an image that is generally used to describe the economy of grace" (my translation)] (74). In contrast to the conventional view of Koster's book as a polemic against mystical body of Christ ecclesiology *tout court*, Napiwodzki argues that Koster specifically finds the predominately christological metaphor of the mystical body of Christ, used in ecclesiological isolation, to tend toward Luther's *Heilspersonalismus* or personal salvation (46ff.). If Napiwodzki is correct, such a critique of mystical body theology as underemphasizing the solidarity related to communal salvation is rather unique.

ghostwriter Tromp, emphasis on the structures of the church was a clear way to emphasize mediation.

Sebastian Tromp and the Roman Stream of Mystical Body Theology

Before discussing Tromp's theology in particular as representative of the Roman stream of mystical body of Christ theology, we must understand how it is that the mystical body theology renewal got to Rome in the first place. As de Lubac's *Corpus Mysticum* illustrates, the language of mystical body has been with the church since the patristic era, though its narrow ecclesiological application did not begin until after Berengar in the eleventh century.[46] After that point, "mystical body" was present in theological reflections from St. Thomas to St. Robert Bellarmine. Its twentieth-century explosion is directly indebted to the nineteenth-century Romantic Catholics at the University of Tübingen, especially Möhler, whom Joseph Ratzinger calls "the great reviver of Catholic theology after the devastation of the Enlightenment."[47]

Characteristically, Möhler developed his mystical body theology by way of deep engagement with the fathers of the church. It emphasized an evolving, organic body, extended through time. Introducing his *Unity in the Church*, Möhler wrote to his friend Joseph Lipp: "A careful study of the Fathers has stirred up much in me. While undertaking [the project] I discovered a living, fresh, full Christianity."[48] Möhler's ideas traveled to

---

[46] Henri de Lubac, *Corpus Mysticum: The Eucharist and the Church in the Middle Ages*, trans. Gemma Simmonds with Richard Price and Christopher Stevens (Notre Dame, IN: University of Notre Dame Press, 2006). Though de Lubac's work had a wider-ranging impact on mystical body theology and is a much more complex piece of scholarship, about a decade before the first publication of that work, Archbishop Edward Myers noted that "mystical body of Christ" was originally ascribed to the Eucharist and not to the church in *The Mystical Body of Christ* (London: Burns and Oates, 1930), 27–28. We will return to de Lubac's *Corpus Mysticum* in chapter 4.

[47] Joseph Ratzinger, *Church, Ecumenism, and Politics: New Endeavors in Ecclesiology* (San Francisco: Ignatius Press, 2008; German orig., 1987), 14.

[48] Quoted in Peter C. Erb, "Introduction" to Johann Adam Möhler, *Unity in the Church or The Principle of Catholicism, Presented in the Spirit of the Church Fathers of the First Three Centuries*, ed. and trans. Peter C. Erb. (Washington, DC: The Catholic University of America Press, 1996), 1.

Rome through Jesuits Giovanni Perrone (d. 1876) and Carlo Passaglia (d. 1887) and down the generations of important Roman College theologians: Klemens Schrader (d. 1875), Johannes Baptist Franzelin (d. 1886), and Matthias Scheeben (d.1888).[49] Their sensibilities were different from the purer manualist theologians that preceded them. Like Möhler, they emphasized the christological, incarnational character of the church, rather than merely its societal aspects. They were, however, still interested in writing theology in the more positive scholastic treatise style, rather than the freer essay/narrative style of Möhler or John Henry Newman.

The Roman College was deeply influential in constructing the schemas for Vatican I and, as Mersch and also Michel would later relish repeating, the tabled schema on the church began with a reflection on the mystical body of Christ. According to Mersch, the schema was criticized by a minority of the bishops in their *vota* for its overly abstract and ethereal qualities and never given full consideration because the Franco-Prussian War precipitated the early conclusion of that council. Mersch remarks that of the one-third of bishops (230 out of 639) whose written opinions are on record, precious few (4) thought that "mystical body" should be left out of the schema entirely. A more substantial but still small number of the respondents (25) were not utterly opposed to the idea of centering the document on the church around the mystical body but nevertheless found it "too complicated, obscure, or vague." A particular problem for the bishops, one deeply significant for the future debates about the composi-

---

[49] Yves Congar, "L'Ecclésiologie, de la Révolution Française au Concile du Vatican, sous le Signe de l'Affirmation de l'Autorité," in *L'Ecclésiologie au XIXe Siècle*, Unam Sanctam no. 34, ed. Maurice Nédoncelle et al. (Paris: Cerf, 1960), 107. In the same paragraph Congar sums up this genealogy pithily: *Moehler genuit Passaglia; Passaglia genuit Schrader; Passaglia et Schrader genuerunt Scheeben et Franzelin.* Augustus Kerkvoorde, OSB, offers a brief overview of the contributions of the Roman College to the mystical body recovery in "La théologie du Corps Mystique au dix-neuvième siècle," *Nouvelle Revue Théologique* 67 (1945): 417–30. Kerkvoorde explains that Scheeben studied in Rome from 1852 to 1859. It was in 1857 that Passaglia and Schrader left and were replaced by Franzelin and Raphaele Cercia. Passaglia left the Jesuits shortly thereafter (423–24). Kerkvoorde describes Franzelin in this way: *Esprit moins brillant que Passaglia, mais plus précis, plus sobre, ennemi de toute exagération, il avait cependant été forme à son école et ne prenait pas encore place parmi les thomistes rigoureux. Il se basait aussi sur l'étude positive, sur l'Ecriture et les Pères* (425). The Roman College would later become the Pontifical Gregorian University.

tion of the mystical body, was that "the concept of the Mystical Body does not coincide perfectly with that of the Church." [50] De Lubac argues that there was quite a range of criticisms among the bishops. For some it was too metaphorical, for others too abstract, and still others too pious instead of dogmatic. [51] Patrick Granfield finds *societas perfecta* to be much more fundamental to the work of Vatican I's preparatory commission and finds much less enthusiasm among the bishops than does Mersch. He writes:

> The theology of the Body of Christ did not permeate the rest of the Constitution. It was used in the text and canons only fifteen times and was not a central, unifying theme. Furthermore, many of the fathers were opposed to it. The French bishops in particular found it "too abstract and mystical," claimed that it belonged rather to mystical theology, and argued that one could not construct a schema on the Church on a metaphorical term. Cardinal Trevisanto, Patriarch of Venice, along with thirteen other bishops (twelve Italians and one Brazilian) questioned the prudence of using "the doctrine of the Mystical Body which the Jansenists used to introduce their own errors." The term "*societas*," however, played a much more significant methodological and theological role in the schema than the Body of Christ. [52]

In this same discussion, Granfield also indicates that it was Schrader who edited the entire schema and left his mark on chapter 1, "The Church Is the Mystical Body of Christ." Granfield suspects that Perrone, who wrote paragraph 5 of the *Syllabus of Errors* on the church as perfect society, was responsible for thematizing *societas* in the schema. Granfield's conclusions indicate the complex character of the Roman School. [53]

---

[50] Mersch, *The Whole Christ*, 564.

[51] De Lubac, *Corpus Mysticum*, 117.

[52] Patrick Granfield, "The Church as *Societas Perfecta* in the Schemata of Vatican I," *Church History* 48, no. 4 (1979): 434–35.

[53] Ibid. Perrone was, after all, the Roman Jesuit that John Henry Newman, upon his conversion, deemed most receptive to his ideas on doctrinal development, favoring Perrone over Passaglia to read his *Essay on the Development of Christian Doctrine*, which he had translated into a scholastic treatise. See John Henry Newman, *Roman Catholic Writings on Doctrinal Development*, trans. and comm. James Gaffney (Kansas City, MO: Sheed and Ward, 1997). The affinities between Newman and Möhler have,

Tromp, Dutch Jesuit and chief representative of the Roman stream of mystical body theology in the twentieth century, had inherited some of the cutting-edge emphases of his forebears in the Roman College but applied them in a different ecclesial and theological context. After Leo XIII's emphasis on Thomistic philosophy in *Aeterni Patris* (1879), and even further after Pius X's condemnation of Modernism with *Pascendi Dominici Gregis* (1907), the next generation of Roman theologians tightened the screws on their custodial bearing of the neoscholastic manual tradition.[54] The Romantic impulses of Möhler's ecclesiological turn were further muted in favor of greater clarity.

Tromp was trained in classics in the Netherlands and then went to the Gregorianum for theological study in the twenties after his ordination. His engagement with the revival of mystical body theology made him more broad-minded than some of his colleagues in Rome. Congar called late nineteenth-century Roman College theology "patristico-dogmatic," and that descriptor fits Tromp's work well.[55] There is in Tromp's work not a slavish parsing of Thomistic commentaries, but an engagement with and appreciation for patristic texts. In a reflection preceding the bibliography of his work on the mystical body of Christ, Tromp speaks highly of his predecessors at the Gregorian University in Rome:

> Because this dissertation was especially intended for students at the Pontifical Gregorian University, special mention should be made of the professors of sacred theology in this University who have shed light on our topic. Nor do I wish to slight those who taught in the Gregorian University in the middle part of the nineteenth century, and who deserve high praise for their part in the revival of the sacred sciences. Anyone who reads the works of Fathers Passaglia, Perrone, Schrader, Franzelin, etc., will see that at the time when Scheeben himself was a student, the professors

---

of course, been well documented. See, for example, James Hennesey, "Leo XIII: Intellectualizing the Combat with Modernity," *U.S. Catholic Historian* 7 (Fall 1988): 395.

[54] Pope Pius X, *Pascendi Dominici Gregis*: On the Doctrines of the Modernists (9 August 1907); Pope Leo XIII, *Aeterni Patris*: On the Restoration of Christian Philosophy (4 August 1879).

[55] Congar, "*L'Ecclésiologie, de la Révolution Française au Concile du Vatican, sous le Signe de l'Affirmation de l'Autorité*," 107.

did more than simply explain the catechism, and were highly versed in the study of the Fathers, especially the Greeks.[56]

Tromp did not have an overly narrow view of theology. He directed the dissertation of Julius Döpfner, future cardinal archbishop of Munich and Freising, on the relationship between nature and the supernatural in Newman.[57] Tromp's bibliography shows that he read widely on the topic of the mystical body, including even so-called *nouvelle théologiens*.[58] Tromp appreciates his formation in the patristic sources of the tradition and wields them competently, but directly, toward the *telos* of his work, reflected in the second part of its title: *Corpus Christi, Quod Est Ecclesia*. The task of Tromp's work is to illustrate why it is that the mystical body of Christ is properly understood as the Roman Catholic Church.[59] Tromp was not without some nuance in this respect:

> Whereas not a few modern writers, when they discuss the structure of the Mystical Body, seem to have in mind almost solely the hierarchical organization, which, it is true, as the perpetual continuation of Christ the teacher, king, and priest, is the primary element in the spiritual edifice of the Church; the ancients enjoyed a much broader vision. . . . To give one example which is rather

---

[56] Sebastian Tromp, *Corpus Christi, Quod Est Ecclesia*, trans. Ann Condit (New York: Vantage Press, 1960), 232. This is the English translation of volume 1 of Tromp's 1946 revised and expanded edition of his 1937 original. Hereafter, Tromp, *Corpus Christi*, English. Cf. Sebastian Tromp, *Corpus Christi, Quod Est Ecclesia*, vol. 1, *Introductio Generalis*, rev. and exp. ed. (Rome: Gregorian University, 1946), 224. Hereafter, Tromp, *Corpus Christi*, Latin rev. The original publication of the work is *Corpus Christi, Quod Est Ecclesia*, vol. 1, *Introductio Generalis* (Rome: Gregorian University, 1937). Hereafter, Tromp, *Corpus Christi*, Latin orig.

[57] Teuffenbach, *Aus Liebe und Treue zur Kirche*, 40. Julius Döpfner, "Das Verhältnis von Natur und Übernatur bei John Henry Kardinal Newman" (STD diss., Pontifical Gregorian University, 1941).

[58] In a section of the bibliography inexplicably not included in the English version of Tromp's *Corpus Christi*, Tromp refers his readers to de Lubac's *Corpus Mysticum*. He explains de Lubac's argument that "mystical body" was not applied to the church until the eleventh century, but disputes de Lubac's reading of Hesychius of Jerusalem, insisting that the latter's references to *corpus mysticum* have ecclesial purchase. Tromp, *Corpus Christi*, Latin rev., 222.

[59] Tromp, *Corpus Christi*, English, 9.

near to us today: matrimony is sometimes called a special "office" in the Body of Christ (cf. Augustine); rather often, a "degree" (ibid.) . . . an "order" (cf. Gregory the Great, Bede, Berengaudus); an "ecclesiastical order" (cf. Theodoret). . . .

The idea I have just explained is absolutely necessary in order that one may properly understand how Catholic Action is related to the total organism of the Church herself; and in order that none may suppose that all organs which belong by right to the Church are jurisdictional organs.[60]

Characteristically Tromp argues here, based on mystical body theology, that the organization of the church is not solely the domain of the hierarchy, as in the framework of Catholic Action, but that organization extends to the rank and file, the laity, who even hold particular offices in the church. In Scripture, Tromp finds incipient traces of this structure: "In Paul's thought the Body of Christ is that visible hierarchical organization such as existed at the time."[61]

Tromp asserts that for Paul, the church is Christ. Aware of the dangers of such an identification, Tromp invokes St. John Chrysostom, "certainly not a man prone to false mysticism [*pseudomysticismum*]," in order to corroborate the identification of the church and Christ in Corinthians.[62] Tromp concludes with a pneumatological resolution: "When Christ is spoken of as the quasi-hypostasis of the mystical Body, the reason is that by means of His Spirit, and through His Spirit He works all supernatural things in all the members of the Church."[63] Of course, the "quasi" is of utter importance in Tromp's theological statement insofar as it provides the distinction between God and human beings that false mysticism does not. For Tromp, however, the problem is wider. In order to emphasize the institutional location of the mystical body, the Dutch theologian is much more comfortable treading near the danger of identifying the church with Christ than he is approaching the opposite error of rendering the church irrelevant by emphasizing the Spirit's work in the world. Tromp's enthu-

---

[60] Tromp, *Corpus Christi*, English, 158; cf. Tromp, *Corpus Christi*, Latin rev., 143–44; cf. Tromp, *Corpus Christi*, Latin orig., 121–22.

[61] Tromp, *Corpus Christi*, English, 196.

[62] Tromp, *Corpus Christi*, Latin rev., 83. Cf. Tromp, *Corpus Christi*, English, 98.

[63] Tromp, *Corpus Christi*, English, 85.

siastic statement to Congar at the Second Vatican Council furthers the point made here. "THEY [the non-Catholic observers] insist on the Holy Spirit because they have eliminated the magisterium. . . . Jesus Christ could have acted on human beings without the Church, through his Holy Spirit alone, but he chose to act on them THROUGH THE CHURCH, by putting his Holy Spirit in the Church."[64]

It is important here to recall that Tromp was a ghostwriter for *Mystici Corporis*. Pius XII's encyclical uses a slightly different Latin phrase also translated as "false mysticism," *falsus subrepit mysticismus*, to describe a tendency of mystical body theology to make Christians into God. Because the exact same Latin phrase appeared in the pre-*Mystici* (1937) edition of Tromp's work,[65] it makes sense to attribute this formulation—"false" or "pseudo" mysticism—to Tromp's own concern about eradicating any difference between God and humans, a concern that, as we have seen, is very important in the encyclical. Along these same lines, *Mystici* echoes Tromp's concern that the Spirit be firmly planted in the visible church, "Hence they err in a matter of divine truth, who imagine the Church to be invisible, intangible, a something merely 'pneumatological' as they say, by which many Christian communities, though they differ from each other in their profession of faith, are united by an invisible bond."[66]

Despite the fact that such debates about the visible and invisible church have been with us at least since the Reformation (and perhaps since the fourth-century Donatist controversy), Tromp's purpose is to ground mystical body theology firmly in the structures of the visible church. For Tromp, there are two major aspects of the church—the spiritual and the juridical: "If we consider the final goal at which the Church aims and the proximate efficient causes of sanctity, she is undoubtedly spiritual; but if we consider those in whom the Church consists and the things that lead to the spiritual gifts, she is external and necessarily visible."[67] Though he spends considerably more time developing the former,

---

[64] This comment is recounted by Congar in *My Journal of the Council*, trans. Mary John Ronayne and Mary Cecily Boulding (Collegeville, MN: Liturgical Press, 2012), 711–12; emphasis original.

[65] Tromp, *Corpus Christi*, Latin orig., 77.

[66] *Mystici Corporis*, no. 14.

[67] Tromp, *Corpus Christi*, English, 10.

ultimately the latter is *terra firma*. Even in his reflections on the spiritual aspect, the bishops hold a primacy of place. Rightly, he concludes, do we identify the bishops, and especially the bishop of Rome, with the head of the mystical body because they serve as Christ's vicar on earth.[68] Tromp says, "The Roman Pontiff is the bridegroom of the Church, by the power of the divine Bridegroom; he is the foundation, by the power of Christ the Foundation; he is the head, by the power of Christ the Head."[69]

The book arrives at its final destination that—in both its spiritual and visible aspects—"the Mystical Body of Christ [on Earth] is the Roman Catholic Church."[70] Tromp says that "although it has not been solemnly defined that the Roman Catholic Church is the Mystical Body of Christ, the matter is so clearly contained in the deposit of faith that denial of it should be said to be heresy."[71] Tromp's emphases are clear. His engagement with the long tradition of the church, and especially with the Fathers, is extensive. Nevertheless, these readings stand in service to illustrate that the mystical body of Christ is firmly grounded in the episcopacy and, ultimately, the pope.

My point here is not that Tromp is objectively wrong in this analysis but rather that his emphasis in elaborating a theology of the mystical body of Christ was that it be strictly identified with the Roman Catholic Church; indeed, evidence certainly suggests that this may have been the real goal of his project. For Tromp, that identification necessarily entails a strong and juridical emphasis on the bishops as the head of the body. The precariousness of mystical body theology was such that it needed to be grounded, to be rooted in some fleshier, concrete matter in order that it not become a false mysticism.

[68] Tromp, *Corpus Christi*, Latin rev., 144–50.

[69] Tromp, *Corpus Christi*, English, 198.

[70] Tromp, *Corpus Christi*, English, 194. This is the title of the final part of the book.

[71] Ibid. It is interesting that even in the revised edition of his work, after *Mystici Corporis*, that Tromp does not understand the identity between the Roman Catholic Church and the mystical body of Christ to have been solemnly defined.

Karl Adam and the German-Romantic Stream of Mystical Body Theology

Of course, a theological lineage of mystical body theology also remained in Germany, most especially among those on the faculty of the Tübingen School.

After stints at Strasbourg and Regensburg, the formidable theologian Karl Adam took on a chair at Tübingen in 1919 and also a good bit of the theological tradition of the university.[72] Adam stood at the vanguard of Catholic theology in the 1920s and 1930s but had been deeply influenced by the German-Romantic movement spearheaded by his nineteenth-century Tübingen forbears. Because of Adam's notoriety and long-lasting influence in Catholic theology,[73] he serves as a suitable representative of the German-Romantic stream of mystical body theology. To acknowledge that Adam absorbed Nazi race rhetoric and found in it firm grounding for the mystical body of Christ is not to say that every German thinker on the mystical body moved in the same direction, although some—such as Karl Eschweiler and the influential ecumenical historian Joseph Lortz—also did. Adam illustrates both the enormous potential of mystical body theology and, at the same time, its danger, detached from the sacramental life of the church, to veer into justification for other more nefarious englobulating visions.

Influenced as Adam was by the Tübingen heritage, he employed mystical body theology to argue against neoscholastic juridicism and individualistic congregationalism, both seen as overly Enlightenment driven, in his early and deeply influential book, *The Spirit of Catholicism* (1927). Adam emphasized the solidarity of the mystical body, members of which share in both sin and redemption by Christ's paschal mystery. His exegesis of St. Paul's exhortation to the Corinthians concerning the different

---

[72] See Robert A. Krieg, *Karl Adam: Catholicism in German Culture*, foreword by Walter Kasper (Notre Dame, IN: University of Notre Dame Press, 1992), 4–27.

[73] Walter Kasper calls him "one of the most celebrated Catholic theologians," "one of the great forerunners of the Second Vatican Council and of the postconciliar renewal of the church" in "Foreword" to Krieg, *Karl Adam*, vii. Pope Benedict XVI lists Adam's work among several "exhilarating" books about Jesus in the 1930s and 1940s in *Jesus of Nazareth: From the Baptism in the Jordan to the Transfiguration* (New York: Doubleday, 2007), xi.

functions of the body produced the insight that "the ultimate meaning of every vital Christian function lies precisely in its close relation to the complete organism, in its solidarity with the whole."[74] Following Möhler, he thinks of the church as an "organic unity" created by God.

Adam's organic unity did not float above history. Rather, he espoused a basic principle of mediation: "The supernatural reality is not manifested in naked truth, as it is in itself, but enters into the particular age and therefore in a form determined by that age,"[75] or, as he wrote in 1939, "the historical *milieu* will . . . be able to impress upon the external development of the Church its own individuality."[76] There were important ecumenical ramifications of the demand that the milieu places on the church. The persecution of heretics, now forbidden by canon law, was not of the church's essence but rather due to the particular character of the Middle Ages, in which "every revolt against the Catholic faith seemed . . . to be a moral crime, a sort of murder of the soul and of God, an offense more heinous than parricide."[77] The church's renunciation of the *auto-da-fé* opens a door of access to Catholicism's embrace of non-Catholic baptism and its broader conviction that the grace of Christ is ultimately unbounded.[78]

There was also a darker side to Adam's mystical body theology, which was rooted in his understanding of the relationship between the natural and the supernatural. In the quotations in the previous paragraph, note Adam's strong language: "determined by the age" and "impress upon." In themselves these statements indicate a robust sense of mediation. Adam's insistence on the appropriate natural conditions for the realization of the supernatural would, however, prove deeply problematic.

In the 1939 essay "The Mystery of Christ's Incarnation and of His Mystical Body," Adam spells out the character of the Jewish, Greek, Roman, and Germanic influences on the church. While the Greek emphasis on philosophical speculation, the Roman on structured authority, and the Germanic on restless profundity all have their advantages and excesses,

---

[74] Karl Adam, *The Spirit of Catholicism*, trans. Justin McCann, Milestones in Catholic Theology (New York: Crossroad, 1929; German orig., 1924), 97.

[75] Ibid., 210–15.

[76] Karl Adam, "The Mystery of Christ's Incarnation and of His Mystical Body," *Orate Fratres* 13, no. 9 (1939): 397.

[77] Adam, *The Spirit of Catholicism*, 170–75.

[78] Ibid., 99.

the Jewish mentality that deeply shaped Christianity's beginnings offered only the negative influence of legalism, Adam argues, which still "endangers . . . certain unenlightened pious souls."[79] In line with Nazi propaganda, Adam saw the Jewish influence as a particular threat to the unity of Christianity in his own day. An influential strain of German writing, including the work of German immigrant Houston Stewart Chamberlain, son-in-law of Richard Wagner, had tried to dissociate Jesus from Judaism completely. As late as 1943 Adam argued, however, that Jesus was indeed Jewish, but a Galilean, and therefore likely of mixed race. Further, because of the immaculate conception, Jesus' mother shared no "physical or moral connection with those ugly dispositions that we condemn in full-blooded Jews."[80] Adam takes Gröber's "devaluation of the historical Christ" in another direction, employing the Marian doctrine to trump Jesus' lineage. Adam had learned this theological twist of the immaculate conception from Richard Kleine, a pro-Nazi priest.[81] Adam went on to help Kleine establish a collective of pro-Nazi priests.[82]

It was essential that he work out some account of Jesus' heritage because, unlike for Pelz, the historical Jesus matters for Adam. The incarnation, Adam says, sets Christianity about uniting heaven and earth, the divine and the human, rather than separating them.[83] But Adam's particular construal of the relationship of nature and the supernatural posited the necessity of a natural unity as a prerequisite to the supernatural solidarity of the mystical body of Christ. Apart from its appalling racism, Adam's position suggests that God's grace is insufficient to bring

[79] Adam "The Mystery of Christ's Incarnation and of His Mystical Body," 397.

[80] Karl Adam, "Jesus, der Christus und wir Deutsche," *Wissenschaft und Weisheit* 10 (1943): 91, quoted in Robert Krieg, "Karl Adam, National Socialism, and Christian Tradition," *Theological Studies* 60 (1999): 447–48. See also John Connelly, "Reformer and Racialist: Karl Adam's Paradoxical Legacy," *Commonweal* (18 January 2008): 11.

[81] Kevin Spicer explains that in a letter Adam responded favorably to Kleine's 1939 essay, "Was Jesus a Jew?" in which Kleine employed the argument. Adam then gave prominence to the argument by including it in his own work. Kevin Spicer, "When Theology and Racism Mix: Catholicism, Anti-Semitism, and the Holocaust" (Ethel LeFrak Holocaust Education Conference, Seton Hill University, Greensburg, PA, 26 October 2015). See also Kevin Spicer, *Hitler's Priests: Catholic Clergy and National Socialism* (DeKalb: Northern Illinois University Press, 2008), esp. 189–90.

[82] Spicer, "When Theology and Racism Mix."

[83] Adam, "The Mystery of Christ's Incarnation and of His Mystical Body," 344.

about supernatural unity without the prerequisite efforts of nationalist purification. Unlike fellow German theologian Eschweiler,[84] Adam never joined the Nazi Party and refused to give the Nazi salutation of "*Heil, Hitler*,"[85] yet he came to see Hitler as the bearer of a rejuvenated national "blood unity"[86] and, therefore, as building the necessary natural foundation to the mystical body of Christ. Hitler was not to be hailed, but he drew attention to the importance of natural unity. The supernatural union of the mystical body of Christ, Adam reasoned, must be predicated on a natural racial-ethnic union of the *Volk*. The supernatural solidarity of the mystical body of Christ is possible only insofar as there is first a natural solidarity of the national body. Eschweiler shared Adam's vision of nature and grace if in an even more extreme form: If the swastika offends some Christians, it is because they hold a negative, Augustinian view of human nature, marred by a dualistic understanding of the relationship between nature and grace, rather than a Thomistic view, which posits an intrinsic union between the natural and supernatural orders.[87]

It is clear that Adam's particular appropriation of mystical body theology led him to some profound ecumenical insights. Further, his theology was not abstracted in the manner of Pelz's; that is, it does not sanction a view of deification in which the Christian *is* Christ *tout court*. Instead,

---

[84] The jury is still out on Pope Pius XII's record during the Second World War. Though we do know that as secretary of state in 1933 Cardinal Pacelli (the future Pius XII) had initiated canonical proceedings against Karl Eschweiler and Hans Barion for their support of Nazi sterilization law. Both were subsequently removed from priestly ministry until they recanted that support (Krieg, *Catholic Theologians*, 50). Eschweiler, who was buried in 1936 in his Nazi uniform, had argued that based on the Thomistic maxim that grace perfects nature, states had the right to sterilize those whom it found unfit to become parents precisely because God's grace cannot make up for such a natural deficiency. This same understanding of the relationship between nature and grace fueled Eschweiler's and Adam's understanding of the doctrine of the mystical body of Christ. As an interesting precursor to *Mystici Corporis*, Krieg notes that Pacelli worked to keep Adam's *The Spirit of Catholicism* off of the Index in the thirties (Krieg, *Karl Adam*, 51).

[85] Krieg, *Catholic Theologians*, 97. Krieg explains that at certain points in his career, especially when he publicly critiqued the neo-pagan strains in Nazism, Adam was even harassed by the SS.

[86] Quoted in Connelly, "Reformer and Racialist," 11.

[87] Krieg, *Catholic Theologians*, 48–49, 166.

Adam was concerned to ground mystical body theology in the concrete, but he did so in the particularity of the German nation—the national unity that would support the supernatural solidarity of the mystical body theology. In 1943, returning to his earlier emphasis on the interaction between the church and its encounter with particular cultures, Adam wrote in a letter to priest friend Josef Thomé, "I have always judged Nazism as a necessary, indeed a healthy reaction to certain excesses inside the Church and inside Christianity. I am thinking here of the Nazis' deep respect for the 'blood,' and in general for the realm of the body and of the senses against the Gnostic-Platonic overemphasis on the purely spiritual."[88] This is an example of the Germanic spirit correcting the Hellenistic.[89]

While Adam discusses the sacraments in many of his writings—his *Habilitationsschrift* was on Augustine's theology of the Eucharist[90]—he rarely, if ever, does so in conjunction with talk about the unity of the mystical body. *The Spirit of Catholicism*, for example, connects the unity of

[88] Quoted in Connelly, "Reformer and Racialist," 11.

[89] Charles E. Coughlin in America also engaged with mystical body theology to support his own anti-Semitism. Coughlin's version of mystical body theology came from Irish Holy Ghost father Denis Fahey. Fahey's (and Coughlin's) mystical body theology requires further research, but it appears that Fahey derived mystical body theology out of the Roman stream. He studied at the Gregorian in the early twentieth century but does not engage any of the key thinkers of that school in his work on the mystical body. See Mary Christine Athans, *The Coughlin-Fahey Connection: Father Charles E. Coughlin, Father Denis Fahey, C.S.Sp., and Religious Anti-Semitism in the United States, 1938–1954* (New York: Peter Lang, 1991), esp. 183–92. See also Denis Fahey, *The Mystical Body of Christ and the Reorganization of Society* (Cork, IE: Forum Press, 1945), 135–240. Fahey describes "the Jewish Nation," along with Satan and the Free Masons, as "organized anti-supernatural forces" of opposition to the mystical body of Christ, while explicitly denouncing any correlation between Hitler's vision and the mystical body of Christ (367). Virgil Michel denounced Fahey's earlier *The Mystical Body of Christ in the Modern World*, explaining that the book is not about the mystical body as such but rather about the cosmic struggle of the church with contemporary "satanic forces of darkness," including not only Rousseau and his disciples, but also "the conspiracy of Jewry, of which the author is overwhelmingly convinced." Michel's one hundred–word review of this 326-page book ends with "Quotations from papal encyclicals constitute much of the text for pages at a time." Virgil Michel, "The Mystical Body of Christ in the Modern World," *Orate Fratres* (1936): 236.

[90] Karl Adam, *Die Eucharistielehre des hl. Augustin* (Paderborn: F. Schöningh, 1908).

the mystical body to the incarnation—the unity of the divine and human natures in Christ—but there is not an intrinsic relationship to the liturgical life of the church. Adam elevates the seven sacraments, which "sanctify all [of life's] heights and depths," and emphasizes that the church, through them, conveys God's grace to the members.[91] When Adam discusses the basis of the mystical body, however, instead of turning to the sacramental action of Eucharist, for example, he turns toward the primary unity of an ethnic-racial people. In order for the mystical body to be truly alive, it must build on "the concrete person with his blood-determined condition."[92]

In contrast to Adam, fellow German Romano Guardini explains the mystical body this way:

> Their fellowship consists in community of intention, thought and language, in the direction of eyes and heart to the one aim; it consists in their identical belief, the identical sacrifice which they offer, the Divine Food which nourishes them all alike; in the one God and Lord Who unites them mystically in Himself. But individuals in their quality of distinct corporeal entities do not among themselves intrude upon each other's inner life.[93]

For Guardini there is, perhaps idealistic, interplay between the unity of the mystical body and the individual, grounded firmly in the liturgical celebration of the church. Guardini criticized Nazism as early as 1935, with an article that impugned Hitler for inserting himself in people's lives in the place that only Jesus should stand.[94] In 1939, the Nazi Party dismissed Guardini from his post at the University of Berlin.[95]

It should be clear that these differences between Adam and Guardini are not reducible to any conventional construal of conservative or

---

[91] Adam, *The Spirit of Catholicism*, 176–92.

[92] Karl Adam, "Deutsches Volkstum und katholisches Christentum," *Theologische Quartalschrift* 114 (1933): 56. Quoted in Krieg, *Catholic Theologians*, 167.

[93] Romano Guardini, *The Spirit of the Liturgy*, trans. Ada Lane, Milestones in Catholic Theology (New York: Crossroad, 1998; German orig., 1918), 42.

[94] Krieg, *Catholic Theologians*, 107.

[95] Romano Guardini, *The Essential Guardini: An Anthology of the Writings of Romano Guardini*, ed. Heinz R. Kuehn (Chicago: Liturgy Training Publications, 1997), 8.

liberal leanings. In fact, Krieg characterizes both, along with Eschweiler, Lortz, and Engelbert Krebs, as "progressive theologians" who "contributed in their respective ways to the fermentation in Catholicism that eventually eroded neo-scholasticism."[96] In other words, all of these theologians challenged the received narrowness of theology as commentary on St. Thomas's commentators and instead argued for a more dynamic theology engaged with the contemporary context. As such, they all have common cause with the *ressourcement* movement in France.

Guardini's deep involvement in the burgeoning liturgical movement connected him not only with the monks at Maria Laach in Germany[97] but also with the other centers of liturgical renewal in Europe. Clearly, with some important variance in context, those involved in the liturgical movement expressed a theology of the mystical body that was, not surprisingly, firmly grounded in the liturgy and sacraments of the church.[98]

Mersch, Beauduin, and the French-Speaking Socio-liturgical Stream of Mystical Body Theology

In the French-speaking sphere, mystical body theology always had a bit of a different cast. It was at the same time less grandiose, less sweeping (and therefore less amenable to the all-encompassing vision of National Socialism), and more theologically pervasive. Theologians such as Marie-Dominique Chenu, Congar, de Lubac, and other scholars of the mystical body stream in France during this period share a general approach with Mersch and Beauduin, who are engaged with mystical body

---

[96] Krieg, *Catholic Theologians*, 172.

[97] Odo Casel's "mystery theology" is an interesting study here. Keith Pecklers claims that Casel's "interpretation of the sacraments gave way to a very positive and rich view of the Church as the Mystical Body of Christ which expresses itself relationally and symbolically through sacramental participation" (*The Unread Vision*, 6). Like Guardini, Casel's involvement in the liturgical movement likely grounded his mystical body theology firmly in the church's public worship.

[98] Keith Pecklers argues that the German liturgical movement was much more intellectualist and elitist, while the Belgian one was aimed at the parish level (*The Unread Vision*, 14). He also mentions Beauduin's somewhat demure regret that "we are aristocrats of the liturgy" (11). Much of Beauduin's work illustrates his attempts to overcome a class gulf.

theology in Belgium.[99] The treatment here focuses on Mersch, however, because he is recognized as *the* major exponent of mystical body theology during this period and on Beauduin because he is the paramount early influence on Michel.

Supernatural Solidarity

Mersch's groundbreaking series of *ressourcement* studies on the mystical body of Christ situated the doctrine in a wider historical context. Mersch was trained in philosophy and then theology at Leuven in the second decade of the twentieth century, where Belgian Jesuits developed a renewal of Thomism in response to *Aeterni Patris*. Two of those Jesuits, Pierre Scheuer and Joseph Maréchal, guided Mersch in his philosophy studies.[100] These influences gave Mersch different theological reflexes

---

[99] For example, Yves Congar writes, "The establishing and unifying of the Mystical Body are, in St. Paul, dependent on sacramental activity," in *The Mystery of the Church* (London: Geoffrey Chapman, 1965; French orig., 1953), 30. Those few words illustrate that, for Congar, mystical body theology was grounded in the sacraments. It brings the differences into sharp relief when placed next to Tromp's line quoted above: "In Paul's thought the Body of Christ is that visible hierarchical organization such as existed at the time." Congar himself did go through some development on the question of the mystical body, as Elizabeth Teresa Groppe ably demonstrates in *Yves Congar's Theology of the Holy Spirit*, The American Academy of Religion Academy Series, ed. Kimberly Rae Connor (New York: Oxford University Press, 2004). Marie-Dominique Chenu, for his part, never tired of emphasizing the social ramifications of a theology of the mystical body that pervaded the Christian life. For example, "The continuing incarnation, the Mystical Body of Christ; such will be the future classic theme of a spirituality in which the world of work will find its level and its place in Christianity, and not by the acquisition of merits alone." See Marie-Dominique Chenu, *The Theology of Work: An Exploration*, trans. Lilian Soiron (Chicago: H. Regnery, 1963; French orig., 1955), 24. Or, again, "The convergence of the tendency to class solidarity and the doctrine of the mystical body of Christ is the perfect example of the just balance of the Christian plan. The divine brotherhood is not something confined to extraordinary mystical cases but is made incarnate from day to day in the most human, most earthly solidarities." See *Faith and Theology*, trans. Denis Hickey (New York: Macmillan, 1968; French orig., 1964), 200. In the beginning of this chapter, Chenu refers to a First Communion feast that transcended the boundaries of social classes and thus, like the early Christians, "made concrete . . . vague aspirations of human solidarity" (185–87).

[100] James Arraj, *Mind Aflame: The Theological Vision of One of the World's Great Theologians, Emile Mersch* (Chiloquin, OR: Inner Growth Books and Videos, 1994),

than those of the Roman stream. Instead of the rationalistic tendencies of neoscholasticism, which led to considerable data cataloguing, Mersch imbibed an approach to revelation that emphasized relational knowledge irreducible to the ideas and doctrines it produces. Mersch became enthralled with the doctrine of the mystical body of Christ after giving a seminar presentation on it in 1917. Pierre Charles, SJ, attended that presentation. When, in 1920, Father General Wlodimir Ledóchowski sent an inquiry to Charles and another Jesuit professor on account of their espousal of Pierre Rousselot's ideas, Mersch wrote to Ledóchowski, taking up their support. A few months after defending his confrères from suspected Modernist tendencies, Mersch received a letter from his provincial that effectively removed him from theological teaching. Assigned to teach philosophy and minister to lay students at the University of Namur, Mersch was disheartened but continued theological research privately.[101]

In 1933, Mersch published *Le corps mystique du Christ: Études de la théologie historique*.[102] At the beginning of what came to be received as the *tour de force* of the twentieth-century renewal of mystical body theology, Mersch anticipates the error that Pelz would make six years later. He describes the false view that the faithful are made really and absolutely into Christ himself. Such a view leads either to disdain for human actions because they are not those of Christ or exaggerated esteem for them because they are those of Christ himself.[103] For Mersch, mystical body theology works against this pantheistic or "panchristic" error.

It is particularly important for Mersch to disavow the pantheistic (or false mystical) position from the start because he follows a line of theological thinking that is rooted in the Eastern patristics and generally foreign to Western theology, especially in his day. Mersch explains two orthodox views of mystical body theology. One emphasizes an ontological union with Christ, "a unity that transcends the biological realties from

---

13–14. As reflected in the title, Arraj's treatment of Mersch is hagiographical, but it nevertheless provides some important details about his life.

[101] Gregory E. Malanowski, "Emile Mersch, SJ (1890–1940): Un Christocentrisme unifié," *Nouvelle Revue Théologique* 112 (1990): 44–45.

[102] Émile Mersch, *Le corps mystique du Christ: Études de la théologie historique*, 2 vols. (Louvain: Museum Lessianum, 1933). Hereafter, Mersch, *Le corps mystique du Christ*, first ed.

[103] Mersch, *The Whole Christ*, 6.

which they are taken." "It must be clearly understood," Mersch continues, "that this term is by no means synonymous with 'nebulous' or 'semi-real.' On the contrary, it signifies something which in plentitude and reality surpasses the things of nature and the positive concepts that our reason can elaborate." [104] Mersch eventually draws on the great opponent of the Nestorians, Cyril of Alexandria, to explain that the Eucharist is the means of effecting the real union of the mystical body. The sacramental action is indeed real but not hypostatic.[105]

The second view, an implicit but clear characterization of the neoscholastic approach, also upholds a real union with Christ but a more tenuous one, a union only in the moral order, a union of accord in Christic action. Applying terms from the *theotokos* debate, Mersch eventually contrasts Cyril's theology with that of Cyprian, whose mystical body theology produces only a moral unity, not realism.[106]

Mersch explains that, while both have their value, he favors the first approach, which is "richer in doctrine," more mysterious, and more in line with Scripture and the long view of tradition. The second has the advantage of greater clarity and "is easier to explain and understand." [107] Mersch's preferences are even clearer when his historical study reaches the scholastics, where he finds little of the richness he found in earlier, especially Eastern, articulations of the theology of the mystical body. "The doctrine," he confesses, "always and necessarily retains a certain vagueness which, to judge from the mentality of many of the Scholastics, was scarcely calculated to win their sympathy." [108] At the end of this

---

[104] Ibid., 9.

[105] Ibid., 346–47, 355.

[106] Ibid., 383. Though Cyril's denunciation of "moral union" comes from his characterization of fellow easterner Nestorius's position on the union of the human and the divine in Christ, Mersch enjoys pointing out that the major difference between the East and the West during this period is that the latter had a "special and profound interest in moral problems and in rules of conduct" (367).

[107] Ibid., 10.

[108] Ibid., 452. Joseph Clifford Fenton wrote a vigorous defense that mystical body theology is to be found in scholastic theology in "An Accusation against School Theology," *American Ecclesiastical Review* 110, no. 3 (1944): 213–22. True to his methodology, Fenton breaks down the doctrine of the mystical body into component doctrinal pieces and then finds them in various scholastic treatises. The following lines sum up his position: "There is not one dogmatic element in the *Mystici Corporis* neglected

section, Mersch sums up his reflections: "Though the picture is more distinct, it is also less vivid. The Scholastics indicate more clearly the nature of the mystery, but they do not describe it with vigor and forcefulness. Their doctrine possesses neither the amplitude and richness in which St. Cyril had clothed it, nor the depth of interior life that characterized it in the writings of Augustine." [109]

Mersch makes an essential point about the French stream here. We should take his discussion of the scholastics as at least a gentle critique of the neoscholasticism dominant in Catholic theology at the time Mersch was writing. While neoscholasticism generally produced remarkably clear treatises and what I have called the Roman stream of mystical body theology gained clarity in grounding the theology in the juridical structures of the church, this juridical emphasis overshadowed the liturgical mystery that grounded the French stream.

Mersch does not engage the work of Möhler substantially, only citing his study of Athanasius in the patristic section.[110] And, though he explores the preparatory schema at Vatican I based on the mystical body, he does not mention the Roman school's recovery of the image, ascribing the schema simply to the "Fathers of the Vatican Council." [111] Mersch does mention Jesuit neoscholastic Josef Kleutgen's revision of the same schema, which served to push the mystical body of Christ to the background.[112]

The most recent source of vibrant mystical body theology is to be found in the early modern French school: "The energy and richness which the doctrine of the Mystical Body loses at the hands of the Schoolmen

---

or overlooked in the standard literature of school theology since the Middle Ages. Obviously not every author taught every point. Again, there were various individual writers and teachers who presented elements of the Mystical Body doctrine imperfectly and incompletely. The charge however is leveled at school theology as such, and that charge cannot be sustained" (215).

[109] Mersch, *The Whole Christ*, 484–85.

[110] Ibid., 250.

[111] Ibid., 560–65.

[112] Ibid., 564–65. Kleutgen was German by birth and served in several Vatican posts in the mid-nineteenth century. He played a large role in the neoscholastic revival and is chiefly known for composing *Aeterni Patris*, which made St. Thomas's philosophy normative for Catholic theology.

is restored by the masters of the French Oratory and of St. Sulpice."[113] Mersch is particularly impressed by—"echoing," as it does, "the words of St. Cyril of Alexandria"—Pierre de Bérulle's account of the Eucharist drawing us into the divine life, making us into Christ's mystical body, "a real and substantial union."[114] For these thinkers, the mystical body of Christ "becomes a sort of system of spirituality" whereby the Christian life is the prolongation of the incarnation. Mersch explains, however, that since Bérulle found Christ's human nature to lack individuality, Christian existence demands a total renunciation of the self.[115] In the end Mersch finds the French school, especially after Bérulle, too negative and too rigorist, but their achievement—a lively theology of the mystical body that pervaded the whole of Christian doctrine and life—was nevertheless an inspiration to Mersch.[116]

On reaching the end of his study, Mersch confesses that initial forays into his topic returned minimal results. He had expected to find scores of references to the mystical body among the writings of the fathers, but, looking primarily at discussions of the church, he found the doctrine "only dimly visible." It was only when, Mersch explains, he broadened his range of vision that he discovered mystical body theology suffused throughout patristic treatises:

---

[113] Ibid., 531. It should be noted that the term "French school" is one disputed by scholars of the vibrant seventeenth century in France. My use of the term follows Mersch's. I intend it in its more restrictive sense to refer to the insights primarily of Bérulle but also of Jean-Jacques Olier, whom the Sulpicians followed, rather than its wider sense to include everyone who added to the spiritual heritage of seventeenth-century France.

[114] Ibid., 536. These latter words are Bérulle's, quoted by Mersch from the former's *Discours de l'eucharistie*, 1, no. 8, 457.

[115] Mersch, *The Whole Christ*, 539.

[116] Ibid., 544. Mersch has an interesting theory about the French school's "degradation of nature." He writes: "Absolute monarchy and enlightened despotism were beginning to assert themselves in politics; the deference and self-effacement of courtiers in the presence of human majesties offered a convenient illustration of the proper attitude to be taken before the King of Kings. At all events, rigorism was in vogue; nature had to be degraded, all but crushed, lest it spoil God's work."

What we discovered was far better than we had hoped for. Life is not something juxtaposed to what it animates; it lies within. Similarly, the truth of the Mystical Body is not restricted to any one part of Christian teaching; it is everywhere. Just as the Christ of whom it speaks is present in all the faithful in order to communicate light and strength to all, so the Mystical Body is somehow present in every dogma, giving each truth a new meaning for the interior life and a new lesson to guide the actions, thoughts, and affections of men. . . .

The fathers taught the truth of our incorporation in Christ in connection with practically every dogma of our faith; or rather, they presupposed this truth in their explanations of dogma. . . . They fought for the dogmas of ecclesiology, of grace, of the Real Presence, of the value of good works; and each time, in order to give these truths a better expression, they have mentioned the Mystical Body. They all followed this method.[117]

In the end Mersch found that the mystical body of Christ was not limited to ecclesiological reflections but pervaded writing on the Trinity, Christology, sacraments, ascetic practice, and deification. Likewise, the mystical body theology of the French stream was not simply an ecclesiological contribution but a fundamental theological category.

This methodological insight explains Mersch's appreciation for the French school, whose mystical body theology is diffuse but lively in contrast to the wooden edifice of scholasticism. In addition to its rigorism, the theology of the French school tended to emphasize the unity of the person with Christ over the union of the person with other persons in Christ. Mersch himself articulates a theology of the mystical body that upholds the role of the individual but emphasizes the union with others that comes with growing closer to, becoming the mystical body of, Christ.[118]

---

[117] Ibid., 580.

[118] Avery Dulles sums up Mersch's approach nicely in scholastic terminology: "Dissatisfied with the Western scholastic tendency to depict the relationship of Christ to the Church in terms of principal and instrumental causality, Mersch adhered to the Eastern patristic tradition, especially Cyril of Alexandria, who stressed the physical and organic union between the head and the members. The Church according to this view is a prolongation of Christ, who acts upon it from within rather than as an external efficient cause" (Dulles, "A Half Century of Ecclesiology," 421–22).

For Mersch, mystical body theology addresses a host of contemporary problems: naturalism, individualism, that "more dangerous and more aggressive egoism which is known as nationalism," and "unbridled economic liberalism." [119] Across seven years (1928–1934), Mersch preached Days of Recollection for the *Jeunesse Ouvrière Chrétienne* (Young Christian Workers) movement in Namur, Belgium. [120] The JOC, as it was commonly known, was founded by Belgian priest Joseph Cardijn as part of his goals to reconcile the church with the labor movement in the 1920s. [121] Since this was the period during which Mersch was writing *The Whole Christ*, it would be surprising if he did not thematize the mystical body of Christ in his JOC retreats, especially since Mersch calls the mystical body of Christ a theological descriptor for the "supernatural solidarity that makes us members of one another." [122] This characterization signifies a key difference between Mersch and Tromp. For Mersch, the mystical body of Christ is not utterly determined by the bounds of the visible Roman Catholic Church. [123] Rather, in terms of act and potency, the mystical body encompasses, in some sense, all of humanity. A translator's note from Mersch's more systematic work, *The Theology of the Mystical Body*, confirms what is implicit throughout his scholarship: "Like the Greek Fathers, Mersch sometimes uses the term 'mystical body' in a wider sense, including not only actual members, but also potential members of the Church." [124]

[119] Mersch, *The Whole Christ*, 573.

[120] Arraj, *Mind Aflame*, 15. See also Malanowski, "Emile Mersch, SJ," 45.

[121] Craig Prentiss, *Debating God's Economy: Social Justice in America on the Eve of Vatican II* (University Park, PA: Penn State University Press, 2008), 126.

[122] Mersch, *Le corps mystique du Christ*, first ed., vol. 2, 345. This translation is my own. In French, *la solidarité surnaturelle qui nous fait membres les uns des autres*. Interestingly, Mersch (or his editor) changed the sentence for the second edition published in 1936, three years after the first. There, the phrase reads, *la solidarité surnaturelle qui fait les chrétiens membres les uns des autres*. From Mersch, *Le corps mystique du Christ: Études de la théologie historique*, vol. 2, second ed. (Paris, Desclée de Brouwer, 1946), 376. Hereafter, Mersch, *Le corps mystique du Christ*. While Arraj does note that Mersch had some back and forth with censors, one can only speculate what precisely led to this textual change.

[123] Mersch, *The Whole Christ*, 50, 480, 487.

[124] Mersch, *The Theology of the Mystical Body*, trans. Cyril Vollert (St. Louis: Herder, 1951), 197. The final version of this work was published posthumously in

Mersch understands the fundamental relationship between nature and the supernatural, a relationship that undergirds his mystical body theology, differently from Adam. Like Adam, Mersch describes the supernatural unity of the mystical body, but unlike Adam, he neither limits the range of what constitutes natural unity nor finds such a firm distinction between the two. He writes, "The 'mystery' is before all else a prodigy of unity. God has raised to a supernatural perfection the natural unity that exists between [*sic*] men."[125] Notice the lack of any particular subset of humanity indicated by these lines from Mersch (except, of course, the typical archaic use of "men" [*les hommes*] to indicate all of humanity). The contrast between Adam's and Mersch's theology of the mystical body is clearly connected to their rendering of the nature/supernatural relationship. For Adam, the supernatural unity of the mystical body is built on the natural unity of the *Volk*. For Mersch, the unity of the mystical body brings to completion the potentiality already present among all human beings. Mersch expresses this even more clearly when he explains that the Stoic and Platonist conceptions of the world as a gigantic body are amenable to the patristic development of mystical body theology. He says, "The supernatural order . . . is not simply superimposed upon the natural order; it takes the natural order, and adapts its elements to its own purposes."[126]

Mersch's project brought together the whispers of the mystical body recovery circulating in the first years of the twentieth century. He brought the depth of the tradition in order to bolster the nascent movement. But Mersch died, tragically, in France trying to help a wounded priest during a German air raid in May 1940. A barely unfinished draft of the third, heavily revised, version of *La théologie du corps mystique* was lost in the suitcases from which he had been separated in the chaos.[127]

Socio-liturgical Reform

His fellow Belgian, Benedictine liturgical reformer Beauduin, had been thinking about the mystical body in the years before Mersch undertook his

---

1944, compiled from several drafts that Mersch left behind. This translation is from the second edition of that work, published in French in 1946.

[125] Mersch, *The Whole Christ*, 3.

[126] Ibid., 100.

[127] Arraj, *Mind Aflame*, 18–19.

major work. Beauduin, who has been called the "father of the twentieth century Liturgical Movement,"[128] saw the recovery of a deeper sense of the liturgy as his primary work, flowing out of the Benedictine monastery at Mont César in Leuven. Beauduin's path to liturgical reformer was somewhat atypical, deeply shaped as it was by his turn-of-the-century role as a labor chaplain with the Congrégation des Aumôniers du Travail (Chaplains of Labor), a local Belgian response to the emphasis on labor in *Rerum Novarum*. Beauduin took that position in 1899, shortly after his ordination, and left to join the Benedictines in 1906, after the Aumôniers ceased direct contact with the workers, that is, when they pulled back in their exercise of concrete solidarity.[129] Founded in 1894 by Théophile Reyn, the Aumôniers emphasized the solidarity of the church with the workers, especially in striving for a just wage.[130] Beauduin in particular oversaw the group's construction of several buildings to provide housing for workers in Montegnée.[131] They were, in a way, precursors to the worker-priest movement in France a few decades later, although, unlike the worker-priests, who set aside clerical garb and formal ministry to labor with dock and factory workers, the Aumôniers kept their formal priestly ministry. Both initiatives responded to the decay of Catholic practice and growth of Marxist ideology among the working classes. Both were controversial. The Aumôniers were eventually endorsed by the Belgian bishops and later received papal recognition, which led to their expansion outside of Belgium. They continue to operate trade schools in several countries today.

Beauduin would later reflect on the christological core of authentic efforts at human solidarity. In 1930, he wrote to his friend Jean Jadot: "The whole of the great supernatural organism, of the tremendous reality of the visible world (but much more real than the visible world), of the mystical body which envelops us, is the glorified body of the risen Christ."[132] This

---

[128] Alcuin Reid, Introduction to Lambert Beauduin, *Liturgy, the Life of the Church*, 3rd ed. (Hampshire: Saint Michael's Abbey Press, 2002), 9.

[129] Kurt Belsole, "Beauduin, Lambert," in *The Encyclopedia of Monasticism*, ed. William M. Johnston, vol. 1 (Chicago: Fitzroy Dearborn, 2000), 117.

[130] Pecklers, *The Unread Vision*, 9–10.

[131] Ibid., 10.

[132] Beauduin to Jean Jadot, 1930. Quoted in Sonya A. Quitslund, *Beauduin: A Prophet Vindicated* (New York: Newman Press, 1973), 256.

all-encompassing vision of Christ's mystical body is what drove Beauduin's efforts at solidarity, but after his Benedictine formation, Beauduin came to see the centrality of the liturgy in supporting the exercise of solidarity. In the context of Benedictine prayer life, Beauduin came to the conclusion that, in the words of Pecklers, "It was the liturgy and only the liturgy that was capable of giving the necessary grounding to Christian social activism." [133] Thus Beauduin integrated the Benedictine emphasis on liturgical prayer as the shape of life with his own earlier social efforts. But more than that, Beauduin sees mystical body theology driving a particularly socially inflected form of liturgical reform.

Methodologically, Beauduin wanted liturgical reform in the vein of the *ressourcement* movement before that movement really developed in the 1940s. [134] He thought that blatant calls for reform would be hasty and shortsighted. Instead, reformers should first strive to understand the liturgy as received in the tradition. This required the methods of history, philology, and archaeology. Having therein discerned the "spirit of the liturgy," obsolescence would fall away. [135] Grasping the Eucharist as the center of the liturgical celebration was a key component of Beauduin's recovery of the "spirit of the liturgy." [136] Pius X's revitalization of the Eucharist in Catholic piety, thought Beauduin, was the beginning of a reorientation of Catholic life, but he was disappointed that Pius didn't emphasize Communion as an integral part of the Mass. Beauduin's biographer recounts the enthusiasm with which he told his students what he had discovered while celebrating Mass—that in the eucharistic celebration the church takes on flesh. [137]

As the church is constituted in the liturgy, the latter is also morally formative; it challenges the worshiping community to live concretely as the mystical body of Christ. Beauduin wrote:

[133] Pecklers, *The Unread Vision*, 11.

[134] Louis Bouyer specifically calls Beauduin's work a "return to the sources" in his *The Church of God: Body of Christ and Temple of the Spirit*, trans. Charles Underhill Quinn (San Francisco: Ignatius Press, 2011; French orig., 1970), 155.

[135] Bernard Botte, *From Silence to Participation: An Insider's View of the Liturgical Movement*, trans. John Sullivan (Washington, DC: Pastoral Press, 1988), 22–23.

[136] Quitslund, *Beauduin*, 17ff.

[137] Ibid., 16.

> There is no doubt that the liturgical books have nothing of the
> scientific exposition about them; they are not treatises, any more
> than are the holy Gospels or the apostolic writings. Dogma is not
> proposed there under the form of canons or theses; revelation is
> not systematized and abstracted but is found in its pristine state—
> as the schoolmen say, *exercita*, intertwined with life itself.[138]

Beauduin clearly grants primacy to the aesthetic quality of the liturgy over
the clarifying function of the scholastic treatise. It is in this aesthetic sense
that the liturgy constitutes an abundant fount for living the Christian life.
The liturgical movement, as Beauduin conceived of it and lived it, exegeted
and worked to develop the liturgy as rich fodder for spiritual growth in
ways that neoscholastic writing could not. Mystical body theology is a key
way of characterizing that richness for this liturgical reformer.

Dissatisfied with what had been written for the Catholic in the pew,
Beauduin began journals for priests and laity, emphasized the connection between liturgy and daily life, and aimed at translating the symbolic
complexities of the liturgy into widely understandable language. The apex
of the liturgy is the celebration of the Eucharist, about which Beauduin
wrote, "The chief aim of our Lord in instituting the Eucharist was not that
of being a permanent Host in our tabernacles, but that of realizing every
day and in every member of Christ the mystery of the death and life of
the head by means of the Eucharistic Sacrifice and Sacrament."[139] His eucharistic theology was not limited to individual piety but flowered into an
impulse toward the union of all of humanity. In the words of Beauduin's
biographer, "The sacred species enflesh Christ in the Christian, initiating
his slow resurrection into Christ's glorified humanity."[140] Since Christ
came for all, Christians, having received the Body and Blood of Christ,
willingly give themselves up for all.

Louis Bouyer explains that Beauduin avoided the extremes of the
apologists who wanted to have "death on the corporal," in order to make
the sacrament real, and those who spiritualized the sacrifice of the altar,

---

[138] Beauduin, "Abbot Marmion and the Liturgy," *Orate Fratres* 22 (16 May 1948): 312.

[139] Lambert Beauduin, *Liturgy, the Life of the Church*, trans. Virgil Michel (Collegeville, MN: Liturgical Press, 1926), 56.

[140] Quitslund, *Beauduin*, 245.

acting as if it were "the affair of disincarnate souls and for the isolated."[141] Beauduin emphasized that as the elements themselves are transubstantiated into the Body of Christ, so too is the church made one symbolic offering. In fact, Beauduin uses the term "mystical body of Christ" interchangeably for Eucharist and for assembly, taking advantage of the wordplay in saying that Christ offers his mystical body on the altar.[142]

Like Mersch's, Beauduin's mystical body theology has a different genealogy than those versions that flourished in Germany and in Rome. In the same year (1906) that he left the Aumôniers, Beauduin joined the monastery of Mont César in Leuven. There, he was inspired and guided by Prior Columba Marmion. Marmion, who was beatified in the same September 2000 ceremony as Pius IX, John XXIII, and William Chaminade, helped to found Mont César and was its first prior before returning to Maredsous in 1909. When Beauduin entered Mont César he was thirty-three years old. He had a developed spirituality that was not particularly Benedictine and, as he would later admit, not very liturgical.[143] Marmion was a key figure in acclimating Beauduin to the Benedictine life. Beauduin called their relationship one of "respectful intimacy"[144] and, even though they disagreed on some matters, it appears that Beauduin received mystical body theology initially through Marmion's spirituality.[145] Marmion provided the intellectual underpinning that led to Beauduin's prayerful insight about the centrality of the liturgy, which Beauduin called "the language of the Church."[146]

---

[141] Louis Bouyer, *Dom Lambert Beauduin: Un homme d'église* (Paris: Casterman, 1964), 78.

[142] Lambert Beauduin, *Mélanges liturgiques : Recueillis parmi les œuvres de Dom Lambert Beauduin à l' occasion de ses 80 Ans (1873-1953)* (Louvain: Centre Liturgiques, 1954), 109–10.

[143] Quitslund, *Beauduin*, 9–11.

[144] Beauduin, "Abbot Marmion and the Liturgy," 303n1. Beauduin critiqued Marmion for being too presentist and static in his approach to the liturgy, for not having enough of a sense of *ressourcement* as it pertains to the liturgy (306). These shortcomings, Beauduin claims, were related to Marmion's insistence on "scrupulous and single-minded adherence to the Church's presentday [sic] law," which "preclude[ed] criticism in any other sphere" (305).

[145] See Pecklers, *The Unread Vision*, 10.

[146] Beauduin, "Abbot Marmion and the Liturgy," 305.

Bouyer, himself an Oratorian, argues that Marmion was the father of the "spiritual movement's" strain of mystical body theology in France, which was centered on divine filiation and emphasized the Christian as *alter Christus* (another Christ).[147] Around 1933, Beauduin read and enjoyed Mersch's two volumes on the mystical body.[148] As we have seen, Mersch argues that the French Oratory and the Sulpicians restored vibrancy to mystical body theology that had been lost by the scholastics. It is from this stream of French spirituality that the mystical body theology of Marmion and, in turn, Beauduin traces its roots.[149]

When in 1907 Beauduin was assigned to teach a course on the church, he developed it around the mystical body of Christ.[150] But fundamentally, for Beauduin, the mystical body of Christ was a broad descriptor of life after the incarnation.[151] Beauduin wrote regarding the incarnation, it "groups all humanity into a vast moral organism of which Christ is the head. . . . His whole terrestrial work is above all collective and belongs

---

[147] Bouyer, *The Church of God*, 154–57. Though he finds "Body of Christ" a very rich image for the church, Bouyer thought that mystical body of Christ theology was sometimes dangerous because it often resulted in a highly spiritualized (ungrounded) ecclesiology that tended toward a devaluation of the visible church and "warps the biblical texts" (165). He laid out these arguments in "Où en est la théologie du corps mystique?," *Revue des Sciences Religieuses* 28 (1948): 313–33. Henri de Lubac calls this article "a study written in reaction against Wikenhauser's unilateral exegesis in *Die Kirche als der mystische Leid Christi nach dem Apostel Paulus* (1937)" in *The Splendor of the Church*, trans. Michael Mason (San Francisco: Ignatius Press, 1986), 120n151. In the article, Bouyer argues that in France, theologies of the mystical body have tended to play fast and loose with the tradition, resulting in a parallel problem to that of Karl Pelz in Germany. Wikenhauser's exegesis in question argues that Paul has a more individualized understanding of deification. Thus, when he discusses "Body of Christ" in 1 Corinthians and Romans, he is referring primarily to the union of the individual with Christ. Bouyer rejects this outright (328).

[148] Quitslund, *Beauduin*, 243.

[149] John Saward, "Bérulle and the 'French school,'" in *The Study of Spirituality*, ed. Cheslyn Jones, Geoffrey Wainwright, and Edward Yarnold (New York: Oxford University Press, 1986), 395n2.

[150] Belsole, "Beauduin," 117–18.

[151] Quitslund, *Beauduin*, 243. Quitslund's analysis of Beauduin's mystical body theology under that heading leaves much to be desired because, like many others, she restricts her consideration to ecclesiology. The more interesting points concerning the mystical body theology arise in her explanation of his Christology.

to the whole of humanity." [152] In this, Beauduin differed from his mentor Marmion in at least two respects: first, Beauduin saw radical liturgical and social implications bound up in the theology of the mystical body; second, Beauduin thought that the profundity of the liturgy could and should be brought to the faithful in the pews, rather than reserved to religious and clergy. [153]

Amid some friction with his Mont César brethren after returning from service in the First World War, Beauduin took a position as a lecturer in liturgy at Sant'Anselmo (Rome) in 1921. Apparently Beauduin's social efforts and emphases began to alarm his brother Benedictines. His biographer reports that "his version of Benedictine spirituality had become overwhelmingly non-Benedictine in their eyes with its emphasis on the social dimensions of human relations." [154] Yet, Beauduin began enthusiastic work on what he understood as the imperative toward Christian unity that flowed from the Eucharist. On the sixteenth centenary of the Council of Nicaea (1925), Pius XI encouraged Benedictines to foster studies and programs that would address the profound division between Roman Catholics and the Orthodox. Beauduin established a priory at Amay-sur-Meuse in order to engage with the East on the common ground of monasticism in their respective traditions. [155] To his friend Olivier Rousseau in 1924, Beauduin described this project as rooted in the mystical body: the *Principe ascétique unique* ("unique ascetic principle") of Amay, he wrote, was *ut unum sint, le Corps mystique* (that all may be one, the mystical Body). [156] In 1926, he

---

[152] Lambert Beauduin, *Notre piété pendant l'avent* (Louvain: Mont César, 1919), 45–46. See Quitslund, *Beauduin*, 254. I have followed Quitslund's translation.

[153] Beauduin even attributes Marmion's lofty sense of the liturgy to his Irish background—that Irish Catholic churches had to be underground and discreet during Cromwell's reign. See Beauduin, "Abbot Marmion and the Liturgy," 308–9. He says further that Marmion's contacts with parishioners were infrequent, that his apostolate was exercised primarily in religious houses.

[154] Quitslund, *Beauduin*, 51.

[155] Ibid., 110–16.

[156] Beauduin to Olivier Rousseau, Rome, 29 May 1924. Quoted in Raymond Loonbeek and Jacques Mortiau, *Un pionnier: Dom Lambert Beauduin (1873–1960): Liturgie et unité des chrétiens*, University of Louvain Works of History and Philology, vol. 1 (Louvain-la-Neuve: Éditions de Chevetogne, 2001), 427. These authors also note the intrinsic connection between the liturgy, the mystical body, and ecumenism for Beauduin: *"Sa docilité a la liturgie, culte du Corps mystique, le conduit inévitablement—*

established the ecumenical journal *Irénikon*. In 1928 Pope Pius XI became concerned about the direction of Beauduin's work and asked him to step down as prior.

The eucharistic-ecumenical emphasis of Beauduin's mystical body theology eventually led him to found another ecumenical monastery, located in Chevetogne, in which Western monks would worship, study, and write about Christian unity as well as make sojourns to Eastern monasteries.[157] Angelo Roncalli (future Pope John XXIII) had met Beauduin on a chance encounter at Sant'Atanasio (Rome) in 1925. Roncalli had just been appointed apostolic delegate to Bulgaria and asked Beauduin about a secretary. Beauduin recommended his friend Constantin Bosschaerts, who served Roncalli throughout his time in Bulgaria and kept his employer abreast of Beauduin's developing work.[158] Roncalli stayed in touch with Beauduin throughout the years. They met several times in southern France while Roncalli was nuncio in Paris, and Roncalli later reflected, "The true method of working for the reunion of the churches is that of Dom Beauduin."[159]

It was in concrete ministries that Beauduin elaborated on the theology of the mystical body, which flowed out of the liturgy. For him, the mystical body impels toward unity, but not a unity grounded in a particular national or racial (i.e., natural) union as a prerequisite of a mystical (i.e., supernatural) union. In a celebration of the twenty-fifth anniversary of Chevetogne, seven years after Pius XII's *Mystic Corporis*, he wrote:

> There is only one doctrine in terms of which we may think about the concept of the union of the churches, if indeed we wish to think about it in all its supernatural profundity and divine richness: it is the doctrine of the Church, the mystical body of Christ. At the base of their spiritual life, the workers of reconciliation must place the growth of the body of Christ; they must realize

---

cela devient pour lui une évidence—a une mentalité œcuménique; il découvre aussi que les célébrations liturgiques orientales constituent un moyen privilégié de pénétrer de l'intérieur l'âme de l'orthodoxie" (546).

[157] Ibid., 115.

[158] Quitslund, *Beauduin*, 54–55.

[159] Thomas Stransky, "L. Beauduin," in *Dictionary of the Ecumenical Movement*, ed. Nicholas Lossky et al. (Grand Rapids, MI: Eerdmans, 1991), 91.

profoundly that the only thing which interests us is the full mea-
sure of Christ. . . .

One may hope that then the day will come when Christians
will have finally relearned what is so familiar to St. John and St.
Paul, the devotion to the body of Christ. . . .

All of our spiritual goods assume immense proportions in the
irradiation of the total Christ; they are integrated into what is
more profound and more authentic in the Christian mystery: the
unity of the mystical body, the Church.[160]

These reflections demonstrate both the way in which mystical body theology supported Beauduin's monastic ecumenical endeavors and its tendency, common in the French stream of mystical body theology, to function
as a theology of the church as well as a more pervasive theological theme.
Indeed, they appear in a section titled "Our Spirited Life."

If Beauduin's reflections on the mystical body sound somewhat abstract and amorphous, we should note that for him the theology did not
collapse the distinction between Christ and Christian. In fact, he lamented
the tendency to limit the mediation of Christ by substituting various other
mediations. Most irritating to Beauduin was the exaggerated cult of Mary
which, in one case, he called "a blasphemy against the whole economy of
the incarnation."[161] Beauduin was fond of repeating what he called "the
great truth," that Christ is the sole mediator between God and humanity,

---

[160] Lambert Beauduin, "Jubilé du Monastère de l'Union (1925–1950)," *Irénikon*
23 (1950): 372–73.

[161] Lambert Beauduin to Charles Moeller, Chatou, 9 April 1951. Quoted in Quitslund, *Beauduin*, 250. The full quotation demonstrates Beauduin's Christocentrism:
"The Holy Virgin is closer to us than our Lord—what a blasphemy against the whole
economy of the incarnation . . . and the effect of this Mariology on our separated
brothers. . . . You probably think I am willing to sacrifice truth for the sake of reconciliation. But this is very serious: there is only one priest . . . one victim, and it is
this singular sacrifice of the only priest which has reconciled us. *No* creature can in-
tervene in order to add some additional efficacy to this redemption by the only eternal
priest . . . Christ *man-mediator* between us and his Father—that is the great truth.
What is serious is that for this unique, visible, human, divine, eternal, priesthood,
they substitute a sanctifying action, invisible and transcendent, in which Mary and
the Holy Spirit collaborate mysteriously outside the visible and priestly economy of
Christ and his Church. . . . It's a kind of Catholic Protestantism" (emphasis original).

an assertion made often by Marmion as well.[162] That Beauduin clung to this "great truth" late in life is fascinating. Beauduin had founded Chevetogne so that Catholic monks might "go to school in the East" in order to foster deeper mutual appreciation. It was, after all, interaction with Orthodox theologians at the Second Vatican Council that fueled Yves Congar's critique of Catholic theology as, at times, Christomonist and his subsequent work on pneumatology.[163] For Beauduin, emphasizing Christ's sole mediatorship meant ecumenical work with the Eastern Orthodox and pastoral work on behalf of labor. It cut against individualism.[164]

Like Adam, Beauduin railed against Docetic tendencies wherever he saw them and did so more and more as his life progressed. He refused to let his fellow Christians forget the importance of Christ's humanity, a tendency he thought the most pressing christological problem of his day. In a letter to Charles Moeller, he called this amnesia "the singular want of modern Christian life; there is no longer any human mediator to go to the Father; therefore there is no longer any Christianity."[165] He thought that St. Thomas tended toward monophysitism when he spoke of Christ's humanity as the instrument of his divinity. And of neoscholastic apologists, he remarked, "The incarnation bothers them."[166] Thus, we

---

[162] Beauduin, "Abbot Marmion and the Liturgy," 312–13. Beauduin shared with Marmion a suspicion of giving Mary the title "Mediatrix."

[163] The term "Christomonism" appears to originate with Paul Althaus's critique of Karl Barth. Congar thematized this term, taken from Eastern interlocutors. See "Pneumatologie ou 'Christomonisme' dans la tradition latine?," in *Ecclesia a Spiritu sancto edocta*: Mélanges théologiques, hommages à Mgr. Gérard Philips, Bibliotheca Ephermeridum Theologicarum Lovaniensium 27 (Gembloux: J. Duclot, 1970), 41–63. Congar understood it to mean a deep neglect of the theology of the Holy Spirit. Barth claimed that the term "was invented by an old friend of mine whose name I will not mention. Christomonism would mean that Christ alone is real and that all other men are only apparently real." Karl Barth, "A Theological Dialogue," *Theology Today* 19, no. 2 (1962): 172. Apropos of Barth's comment here, the critique leveled against him was usually oriented toward his theological anthropology and theology of grace rather than his doctrine of God.

[164] Beauduin, "Jubilé du Monastère de l'Union," 375–76.

[165] Lambert Beauduin to Charles Moeller, Chevetogne, 18 March 1953. Quoted in Quitslund, *Beauduin*, 253.

[166] Lambert Beauduin to Charles Moeller, Chevetogne, 30 March 1953. Quoted in, and trans. Quitslund, *Beauduin*, 255. In an earlier letter, Beauduin baldly stated

can see that Beauduin's mystical body theology was paired with a robust sense of the humanity of Christ and yet presented a challenge to a singular emphasis on the operative power of the hypostatic union. "He is a man, not a human nature," Beauduin wrote.[167]

Unlike Adam, who found a remedy in the concrete German *Volk*, Beauduin emphasized the liturgy. Raymond Loonbeek and Jacques Mortiau discuss a gradual development in Beauduin's mystical body theology from 1911 to 1926. What was present only in seed in his 1911 course outline was more fully developed and integrated by 1926.[168] Christ's mediation was found most viscerally and truly in his mystical body, which was firmly grounded in the liturgy. More than once, Beauduin relayed insights that he had gained while celebrating Mass; most of them were related to the social nature of the Eucharist.

Conclusions

In this chapter we have uncovered three sources for the tensions within *Mystici Corporis*: (1) the slipperiness of the use and application of mystical body of Christ, (2) the situation in Germany, and (3) the wider, variegated landscape of mystical body theology that surrounded the encyclical. This last element has led us to a key point: there were three major streams of mystical body theology in the early twentieth century. These streams are not univocal but can be distinguished by how they explicitly or implicitly avoid the error of false mysticism by grounding mystical body theology in something more concrete.

The tendency of mystical body theology to become mystified, to float free of mediation, as *Mystici Corporis* recognizes, and as Pelz proves, is a real danger of the theological image. Each stream evinces a different way of grounding mystical body theology in the particular. Those in the Roman stream, represented by Tromp, planted the mystical body firmly

---

the failure of neoscholastic theology to support a robust life of faith: *Je crois vraiment que si ma foi était basée sur la théologie des grands séminaires, sur le traité de l'Eglise, . . . je l'aurais depuis longtemps perdue: heureusement, tout cela c'est de la contrefaçon* (Beauduin to Jadot, 1933, quoted in Loonbeek and Mortiau, *Un pionnier*, 547).

[167] Lambert Beauduin, "Sur le sens des mots 'présence sacramentelle,'" *Les Questions Liturgiques et Paroissiales* 27 (1946): 152.

[168] Loonbeek and Mortiau, *Un pionnier*, 540–45.

in the Roman Catholic Church (and ultimately in its pope). Several in the German-Romantic stream, represented by Adam, insisted that the supernatural unity of the mystical body required a natural, even racial/ethnic, unity of the German nation. Thus, the organic fleshiness of the body image fit nicely with Nazi race rhetoric. And finally, the French socio-liturgical stream, represented most profoundly by Beauduin, grounded mystical body theology in the celebration of the Eucharist. While, across the board, mystical body theology buttressed strides in Catholic ecumenism, the mystical body theology of Beauduin, and others in the French stream, was particularly precocious because of its intrinsic link to the sacramental, liturgical life of the church. This not only disabled false mysticism but, in the case of Beauduin, also radiated into concrete social action.

All three streams of mystical body theology manifest a universalizing tendency but do so in different ways. The Roman version is universalizing in the sense of a *philosophia perennis*; it is appropriate and valid in all times and places. Thus Pope Pius XII writes, "We shall find nothing more noble, more sublime, or more divine than the expression 'the Mystical Body of Christ.'" [169] For its part, the German-Romantic version is all-encompassing in the Romantic sense of the mystical body of Christ standing at the culmination of history. For Adam, and others, the christological moment of the doctrine is less fundamentally transformative of the natural order, that is, national unity. In retrospect we can see that his mystical body theology, and that of some others of the German stream, held too much sanguinity with respect to the correspondence between the natural and supernatural orders. Finally, the French-liturgical stream, as noted in the examples of both Mersch and Beauduin, tends toward a pervasive theology in terms of how Christians live all of life. It is a vision through which all Christian life makes sense, and it does so with "a sacramental emphasis, helping to explain the inner and the outer, formal realities of the Church and of Christian life." [170]

In *The Catholic Counterculture in America 1933–1962*, James T. Fisher argues that Day's articulation of mystical body theology was idiosyn-

---

[169] *Mystici Corporis*, no. 13.
[170] Scully, "The Theology," 58.

cratic.[171] She used what was the dominant symbol of "triumphalist exclusion" in a radically egalitarian way. Indeed, she did. But she was not alone. As we cross the Atlantic in the next chapter to take a deeper look at how Michel, one of Day's good friends, developed the French stream in the United States, it is important to keep in mind that Beauduin, Mersch, and the others in the French stream articulated a mystical body theology that did not begin Catholic Worker houses but did support radical movements and challenge ecclesial juridicism even as it hewed closely (as did Day) to the liturgy and sacraments of the church. Fisher notes Mersch's surprise, when he turned to the patristic era, to find only a few mentions of mystical body theology.[172] Indeed, he was surprised. But Fisher fails to note how Mersch exclaims that it was only in looking to reflections on various other elements of Christian doctrine—beyond treatises related to the church—that he found mystical body theology in abundance.[173] Michel will develop this key aspect of the French stream: mystical body theology was not limited to the contours of the ecclesiastical or even ecclesiological but pushed a more integrated vision of the Christian life that necessarily included other doctrinal questions, and certainly ethical ones.

---

[171] James Terrence Fisher, *The Catholic Counterculture in America 1933-1962* (Chapel Hill: The University of North Carolina Press, 1989), 50-51.

[172] Ibid., 48.

[173] Mersch, *The Whole Christ*, 580.

CHAPTER 2

Journeyed Body

The Case of Virgil Michel

here has been no shortage of scholarship on Michel and the liturgical movement that he popularized in the United States. That work has included no shortage of discussion of the mystical body of Christ theology that was integral to Michel's apostolate. What more needs to be said about Michel and mystical body theology?

Michel scholars have generally assumed that the best way to understand Michel's appeal to the mystical body of Christ is to consider it under the lens of ecclesiology. Benedictine Sister Jeremy Hall's excellent 1973 book elaborating the ecclesiology of Virgil Michel is a case in point. She argues that for Michel the church was fundamentally a mystery best expressed in a variety of images, and that "Mystical Body of Christ" was the most substantial of the images he employed for the church.[1] Hall's approach clearly reflects the first chapter of Vatican II's Dogmatic Constitution on the Church, *Lumen Gentium*, promulgated in the decade before her book was published. That document famously begins by defining the church as fundamentally a mystery before proceeding to enumerate more than a dozen images for the church. During the postconciliar moment of American Catholic historiography, scholars regularly sorted out the ecclesiology of important figures who were not, strictly speaking, theologians. In Michel's case this approach illuminates aspects of his thinking but obscures some of the richness of what exactly mystical body theology was and did for him.

---

[1] Jeremy Hall, *The Full Stature of Christ: The Ecclesiology of Virgil Michel* (Collegeville, MN: Liturgical Press, 1976).

The much different and more recent work of David Fagerberg demonstrates that mystical body of Christ was for Michel an integrative principal between liturgy and social justice. Fagerberg consistently calls it an "ecclesiology."[2] Doubtless it was. But for Michel it was an even more fundamental theological category—a way of seeing the world and acting within it—that blossomed into an ecclesiology. Pecklers sees this in his unmatched history of the liturgical movement in the United States, writing, "Michel viewed the theme of the Mystical Body . . . as a spirituality, as a way of living in society," but then Pecklers continues, "more . . . than as a theological doctrine."[3] For Michel it was both. It was not "pre-theological," as Koster, the German critic of the mystical body revival, called the doctrine in 1940[4] but very much about God's work in the world. For Michel, though, the mystical body of Christ was, at least conceptually, pre-ecclesiological, if also ecclesiological.

"Mystical body of Christ" was the fundamental theological category from which Michel's integrated Catholic vision of liturgical and social action flowed. It describes deification with a thick sense of liturgical and corporate mediation. In short, it is solidarity rooted in Christ. There are three key aspects of Michel's reception and development of mystical body theology. First, Michel remained a scholastic thinker while jettisoning the dominant neoscholastic theology of early twentieth-century Catholicism. Second, Michel imbibed the French-speaking socio-liturgical stream of mystical body of Christ theology on the continent. Third, on bringing it to the United States, Michel saw that mystical body theology held together the diverse arms of his apostolate. We will consider each of these in turn.

---

[2] David W. Fagerberg, "Liturgy, Social Justice, and the Mystical Body of Christ," *Letter & Spirit* 5 (2009): 193–210. See also Kenneth R. Himes, "Eucharist and Justice: Assessing the Legacy of Virgil Michel," *Worship* 62 (1988): 201–24, and Michael J. Baxter, "Reintroducing Virgil Michel: Towards a Counter-Tradition of Catholic Social Ethics in the United States," *International Catholic Review: Communio* 24 (Autumn 1997): 499–528. All three of these commentators, in different ways, attend to the broader implications of "mystical body of Christ" for Michel, but all follow the pattern that "mystical body of Christ" is Michel's ecclesiology.

[3] Pecklers, *The Unread Vision*, 132.

[4] McNamara, "The Ecclesiological Movement in Germany in the Twentieth Century," 350.

Michel the Scholastic

In February 1924, Alcuin Deutsch, abbot of Saint John's in College-ville, Minnesota, sent a promising English and philosophy professor to study in Rome. Deutsch needed a monk to teach the scholastic method to undergraduates, and Michel's restless inquisitiveness and sharp intellect proved a perfect fit. The scholar-mentor Deutsch had in mind for Michel was Joseph Gredt, OSB, at Sant'Anselmo. Gredt was a Luxembourgian neoscholastic philosopher, trained at the Angelicum. Among his teachers were the former apostolic delegate to the United States, Francesco Sa-tolli, and Giuseppe Pecci, Pope Leo XIII's brother. Shortly after arriving in Rome, Michel expressed his overall lack of interest and especially his disappointment with Gredt and other towering neoscholastics. In Michel's view, Gredt was "no teacher at all"; he was "simply his book, no more, no less," and he expected a good student to be "an intellectual slave." [5] Of towering Dominican neoscholastic Garrigou-Lagrange, OP, Michel said, "The whole could be boiled down to ten minutes." [6]

It was not scholasticism per se that Michel found so off-putting but rather the particularly dry manner of engaging the high scholastics, es-pecially Thomas Aquinas, characteristic of Gredt, Garrigou, and others. In fact, Michel considered himself a proponent of the scholastic method and a participant in its renewal throughout his life. We saw in chapter 1 that the dominance of Catholic neoscholastic theology in Europe was the backdrop for the mystical body revival. So too in the United States. Unlike the proponents of *la nouvelle théologie*, however, Michel and others in the United States participated in theological renewal standing outside the field of theology proper, which makes his contributions less obvious but no less significant. Indeed, understanding the theological import of Michel's opus is one benefit of Hall's work and others like it.

Michel thematized his critiques of dominant Catholic approaches to scholasticism in three articles shortly after he returned to the United States in September 1925 and digested his experience of Thomism on the continent. In these essays Michel worked out his own reception and

---

[5] Michel to Alcuin Deutsch, 19 March 1924. Cited in Paul Marx, *Virgil Michel and the Liturgical Movement* (Collegeville, MN: Liturgical Press, 1957), 26.

[6] Michel, Diary, 24 May 1924. Cited in Marx, *Virgil Michel*, 26.

application of the scholastic tradition. He emphasized the boldness of St. Thomas's own (and, more broadly, the University of Paris's) adoption of Aristotle into the curriculum "in the face of ecclesiastical prohibitions," calling Aquinas "a bold innovator" who "suffered . . . episcopal condemnations in his day."[7] Here, Michel was taking a bit of his own advice. In 1926, he had written to Patrick Cummins, OSB, his good friend and associate editor of *Orate Fratres* (the fledgling journal of the US liturgical movement), thanking him for a fine contribution. This was not something that Michel did regularly. In fact, the correspondence between the two is filled with playful jibes and Michel's relentless criticism of Cummins's writing. He thanks Cummins for making a positive case for mysticism instead of writing "a mere scholastic polemic against existing conditions in seminaries." "If we state our views positively, the negative criticism follows without our stating it."[8] In contextualizing and extolling St. Thomas's innovation, Michel's critique of reigning neoscholasticism followed without his stating it.

Nevertheless, Michel cannot help hurling a few direct barbs at his contemporaries on occasion. For example: "It is ever in an all-embracing synthesis, whose disharmonies do not outweigh the harmonies, that alone [the scholastic] finds himself secure. Perhaps too secure at times." Scholastics' occupational hazard is to hole themselves up, to "become too self-satisfied," to "encase [themselves] within [their] own traditional phraseology

---

[7] Virgil Michel, "Why Scholastic Philosophy Lives," *The Philosophical Review* 36, no. 2 (March 1927): 169.

[8] Michel to Patrick Cummins, 20 October 1926, Patrick Cummins Collection, Conception Abbey Archives (CAA), Box 72, Folder: "Patrick, Liturgical Press Correspondence." In fact, after Cummins had made a sojourn to Italy, Michel joked that when Cummins became sufficiently "re-Americanized" he would become more concrete and fastidious in his writing (Michel to Cummins, 15 August 1926). In giving advice, Michel often encouraged Cummins to ground the ethereal tendency in his writing by making concrete references to the liturgy. For example, in the same letter, he writes concerning an article that Cummins had submitted: "In some ways, the article gave the impression of being in the air, instead of coming down to mother earth. Would not concrete references and illustrations, taken from the liturgy, help to avoid this?" It is surprising that Cummins would go on to translate Reginald Garrigou-Lagrange's *Reality: A Synthesis of Thomistic Thought* (St. Louis: Herder, 1950). Michel's impressions of Cummins's work, as well as Cummins's own estimation of its inexactitude, contrast sharply with Garrgiou's Thomistic synthesis.

and ideology," to "forget the social missionary aims of philosophy as of life" and fall, therefore, into "a narrow and fruitless 'commentarism.'"[9] The neologism captures neoscholastic indebtedness to early Modern commentators on Aquinas's work, such as Thomas Cajetan, Francisco Suarez, and John of St. Thomas. To repeat their insights as if nothing had changed over the four hundred intervening years was, according to Michel, to miss the point of Pope Leo XIII's 1879 call for a Thomistic revival. Of the scholastic method itself, Michel wrote, "A philosophy based on contact with facts must expect to be in continuous readjustment insofar as contact reveals new or more definite details of the world of facts."[10] In terms of Leo's call for a return to the philosophy of Aquinas in response to the intellectual problems posed by modernity, Michel says that Pope Leo desired thinking in "the spirit of Thomas" and that he "argued for a complete rejection of past views that were no longer to the point, or had been rendered untenable by the advance of time."[11] In pen on the back of a typewritten draft titled "The Mansions of Thomistic Philosophy," Michel jotted, "Task of today, *not literal*" and "most important that Preface of Editor = convincing and modern language."[12] He was reminding himself of the importance of the task of bringing the Thomistic revival into the contemporary context.

For the Leonine renewal to be successful, it needed to attend to two shortfalls of much theology of Michel's day: It had to disavow the quaintly Modern assumptions of Thomas's commentators, which Michel characterized as "oppos[ing] rationalism, by rationalistic method."[13] Second, it needed to attend to the particular questions of the day, questions that involved day-to-day living as a Christian in the Depression era. Michel's emphases are in line with Jean Daniélou's famous critique of the neoscholastic response to the Modernist crisis: that it failed to address the

[9] Virgil Michel, "Why Scholastic Philosophy Lives," 172. The last quotation Michel takes from Timothée Richard, *Introduction à l'étude et à l'enseignement de la scholastique* (Paris: Maison de la Bonne, 1913), 171.

[10] Michel, "Why Scholastic Philosophy Lives," 172.

[11] Ibid., 169.

[12] Virgil Michel, "The Mansions of Thomistic Philosophy" (unpublished manuscript, SJAA, Series Z, Box 33, Folder 8).

[13] Michel's Retreat Notes, SJAA, Series Z, Box 31. Handwritten in the margin is "Diocesan Retreat" (1937?), Introduction, 3.

important contemporary questions raised by the Modernists and instead recoiled into a rarefied discourse inaccessible, or at least uninspiring, to the average Catholic parish priest and layperson. In other words, to quote Daniélou, much neoscholastic theology failed in *"le contact avec la vie."*[14]

Michel first critiques the assumptions embedded in the early Modern commentaries themselves. Cajetan and the others had read Aquinas through their own lens of nascent Modern philosophical questions, especially a certain mind-body dualism that prevented a full appreciation of St. Thomas's own writings. Michel wrote in 1928, "The modern scholastic is very prone to read into [Thomas's] words variations of meaning that have developed in scholastic tradition only after the thirteenth century."[15] He thought that hidebound neoscholastics locked in on a contextual reality (Aquinas's corpus) and decontextualized it (read it as if it were any other Modern text). "Is it saying too much," Michel asked in 1928, "to aver that many of us champion as traditional in the *philosophia perennis* views which are really quite contrary to the spirit of this philosophy?" "The writer well remembers the mixed horror and surprise with which he was reproached not many years ago: 'Why, you wouldn't think of teaching

---

[14] Jean Daniélou, "Les orientations présentes de la pensée religieuse," *Études* 249 (April 1946): 17. The term "modernism" itself was a creation of ghostwriter Joseph Lemius to describe "the synthesis of all heresies" (*Pascendi*, no. 39). Who exactly was a modernist is a controverted question, but George Tyrrell's "The Relation of Theology to Devotion," *The Month* (November 1899): 461–73, and Alfred Loisy's *L'évangile et L'église* (Paris: A. Picard et fils, 1902) are generally acknowledged as representative of the major issues raised in the controversy. The crackdown and its aftermath resulted in theological trepidation in both Europe and the United States. Much has been written about the Modernist controversy. William L. Portier's *Divided Friends: Portraits of the Roman Catholic Modernist Crisis in the United States* (Washington, DC: The Catholic University of America Press, 2013) provides an excellent window into the crisis, with an emphasis on its stateside impact.

[15] Virgil Michel, Translator's Preface to Martin Grabmann, *Thomas Aquinas: His Personality and His Thought* (Collegeville, MN: Liturgical Press, 1928), vi. While many continue to hold Michel's critique today, there have been several important challenges to this reading of the commentatorial tradition. See, for example, Romanus Cessario, *A Short History of Thomism* (Washington, DC: The Catholic University of America Press, 2005). For a good overview of the current debate on this score see *Josephinum Journal of Theology* 18, no. 1 (2011) dedicated to "Thomism and the *Nouvelle Théologie*," which republishes important essays from the early twentieth century along with some contemporary commentary on the question.

special metaphysics *before* general metaphysics, would you?' To which the only practical answer is: 'Wouldn't I!' " [16] Michel chafes at the organization of scholastic philosophy textbooks (often used in seminaries) that begin with metaphysics as such and move to the various branches of special metaphysics (psychology, natural theology, etc.) especially because that deductive method is more indebted to eighteenth-century rationalism than to scholasticism as such. It insists on working out a metaphysic before any practical questions can be addressed.

Such an injunction, Michel thought, admits of a deep divide between the rational and practical, one foreign to human life and the deeper Catholic tradition. Instead, he offers a defense of beginning with philosophical psychology (a discipline of special metaphysics) because we have good reason to "doubt whether the customary cleavage, made almost universally, between cognitional and emotional processes, holds of reality." Further, "The *body* as apart from the living and thinking substance and the *mind* as apart from the living and thinking substance are abstractions." [17] Rather, Michel insisted: "The body is a living human body, not because in some small spot of it there is a soul, but because the soul transfuses and permeates the whole body and makes it to be alive. So close is the living union of body and soul in man that all man's actions are performed by both body and soul together." [18] This integration of body and soul made a practical difference, theologically speaking. Instead of asserting that one celebrated liturgy for the soul, which governed the body to keep it from sinning, Michel emphasized that the entire person celebrated, worked, played, and failed together.

Unlike some of his contemporaries, Michel did not think that this methodological shortsightedness was endemic to scholasticism per se. Michel appreciated the rigors of the scholastic method, its coherence. Yet, neoscholastics who opposed the challenges of modernity made key

[16] Virgil Michel, "Reflections on a Scholastic Synthesis," *The New Scholasticism* 2, no. 1 (January 1928): 2. Michel does not tell us, but it would not be hard to believe that his reference here is to Joseph Gredt.

[17] Ibid., 8, 9.

[18] Virgil Michel in collaboration with the monks of Saint John's Abbey, Collegeville, Minnesota and the Sisters of the Order of St. Dominic, Marywood, Grand Rapids, Michigan, *Our Life in Christ*, The Christian Religion Series for College (Collegeville, MN: Liturgical Press, 1939), 76.

mistakes in granting the Modern rejection of faith as irrelevant to reasonable inquiry and the Modern grasp of history as mere contingency. Ceding this ground resulted in dualisms between faith and reason, truth and contingency, mind and body, rationality and emotion.

This brings us to Michel's second critique: Much neoscholastic theology, he argued, left many parish priests and laypeople uninspired and misled. Dry and abstract, even dualistic, theological education was a problem for the pastoral vocation of those trained in early twentieth-century seminaries. In some preparatory notes for a diocesan retreat Michel gave toward the end of his life, he writes:

> For generations: Formalistic in religion. What mean? Religious knowledge, possessed intellectually, definite formulas. Had to oppose rationalism, by rationalistic method. What did theology mean to us in seminary, as inspirational for life. Set forms to be believed and memorized. Karl Adam says even educated Catholics know little of fundamental life-giving truths of Christianity. Could add, many priests do not.[19]

Michel saw in forms of neoscholastic theology a tendency to over-rationalize not just theology but the entirety of the Christian life. The efficaciousness of the liturgy was often limited to the calculation of an amount of grace refilling the soul or the precise mechanics of confecting the Body and Blood of Christ from the eucharistic elements of bread and wine. In the process, its educative and aesthetic elements were often undervalued. Mobilizing parish priests to his cause for social action rooted in the liturgy required a richer theological account of the necessary interconnection of the two, as well as the interconnection of people. A key to invigorating Catholic life was to help fellow priests understand the avant-garde in Catholic intellectual life.

It becomes obvious how neoscholastic indebtedness to peculiarly Modern forms of discourse, perhaps ironically, leads to a lack of rooted attention to contemporary Catholic life. The linchpin, for Michel, was a pervasive individualism—in Modern academic discourse, and therefore in much neoscholastic theology, in economic structures, and in some

[19] Michel, "Diocesan Retreat" (1937?), Introduction, 3.

forms of Catholic devotion. The latter two individualisms will merit consideration later in this chapter. Concerning the first, Michel regrets that contemporary academic inquiry has become so diffuse and atomized. He elaborates: "Everything has been split up into elements, of which the whole, no matter how organic, has been considered merely the sum." "Society has long been considered a mere aggregate of individuals." [20] That it runs counter to academic hyper-specialization is what Michel finds ultimately valuable about the scholastic synthesis at its core. Its integrative potential is also what Michel would find stirring and attractive about the theology of the mystical body of Christ.

Michel's analysis of neoscholasticism is not, of course, entirely unique. Such critiques, rumbling underground for a decade or more, burst onto the surface in France, for example, after the publication of Henri Godin's *France, pays du mission?* in 1943. The context was different. Godin argued that the French church was bleeding members largely because of its inattentiveness and therefore increasing irrelevance to the working class. Therefore, it had become mission territory. During Michel's lifetime, the growing US church was still contending with its outsider status in American society. It was, in fact, only a few decades removed from official status as mission territory, a designation lifted by the Vatican in 1908. Nevertheless, the theological emphases of "new social Catholics," such as Michel, and French reformers converged. *Ressourcement* theologians emphasized the necessary connection between theology and the lived Christian life. Chenu, whose scholarship on Aquinas emphasized the angelic doctor as a contextual thinker, denounced the fragmentation of theology, including its divorce from *la vie spirituelle*.[21] Chenu argued that the "speculative formulae and explanations which we find in the textbooks . . . must be considered in the actual *milieu* which is proposed to our faith, that is the living Church of today, where these truths find their

[20] Virgil Michel, "The Intellectual Confusion of To-day and the '*Philosophia Perennis*,'" *The Fortnightly Review* 33, no. 10 (15 May 1926): 211.

[21] See, for example, M.-D. Chenu, "Position de la théologie," *Revue des Sciences Philosophiques et Théologiques* 24 (1935): 252. Chenu's corpus on St. Thomas is highly regarded and extensive. Indicative of his contextual approach to St. Thomas, which emphasized the socially radical character of the Order of Preachers, is his *Aquinas and His Role in Theology*, trans. Paul Philibert (Collegeville, MN: Liturgical Press, 2002; French orig., 1959), esp. chap. 1.

natural surroundings, their context and their synthetic sense."[22] On this side of the Atlantic, Michel conceived Liturgical Press to combat this precise problem by delivering lively theological insights to Catholics in readable form.

In fact, Michel's approach to Thomas, and to scholasticism more generally, was deeply indebted to German thinker Martin Grabmann, a historical theologian who, like Chenu, provided fodder for those wishing to circumvent the hegemony of neoscholastic interpretations of Aquinas.[23] One of the first monographs that Liturgical Press published, after translations of Beauduin's *Piété d'église* and Italian liturgist Emmanuele Caronti's *La pietà liturgica*, was a translation of Grabmann's *Thomas von Aquin: eine Einführung in seine Persönlichkeit und Gedankenwelt* (1912).[24] Michel deeply admired Grabmann's work because it was prescient and more relevant than Gredt's or Garrigou's. In his preface, Michel dubbed Grabmann "the foremost Thomistic student and research scholar of modern times."[25] As many have noted, *Aeterni Patris* spurred not only those theologians and philosophers who were heavily dependent on Thomas's modern commentators but also those who undertook fresh historical looks at Thomas in his own milieu. Grabmann was caught in the ambiguous middle of this burgeoning Catholic theology. Called "the

---

[22] R. P. Chenu, "Catholic Action and the Mystical Body," in *Restoring All Things: A Guide to Catholic Action*, ed. John Fitzsimmons and Paul McGuire (New York: Sheed and Ward, 1938), 1.

[23] Despite the differences between them, Chenu and Grabmann inhabit the same large group of scholars who challenged the abstraction of neoscholastic readings of Thomas on the basis on Aquinas's own writings. See Thomas G. Guarino, *Foundations of Systematic Theology* (New York: T&T Clark, 2005), 287; David Tracy, "The Uneasy Alliance Reconceived: Catholic Theological Method, Modernity, and Postmodernity," *Theological Studies* 50, no. 3 (September 1989): 552–53; David B. Burrell, "Perspectives in Catholic Philosophy II," in *Teaching the Tradition: Catholic Themes in Academic Disciplines*, ed. John J. Piderit and Melanie M. Morey (New York: Oxford University Press, 2012), 86; Jean-Pierre Torrell, *Saint Thomas Aquinas*, vol. 1: *The Person and His Work*, rev. ed., trans. Robert Royal (Washington, DC: The Catholic University of America, 2005), xix, 19.

[24] Michel also translated an article of Grabmann's: "The Influence of Medieval Philosophy on the Intellectual Life of Today," trans. Virgil Michel, *The New Scholasticism* 3, no. 1 (January 1929): 24–56.

[25] Michel, Translator's Preface to Martin Grabmann, *Thomas Aquinas*, v.

greatest Catholic scholar of his time" by his student Ludwig Ott, Grabmann was involved in a deep recovery of Thomas's own texts and contexts for twentieth-century Catholic theology.[26] James Weisheipl groups him with Jacques Maritain, Étienne Gilson, and Congar as a Thomist (but not a neo-Thomist or neoscholastic).[27] Like Gilson after him, Grabmann emphasized the similarity in method (not content) among scholastics.[28] Following Grabmann, Michel was convinced of the liveliness of the scholastic method if one breathed contemporary life into it.[29] In tune with Chenu, Grabmann argued that the fourteenth century was preoccupied with dialectic to the neglect of the scriptural and mystical elements of the faith, a fall from the high scholastics. Thus, the fourteenth-century environment, with the introduction of nominalism, paved the way for the early modern, often rationalistic, defense of the faith from the rationalists.

For Michel, it was necessary that theological questions pertain to those of the day but even further that a concerted attempt be made to illustrate these connections for the laity. While in Europe, he wrote that despite the Benedictine "flight from the world," a good monk still had to keep abreast of worldly developments in order to be able to address them, especially to educate others.[30] Failing to take stock of the real needs of the contemporary church results in a failure to reach the people in the pews. The lack of vibrancy and concern for the embodied lives of early twentieth-century Christians ultimately led Michel to embrace a popularizing vocation as a thinker in the church, which included education and coaching at Saint John's, the US liturgical movement aimed particularly at parish priests and

---

[26] See Phillip W. Rosemann, "Martin Grabmann," in *Medieval Scholarship: Biographical Studies on the Formation of a Discipline*, ed. Helen Damico, vol. 3: *Philosophy and the Arts* (New York: Garland, 2000), 55. Rosemann explains that Grabmann directed Ott's doctorate and became a dear friend of his (58). Ott has the distinction of writing the last major theological manual, widely distributed through the 1960s: *Fundamentals of Catholic Dogma* (Cork, IE: Mercier Press, 1955). After going through four editions, it was brought back into print by TAN Books in 2009.

[27] James A. Weisheipl, "Scholasticism," in *The Encyclopedia of Religion*, ed. Mircea Eliade, vol. 13 (New York: Macmillan, 1987), 118.

[28] José Ignacio Cabezón, "Conclusion," in *Scholasticism: Cross-Cultural and Comparative Perspectives*, ed. José Ignacio Cabezón (Albany: State University of New York, 1998), 249n5.

[29] Roseman, "Martin Grabmann," esp. 62–66.

[30] Virgil Michel, Diary, 26 February 1924, SJAA, Series Z, Box 22, Folder 1.

laypeople, and numerous retreats for priests and sisters. Thus, Michel's foreword to the very first issue of *Orate Fratres* describes the program of the journal as filling a void:

> Our general aim is to develop a better understanding of the spiritual import of the liturgy, an understanding that is truly sympathetic. This means that we are not aiming at a cold scholastic interest in the liturgy of the Church, but at an interest that is more thoroughly intimate, that seizes upon the entire person, touching not only intellect but also will, heart as well as mind.[31]

At its heart, Michel understood the liturgy—and we must not forget that for Michel this was the Tridentine usage of the Roman Rite—not as a bourgeois exercise in mystification but as the "work of the people" in a popular sense. In a discussion question for a course he taught, Michel wrote: "The liturgy is essentially not the religion of the cultured (which often expresses itself by abstract ideas and logical developments) but the religion of the people (which expresses itself by being and action, by imagery and ritual). How well is this concept of the liturgy being carried out in the parishes you are familiar with in the United States?"[32] His own answer to that question was "not well enough," hence the liturgical apostolate.

Neoscholastic theology tended to distinguish the "mystical body of the Church"[33] from the "mystical body of the state," employing the phrase in a

---

[31] Virgil Michel, "Foreword," *Orate Fratres* 1, no. 1 (28 November 1926): 1.

[32] Virgil Michel, "Course in Catholic Backgrounds and Current Social Theory, First Semester, Christian Sociologists, Writings of Dawson, Maritain, E.A., The Personalist and Communitarian Movement" (Unpublished, 1937, SJAA, Series WP, Box 198), 43.

[33] Paul Marx calls it "strange" that the brief 1911 *Catholic Encyclopedia* article on the topic bore this title (82). See George H. Joyce, "Mystical Body of the Church," in *The Catholic Encyclopedia: An International Work of Reference on the Constitution, Doctrine, Discipline, and History of the Catholic Church*, ed. Charles G. Herbermann, et al., vol. 10 (New York: Robert Appleton Company, 1911), 663. British theologian Joyce begins with the church as a "moral union" but moves beyond that unity to discuss a "supernatural" unity with Christ. He cites Franzelin, Passaglia, and German manualist Christian Pesch, SJ. Interestingly, Francis Schüssler Fiorenza describes the topic of Pius XII's *Mystici Corporis* as "the mystical body of the Church" in "Vatican II and the Aggiornamento of Roman Catholic Theology," in James C. Livingston et al., *Modern Christian Thought: The Twentieth Century*, 2nd ed. (Minneapolis: Fortress

merely moral sense, that is, describing people bound together in common action. Thus, mystical body was simply another union of people across space. As we have seen, Mersch was critical of this usage. Michel thought that such a definition of the mystical body of Christ was too restrictive, too cold. In an unpublished manuscript, he wrote:

> That the mystical body is not merely a figure of speech for denoting a moral union between the members of the Church, that it is not merely such a union of mind and will, of intention and aim, as exists between members banded together in any earthly society, no longer needs to be stressed. The mystical body of Christ, far from being a mere figurative expression for such a moral union, refers to a most real and intimate supernatural union by which all the members of the fellowship constitute with Christ a living organism. As a living social organism it must express its nature and being in the immanent activity that is characteristic of all living beings, and it does this in the liturgy of the Church.[34]

Michel describes the scholastic method in organic terms: "It grows and therefore changes; but it also remains itself amid the variety of changes endured in its growth."[35] In the early Modern examples, Michel thought that scholasticism was no longer true to itself. It is striking how this

---

Press, 2006), 239. Joyce's is one of the earliest articles to appear on the topic in English. He appears to be preceded by: B. Conway, "The Communion of Saints," *Homiletic and Pastoral Review* 7 (1907): 592–600, who deals with the mystical body as related to the communion of saints; and what seems to be the first English-language article, Joseph McSorley, "The Mystical Body of Christ," *Catholic World* 131 (1905): 307–14. In the throes of the Modernist controversy, McSorley's mystical body theology is rather Docetic. For him, the mystical body of Christ is a refuge of enduring faith, walled off from critique and safe from the perils of deep historical digging and scientific theories, a bastion of faith untouched by the dictates and conclusions of reasoned inquiry. McSorley calls the church "purely sacramental," by which he means nearly dualist—what we see in the vicissitudes of history is simply "the human vessel," "the material embodiment" (310). On McSorley, his contributions, and struggles during the Modernist crisis see Portier, *Divided Friends*, esp. chaps. 9, 11, and 13.

[34] Virgil Michel, "The Liturgy and Catholic Life" (unpublished manuscript, SJAA, Series Z, Box 33, Folder 3A). Internal evidence dates the manuscript to 1936.

[35] Michel, "Why Scholastic Philosophy Lives," 173.

description of scholastic philosophy would also come to characterize Michel's understanding of the liturgy. Those who stifled the development of the scholastic method in the twentieth century, who preferred simply to reiterate the commentaries on Thomas, were also often the ones who were suspicious of the work of the liturgical movement.

The Fruit of European Study

Despite his critiques, Michel did encounter quite a bit that he found worthwhile while in Europe. Judging by how quickly he undertook to translate Grabmann's book, it is likely that Michel had encountered his work while there.[36] He found the first rumblings of what would blossom into the *ressourcement* that informed Vatican II as well as the liturgical movement. As soon as he had the opportunity, he traveled throughout Italy, France, Spain, Germany, Austria, and Belgium, especially to the Benedictine monasteries, which also happened to be the centers of the budding liturgical movement. Michel was fascinated.[37] These travels were, of course, the beginnings of Michel's commitment—with Deutsch's endorsement—to make Saint John's the center of the liturgical movement in the United States.

The most formative of those trips was to Mont César in Leuven. While studying at Sant'Anselmo, Michel encountered Beauduin, who was teaching apologetics, liturgy, and ecclesiology. Beauduin's classes were the opposite of Gredt's—interesting, perceptive, and engaging.[38] Michel had many private conversations with Beauduin and requested that Beauduin arrange for him to spend holidays at Mont César. Michel would later write in his diary that Mont César was the "center of new liturgical movement."[39] "Undoubtedly," Paul Marx writes, "one of Michel's greatest discoveries in Europe had been the reality of the Church as the Mystical Body of

[36] Paul Marx explains that he received permission to translate Caronti's work and often remarked to his abbot that he looked forward to completing several translations. Marx, *Virgil Michel*, 28.

[37] It is very possible that Abbot Alcuin had intended Michel to encounter the liturgical movement. He had, after all, handed him a copy of Romano Guardini's *Vom Geist der Liturgie* in 1920. See Marx, *Virgil Michel*, 25.

[38] Marx, *Virgil Michel*, 27.

[39] Virgil Michel, Diary, 26 February 1924, SJAA, Series Z, Box 22, Folder 1. Quoted in Marx, *Virgil Michel*, 43n3.

Christ—a doctrine little stressed in the United States at this time." [40] It was Beauduin, claims Marx, who "fired Father Virgil's interest in the liturgy and in the doctrine of the Mystical Body." [41]

Of all that he saw in Europe, it was Beauduin's vision that Michel found most attractive and formative. "No one in Europe influenced [Michel] more than this scholarly and zealous Belgian monk." [42] Michel found Beauduin's approach to the liturgy so absorbing because it was engaged with social questions and, in contrast to Maria Laach in Germany, for example, aimed for a parish-level audience. It is striking how Beauduin's and Michel's descriptions of the method for liturgical movement mirror one another. They both understood the goal of the movement to lay the groundwork for a reform sanctioned by Rome, rather than to demand immediate change. They wanted to elaborate upon the richness of the liturgy in order to cultivate a fuller understanding in the pews. Therefore, they aimed at the parish priest and his parishioners. [43] Michel was captivated by the importance of taking the newest ideas flowing from the mind of the church all the way to the pews.

That Beauduin's mystical body theology influenced Michel is clear from the link that it served for him between liturgy and social questions. In a letter dated exactly one month before his death, Michel was asked by a chaplain at the Catholic center at LSU for the best book on the mystical body of Christ. The chaplain had noticed Michel's letter to the editor concerning a review of Mersch's book. Michel thought of Beauduin's fellow traveler in the French stream, jotting in the margin of the letter, "*The Whole Christ' (Bruce)—Mersch.*" [44] As noted above, both Mersch and Beauduin were enamored of Bérullian spirituality. Beauduin

---

[40] Marx, *Virgil Michel*, 36.

[41] Ibid., 27.

[42] Ibid., 28.

[43] Beauduin wrote, "The action of the liturgy is not reserved to an élite. . . . It must penetrate deeply into the great mass of the faithful" ("Abbot Marmion and the Liturgy," 307).

[44] Schexnayder to Michel, 26 October 1938, SJAA, Series Z, Box 27, Folder 5. Cited in Hall, *The Full Stature of Christ*, 113n22. Of course, Michel could have simply been reminding himself that his letter to *Commonweal* (cited below) appears to defend Mersch's book from the characterization of the reviewer. There is no way to know exactly what he meant.

encountered the spirituality predominantly through Marmion's Benedictine inflected strain of it, from whom he also first encountered mystical body theology.[45]

At the beginning of the chapter, we noted Pecklers's description of Michel's mystical body theology as a spirituality. As mentioned above, Pecklers is right to emphasize this aspect of Michel's mystical body theology, especially insofar as Pecklers shifts the primary locus of that theology out of the realm of mere ecclesiology. Years earlier Marx had used a similar descriptor for Michel's mystical body theology while speaking specifically in the realm of ecclesiology:

> When *Orate Fratres* began its publication in 1926, the *spiritual nature* of the Church as the Mystical Body of Christ seems to have been given little attention in seminaries, to say nothing of being almost unknown among even informed and intelligent Catholic laymen. The very term "Mystical Body" was for a time suspect. Today [c. 1957] the doctrine of the Mystical Body is much better understood and lived.[46]

Marx seems to contrast spiritual here with a merely temporal/juridical approach to the church. A sense of this tension between "mystical body of Christ" and "structured, ordered, defined church" was widespread. Marx also relays that "Msgr. Reynold Hillenbrand recalled that a retreat

---

[45] These connections were further elaborated in chapter 1. Marx explains that Michel was instrumental in Saint John's hiring Ermin Vitry, OSB, a Marmion disciple and chant expert whom Michel hoped would take over the editorship of *Orate Fratres* from him (*Virgil Michel*, 40). That latter hope would never be realized. Nevertheless, it reinforces Michel's appreciation for the strain of liturgical thought associated with Marmion. *Orate Fratres* published several of Vitry's articles, predominately on liturgical music; about half of those were under Michel's editorship. Shortly after Michel's death, *Orate Fratres* published Vitry's "The Spiritual Doctrine of Abbot Marmion," *Orate Fratres* 15, no. 1 (December 1940): 7–11. Vitry had been formed as a monk at Maredsous and was then sent to study at, while serving as organist for, Mont César, the French-speaking Benedictine center of liturgical-theological formation of the era. There, Vitry encountered both Marmion and Beauduin, who were influential on him. See Kathleen Agnes Bolduan, "The Life and Work of Dom Ermin Vitry, O.S.B." (PhD diss., Washington University, 1976), 13–14.

[46] Marx, *Virgil Michel*, 408; emphasis mine.

master that summer [1951] had preached that too much was being said about the Mystical Body and too little about the Church." [47]

"Spirituality" is, in contemporary discourse, a controverted word. Especially in a cultural context that has seen a wide appeal to the attractiveness of spirituality over religion, sensitivities have been rightly raised over the word's use and appeal. Theologically speaking, there has been a wide array of studies on spirituality, which usually undertake one of two tasks: either they reflect on the contributions and charism of a particular religious way of life (e.g., Benedictine spirituality as a particular way of living out the gospel as distinct from Ignatian spirituality) or they engage in what is otherwise called mystical theology (i.e., reflection on the theology of those great souls who have dedicated their lives to cultivating an intimate relationship with God through intense affective prayer). [48]

[47] Ibid., 83. Marx cites Hillenbrand's "The Priesthood and the World," National Liturgical Week: *Proceedings* [1943], 14. Throughout the University of Dayton's copy of Friedrich Jürgensmeier's *The Mystical Body of Christ as the Basic Principle of Religious Life*, trans. H. Gardner Curtis (Milwaukee: Bruce, 1939), the previous owner, a "Kieran" who received the book as a gift "from Fr. Provincial, Christmas 1945," makes numerous corrections to the text based on Francis Connell's review of it in *Franciscan Studies* 6 (September 1946): 380–81, which is cited on the first page. The lined-out paragraphs are those that elaborate on the porous lines of membership in the mystical body of Christ as well as those that heavily emphasize the humanity of Christ (182). An example of the former: "According to her principle, the Church as the mystical body of Christ embraces the whole human race" (149). Jürgensmeier makes the classic reference to Aquinas's *Summa Theologiae* III.8.3.Resp. in which Thomas discusses membership of the mystical body in terms of act and potency. Malachi J. Donnelly's review, "Magnetic Power of Christ," in *Review for Religious* 5, no. 4 (July 1946) blames what he determines to be the book's lack of theological accuracy on Curtis's translation: "phrases, clauses, whole sentences have been omitted." A review in *America* by W. J. Garry, on the other hand, finds "both the summary of the doctrine and the application of it . . . excellently done." See *America* 62, no. 3 (28 October 1939): 80.

[48] Two famous examples of studies in spirituality are Bernard McGinn, John Meyendorf, and Jean Leclerc, eds., *Christian Spirituality: Origins to the Twelfth Century* (New York: Crossroad, 1987); and Bruce H. Lescher and Elizabeth Liebert, eds., *Exploring Christian Spirituality: Essays in Honor of Sandra M. Schneiders* (Mahwah, NJ: Paulist Press, 2006). Sandra Schneiders wrote the landmark essay that made spiri-

From Pecklers's description of Michel's mystical body theology, it appears that he intends spirituality not as a particular comment on Michel's appropriation of the Benedictine charism but as a way of marking it a more fundamental category for Michel. It is notable that several others use language for the (mystical) body of Christ that pushes it either out of the realm of ecclesiology per se or out of theology altogether. Bernard Lee is an example of the latter. He writes, "Body of Christ is not 'merely' a metaphor. It is a physical reality, a new being brought into existence among the disciples of Jesus in the resurrection of Jesus Christ into which we are baptized. Body of Christ is not a theology. It is a way of being in the world with one another and with Christ because of who God is." [49] Debra Campbell is an example of the former. She writes:

> The new apostolates nurtured an alternative to the individualistic, devotion centered spirituality fostered within the parish and reinforced in the large Catholic organizations. This alternative spirituality recognized the connection between the work individual members did in the secular arena and their faith, expressed most directly by their participation in the liturgy. Along with the connection between liturgy and work, it underscored the need for the laity to adopt an active rather than a passive posture in the papal strategy of "restoring all things in Christ." The emergence of this new spirituality was catalyzed by three European Catholic movements that had been imported to America by the 1930s. These included: the theology of the Mystical Body of Christ, with its emphasis upon the radical interdependence of all of the members (laity included), the liturgical renewal popularized by Virgil Michel's journal *Orate Fratres* from 1926 on, and the Jocist movement, which challenged Catholics to form small groups in the workplace and discuss ways to apply the gospel in the service of concrete ongoing, social change. Members of the small-group apostolates gradually adopted an activist spirituality that took for granted the crucial connections between liturgy and work,

---

tuality its own discipline. See Sandra M. Schneiders, "Spirituality in the Academy," *Theological Studies* 50, no. 4 (1989): 676–97.

[49] Bernard J. Lee, "Body of Christ," in *New Dictionary of Catholic Spirituality*, ed. Michael Downey (Collegeville, MN: Liturgical Press, 1993), 104.

and the link between the human solidarity, affirmed in both the Mass and the Mystical Body theology, and the mandate for social change.[50]

Campbell mentions both Michel and the revival of mystical body theology as factors in developing a more all-encompassing spirituality, yet it is still unclear how the three—Michel, mystical body theology, and spirituality—might relate to one another. The influence of the French school on Michel helps to elicit a bit further what Pecklers might mean in claiming mystical body theology as a spirituality for Michel.

In fact, the *Dictionnaire de spiritualité* explains that by the early twentieth century, the Latin substantive *spiritualitas*, with its religious (contra *carnalitas*), philosophical (contra *corporalitas*), and political (contra *temporalitas*) senses had in French scholarship developed into *spiritualité*.[51] The substantive still retained its force as contrary to what was "of this world." Employing the adjectival form, we saw how Chenu critiqued the theology of his day as disconnected from *la vie spirituelle*. He and Michel shared a commitment to theology integrated with the pursuit of holiness. This is precisely what Michel understands the theology of the mystical body to mean. In fact, it is possible to read Michel's apostolate as a precursor to the "universal call to holiness" embraced by *Lumen Gentium*, especially the goal of the liturgical movement in the United States to bring to the laity the connection between the celebration of the liturgy and the wider Christian life that had been far more obvious to the monks, whose daily lives were shaped by Mass and the hours.

While Pecklers is perceptive to see more than an ecclesiology in Michel's repeated appeals to the mystical body of Christ, he misunderstands the ways in which Beauduin influenced Michel. He concludes that the liturgical movement was generally more successful among Germans and, more specifically, the link between the liturgy and the social: "It was Germans and German-Americans who were the first to grasp the intrinsic connection between liturgy and social justice,"[52] but in his overview of the German litur-

---

[50] Debra Campbell, "The Nunk Controversy: A Symbolic Moment in the Search for a Lay Spirituality," *U.S. Catholic Historian* 8, no. 1/2 (1989): 83–84.

[51] Michel Dupuy, "Spiritualité," in *Dictionnaire de Spiritualité, Ascétique et Mystique*, ed. M. Viller et al. (Paris: Beauchesne, 1990), 1142–73.

[52] Pecklers, *The Unread Vision*, 283.

gical movement in the first chapter of his book, Pecklers does not mention the social question, giving credit instead to Beauduin in Belgium, as well as Pius Parsch in Austria, for eliciting those connections. Sure, the monks of Saint John's, and Michel himself, were of German heritage, but understanding the influence of the French-speaking Belgian Beauduin is necessary for understanding not only the connection between the liturgy and the social question but also the doctrine that facilitated it: the mystical body of Christ.

Elaborating on the distinction that he drew between spirituality and theological doctrine, Pecklers says of Michel, "In this way, he differed from his colleagues in Germany from whom he had borrowed the concept in the first place."[53] Pecklers is here referring to Möhler and the nineteenth-century Tübingen theologians (rather than Michel's contemporaries, such as Guardini and Adam) who were midwives to the entire mystical body revival in the twentieth century. While Michel mentioned Adam and Franzelin often,[54] he read them through the liturgy. That is, their insights were absorbed by Michel within the framework of his overall goal of liturgical pedagogy. For this reason, Marmion and Beauduin, as Benedictines, were ultimately more formative upon Michel. His way of understanding the theology of the mystical body of Christ—as a way of living in the world—is connected also to Beauduin's more populist approach to liturgy. Pecklers credits this achievement to the movement on this side of the Atlantic: "Unlike the European movement that was centered in or around monasteries, the movement in the United States was more pluralistic, surfacing on college campuses and in Catholic bookstores, in social outreach centers and adult study groups."[55] Whether or not he succeeded, this was also Beauduin's goal, as Pecklers himself writes earlier in his book: "Unlike the emerging liturgical movement in Germany, which was primarily the work of an intellectual, monastic elite, the Belgian movement was thoroughly pastoral, aimed at the grassroots level: parish communities."[56] Michel's relative successes with *Orate Fratres*,

---

[53] Ibid., 132.

[54] We saw one example in the retreat notes above. Michel refers favorably to Franzelin in "The True Christian Spirit," *Ecclesiastical Review* (February 1930): 139. Several of Michel's course outlines include these two thinkers on the mystical body, among many others. Jeremy Hall confirms this observation in *The Full Stature*, 91–92.

[55] Pecklers, *The Unread Vision*, 281.

[56] Ibid., 14.

Liturgical Press, and the propagation of the theology of the mystical body demonstrate not only his doggedness in pursuit of the cause but also the favorable conditions in the United States that made Beauduin's vision for a "democratization of the liturgy" realizable in America.[57]

Traversing the Sea

H. A. Reinhold, who took over Michel's "Timely Tracts" column in *Orate Fratres* after the latter's death in 1938, writes of Michel, "Instead of dragging his find across the border as an exotic museum piece, he made it as American as only an American mind could make it." "Besides, his clear realism and his burning apostle's heart had one urge none of the great masters in Europe seemed to see: the connection of social justice with a new social spirituality."[58] Patrick Carey also asserts that Michel's deep interest in the social question was the uniquely American characteristic of the liturgical movement.[59] As the various liturgical movements developed, indeed it was. The social aspects of the liturgical movement, however, were not born in the United States. Rather, as we have seen, the seeds of the interconnection between social questions and liturgical celebrations were planted in Michel's head by Beauduin. That social emphasis garnered wider support in the United States than it ever did in Europe.

Formed by the Liturgy

When Michel returned from Europe, he jumped in—almost immediately—to preparing the various arms of the liturgical apostolate at Saint

---

[57] Quitslund, *Beauduin*, 16. Some scholars have critiqued the liturgical movement centered at Saint John's as ultimately unsuccessful in its popularizing mission. Surely, it did not create a deep liturgical sense within every Catholic in the pew. Yet, more recent research, such as Katharine E. Harmon's *There Were Also Many Women There: Lay Women in the Liturgical Movement in the United States, 1926–59* (Collegeville, MN: Liturgical Press, 2012), exposes some of the biases inherent in those conclusions by telling the stories of many women involved in the liturgical movement, some of whom played a key role in popularizing the movement, and some of those by working to integrate it into Catholic households. See especially pp. 313–17.

[58] H. A. Reinhold, "Denver and Maria Laach," *Commonweal* 45 (1946): 86–88.

[59] Patrick W. Carey, *American Catholic Religious Thought: The Shaping of a Theological and Social Tradition* (Milwaukee: Marquette University Press, 2004), 423.

John's. Deutsch had suggested, in a transcontinental letter to Michel, the possibility of a liturgical review centered at Saint John's. Michel replied to his abbot that the suggestion had "kept [him] awake for the greater part of two nights" and that he had sketched out full plans for the review, including associate editors, topics, and layout.[60] Nevertheless, Michel expected to be in charge of the liturgical apostolate for only a limited time, after which he would return to philosophy, entrusting the review and press to a confrere. But over the years he had given himself over to the work with the gusto he expected any Christian to have in pursuing God's calling. So tireless he was that several brother Benedictines even wondered if he worked himself to his untimely death.[61]

Michel knew that the doctrine of the mystical body of Christ that he found so enlivening on the continent was neither sufficiently known nor understood in the United States. "Many today," he writes, "have not heard of it; and for many who have heard of it, it is not a doctrine, but merely a Scriptural figure of speech!"[62] Such a misunderstanding of the mystical body as simply a metaphor or manner of speaking led Catholics to miss its depth.[63] Judging by his commitments to scholasticism, one might expect

[60] Michel to Deutsch, Maredsous, 25 April 1925. Quoted in Marx, *Virgil Michel*, 39.

[61] Marx, *Virgil Michel*, 386–87.

[62] Michel, "The True Christian Spirit," 131.

[63] Years later, Michel responded to a review of Mersch's *The Whole Christ* in *Commonweal*. The reviewer had written, "When we speak of the Mystical Body of Christ we are using a metaphor to designate the unity that should exist between Christ and all mankind." Michel asked: "Is it correct to refer to the Mystical Body of Christ as a metaphor? . . . Would it not be much more correct to speak of the doctrine of the Mystical Body of Christ, or of the sublime supernatural reality of it, which we picture to ourselves under the figure of the human body? And is the M.B. merely used to indicate or declare the unit that 'should' exist between Christ and all mankind, and not rather the most real and living union that does actually exist between the head Christ and His living members?" ("The Mystical Body," Letter to the Editor, *Commonweal* 29 [28 October 1938]: 18). Michel was tapping in to a much larger issue here. As discussed in the previous chapter, the major critique of mystical body theology by Mannes Koster was that it was "merely a metaphor." Several theologians reacted strongly to that proposition throughout the years. Mersch takes up the issue in a nuanced way at the beginning of *The Whole Christ*: "That one should refuse to accept the words 'Mystical Body' and 'members and Head' as the statement of a thesis whence all possible consequences can be drawn—nothing could be wiser; these

that Michel would ground the mystical body so discursively as to mute its more intuitive, suggestive, even nebulous aspects. He does not. Like his forebears in the French stream, he grounds mystical body theology in the liturgy, which provides a center of gravity for his extrapolations on social questions, but also an *espirit de finesse*, to borrow Blaise Pascal's term, resulting from that connection. Pinning down Michel's mystical body theology is difficult precisely because of this aesthetic dimension, the phenomenological excess built into his liturgical imagination. In this regard, Michel's aims are akin to Mersch's, whose work on the mystical body aimed not at writing an ecclesiology but rather a fundamental theological treatise, and who averred that "the doctrine always and necessarily retains a certain vagueness."[64]

Michel's understanding becomes clearer by contrast with Joseph Clifford Fenton, America's consummate neoscholastic theologian. In 1939 Fenton argued with British theologian Joseph Brodie Brosnan in the pages of the *Ecclesiastical Review* about action in the mystical body. "The proper act of the Mystical Body is not different from the proper act of Christ Himself," wrote Fenton.[65] While he avoids identifying the acts of Christ and the mystical body completely, Fenton nevertheless does not allow much room for mediative distinction. As the mystical body acts, so does Christ. By subtle, but important, contrast Michel writes, "Christ lives and acts in His mystical body as truly as He lived and acted in His physical

---

metaphors, for such they are, merely indicate a unity that transcends the biological realities from which they are taken. It is best to retain the traditional name and call it a 'mystical' union. However, it must be clearly understood that this term is by no means synonymous with 'nebulous' or 'semi-real'" (9). As Mersch indicates here, the issue is that, if mystical body is not a metaphor, then it can be too closely identified with Christ's physical body. If it is a metaphor, then it is not real. Michel's contemporary Paul Hanly Furfey, in *Fire on the Earth*, walks a similar line on the question, calling mystical body a "similitude" (42), but then emphasizing: "The Mystical Body is real. It is called *mystical* to distinguish it not from what is real, but to distinguish it from what is visible and physical" (43). We shall have occasion in chapter 4 to consider this issue further, especially as it pertains to the work of Henri de Lubac.

[64] Mersch, *The Whole Christ*, 452. On the first point, see Malanowski, "Émile Mersch, SJ," 47–48.

[65] Joseph Clifford Fenton, "The Act of the Mystical Body," *Ecclesiastical Review* 100 (1939): 400.

body while on earth." [66] Fenton and Michel voice a similar sentiment here, but Pascal's *esprit de finesse* animates Michel's prose by his simultaneous emphasis on Christ *living* in his mystical body. In Michel's thinking, one needs the discernment to find where and how Christ lives and acts in the mystical body. Surely Michel's way of describing this relationship was deeply informed by his years of reflecting on its liturgical character. The liturgy is nothing if not mediative. "The liturgy," writes Michel, "is essentially the external embodiment of an interior soul and spirit. In fact in its sacramental mysteries it is above all else an incarnation of the truly Divine, the making present of the supernatural in its own mystical but real actuality." [67] In Michel's way of speaking, the mystical body clearly mediates Christ. There is no danger of simple identification.

In fact, for Michel the liturgy is the *sine qua non* of the mystical body of Christ. "Without the liturgy," he explains, "there would be no Church such as Christ has instituted. Without the liturgy there would be no mystical body of Christ, in which the divine mission of Christ continues." Michel carries on Beauduin's emphasis on Christ as mediator by identifying the rites of the church as the locus of Christ's ongoing mediation. "It is above all in the official acts of the Church that Christ himself lives and acts. In them He continues his active mediatorship between God and man. . . . It is through the liturgy that the redemption of Christ is extended through all time for the constant glory of God and salvation of souls. *The liturgy is* thus officially *the life of the mystical body of Christ.*" [68] One of Michel's favored ways of discussing what it meant to be a Christian was to live the "Christ Life." And his task in the textbook from which the above quotation comes is reflected in its title: to exposit on *Our Life in Christ*.

The liturgical, spiritual depth of Michel's appropriation of the mystical body of Christ is connected to its genealogy. In the same article in which Michel bemoans the widespread lack of appreciation for the mystical body, he insists that imitation of Christ is not a lofty enough goal for the Christian. After all, an agnostic could imitate him. [69] Rather, as Michel

---

[66] Michel et al., *Our Life in Christ*, 36.

[67] Michel, *The Liturgy of the Church: According to the Roman Rite* (New York: MacMillan Co., 1937), 317. It is of note that Michel is discussing art and the liturgy here.

[68] Michel et al., *Our Life in Christ*, 50–51; emphasis original.

[69] Michel, "The True Christian Spirit," *Ecclesiastical Review* (February 1930): 131.

spells out in his notes for a retreat given to his sister community in Saint Joseph, Minnesota, the mystical body calls us to a supernatural transformation: a "wholehearted oblation of self in union with Christ . . . linked with sacrifice of altar." [70] There are clear echoes of Bérulle. "For Bérulle, participation in the mystery of Christ is not simply 'imitation of Christ,' which would be something purely external; it is a union with Christ's own life and actions." [71] Bérulle's work influenced Marmion and it is the latter whom Michel cites in his retreat notes. Michel's description of Benedictine asceticism in the retreat notes directly follows his explication of the mystical body of Christ—that one cannot separate one's "own spiritual life from that of fellowship in Christ." [72]

Bérulle called for self-annihilation—a controverted concept in his work—but Michel will have no obliteration of the individual in the mystical body. [73] In a posthumously published article, arguing that the liturgy is the foundation of religious experience for "member[s] of Christ," Michel clarifies the point:

> The religious experience of the liturgy, more than any other, is calculated to enrich the individual for the sole reason that it brings him into such intimate real contact with Christ, the true way and life. *The liturgy begins and ends with Christ as the sole mediator between God and man.* The more fully the soul enters into the liturgical action, the more intimately is it united with the fellow-members of the mystical body, but only through the head Christ. The liturgical action is ever a sacrifice of oneself to God, the rendering of a proper homage to Him. In its repeated participation there is an ever closer personal union effected with Christ, the consciousness of Christ ever grows in the soul. This is the ultimate reason for the increasing growth of the individual soul, despite the fact that it seems to give up its own individuality

[70] Virgil Michel, Notes for Retreat given to the sisters at St. Benedict's in Collegeville, 1937, SJAA, Series Z, Box 31, Folder 4.

[71] Jordan Aumann, *Christian Spirituality in the Catholic Tradition* (San Francisco: Ignatius Press, 1985), 225.

[72] Virgil Michel, Notes for Retreat given to the sisters at St. Benedict's in Collegeville, 1937, SJAA, Series Z, Box 31, Folder 5.

[73] William M. Thompson, *Bérulle and the French school: Selected Writings* (Mahwah, NJ: Paulist Press, 1989), xvi.

in entering into the collective action of the fellowship. Christ is indeed infinite in His being and life. Yet the union of the finite individual with Christ, while it is a sinking of self in Him, is not a destruction of self. Rather it is the losing of one's life in order to find it on a higher level. It is an ennobling of self, a sort of divinization of self, in which the best characteristics of the self are not destroyed but transformed into a higher supernatural richness of being. *Liturgical action means the oblation of self, it is true, but never the annihilation of self except in the sense just explained.* It is an oblation that has as its effect the receiving of sevenfold in return. It is a happy exchange of gifts between God and man, in which by the very nature of the case man becomes infinitely enriched. All the members participating in the common action become thus enriched, each becomes a new man in Christ, and all are assimilated to one and the same transcendent Christ. And yet all the members thus ennobled remain ever different among themselves, truer and higher individual personalities than before.[74]

The second sentence of this long quotation is Michel repeating one of Beauduin's favorite lines. As mentioned in the last chapter, Beauduin was indebted to the French school of spirituality, though he had critiques of Marmion, and never tired of emphasizing Christ as the sole mediator, challenging an overemphasis on the Blessed Mother or the pope.

Reacting explicitly to Friedrich Nietzsche and his accusation of Christian morality as slave morality, Michel rejects a juridical understanding of the church, which is connected to a juridical understanding of sacrifice. This "destruction theory" of sacrifice whereby we celebrate the Mass to "appease [God's] anger" easily results in a faulty, extrinsic conception of our relationship with God. Therefore, the understanding of the role of sacrifice in daily living tends toward a slave mentality, wherein one is obliterated by the Master.[75] Instead, Michel offers the mystical body of Christ: "Thus membership in the Church is not confined to the minimum discharging of a debt, but implies an active participation in the life of the

---

[74] Virgil Michel, "Religious Experience: Liturgy Depersonalizes Piety?," *Orate Fratres* 13, no. 11 (1 October 1939): 494; emphasis mine.

[75] Michel, "The True Christian Spirit," 137.

Church. To be a member of the mystic body of Christ means always to be a living member, and to cooperate actively in the life of the whole. . . . There is in his calling nothing of the status of the slave and there is in his service of God naught of the attitude of slave morality."[76]

Because the self is not obliterated or subjugated, individuality remains. In a letter to Cummins more than a decade earlier, Michel wrote: "You believe the liturgy is all-comprehensive; you also must believe that every man is individual and very limited. Is not the inevitable conclusion that we must agree to look at different angles of such a catholic thing as the liturgy without feeling strangers?"[77] The liturgy, the expression of the mystical body, admits of individuality that spills over into our particular appropriation of it. We grasp different sides of the jewel but remain unified in our encounter with the beauty of God.

The Eucharist, the apex of the liturgical celebration, was oftentimes where the problem of unresolved individualism became most acute. As Michel writes:

> Christ indeed enters into individual souls according to our way of speaking. But Christ is not multiplied in the process, He is ever one and the same Christ, so that Communion is rather the more intimate union of souls in Christ. This is the teaching of the Church. St. Thomas, prince of theologians, expresses it by saying that the effect of the Eucharist is the Mystical Body of Christ, i.e., the more intimate union of members with their divine Head.[78]

For Michel, the mystical body communicates participation—participation in the life of Christ by each of his members. He highlights activity—"that which the liturgy offers should be translated into action"[79]—over the dominant conception of passivity, of simply having one's empty soul filled with grace or of merely hearing a Mass. Any approach that places the laity simply on the receiving end of teaching and sacramental grace fails

---

[76] Ibid., 140.

[77] Michel to Cummins, 8 September 1926, CAA, Patrick Cummins Collection, Box 72, Folder: "Patrick, Liturgical Press Correspondence."

[78] Michel, *Our Life in Christ*, 10–11.

[79] Virgil Michel, Review of *The Church Catholic and the Spirit of the Liturgy*, *Orate Fratres* (1936): 238.

to exemplify the extent to which the Christian life is really a participation in Christ's life that elevates us.

Michel had learned from Beauduin that liturgy was the true source of the mystical body of Christ and that one enters into the mystical body by way of it. The liturgy is, of course, sanctifying, but sacramental grace does not eliminate the need for education. Therefore, a primary aim of the liturgical apostolate in the United States was liturgical education—to help pastoral workers and laypeople see the richness of the liturgy. According to Michel, that education could proceed in two ways. It could begin with the various concrete elements of the liturgy and proceed didactically. Or, instead, "it may work at a deeper understanding of the focal concept of the liturgy, of the supreme supernatural reality of the Mystic Body of Christ," which ultimately lights "a new flame of religious love at work in the soul." [80] Such a flame, Michel insisted, cannot but result in a deeper love of Christ encountered in the liturgy. In terms of rational explanation, Michel claimed that "without an understanding of the mystical body of Christ it is impossible to understand the true social nature of the liturgy as the life of that body." Because the liturgy is "essentially the expression of the inner supernatural reality of the fellowship of all the souls that constitute the mystical body," [81] however, one could garner an understanding of the mystical body by participation in the liturgy. "All parts of the liturgy," Michel explained, "increase knowledge of the organic fellowship in which all men are actually, or by destiny, true members with Christ of His Mystical Body, and help the mind more readily to see Christ in all men, and to serve God in them." [82] Thus, when Michel wrote that the mystical body of Christ "can hardly be described by those who do not understand, but it is understood by all who have experienced it," [83] he was thinking primarily of the liturgy but also of the other components of living the Christ life, which include the works of mercy and other work for justice.

---

[80] Michel, "With Our Readers," 186–87. Michel wrote, "The liturgy is the embodiment of God, who has in the liturgy descended from heaven and eternity into time and this earth of ours, and who abides and acts there throughout all time." See Virgil Michel, "The Liturgy and Catholic Life."

[81] Michel, "The Liturgy and Catholic Life," 119.

[82] Ibid.

[83] Michel, "With Our Readers," 187.

It seems appropriate to end this section on liturgical roots of Michel's mystical body theology by noting that one of the challenges he and his liturgical movement companions faced in their popularizing program for the liturgy was a tension between private devotions and liturgical reform. Scholars of the liturgical movement have long pointed out that a key goal of the movement was to reorient all devotions to the liturgy and to eliminate devotional exercises during Mass altogether. As noted, on his return from Europe Michel did not find many Catholics familiar with mystical body theology. Yet, to the extent to which the mystical body was known among the laity in the early twentieth century, it came from devotional practices of mostly religious men and women, indebted to, or adjacent to, the seventeenth-century French school. St. Vincent de Paul's emphasis on daily dedicating oneself to the incarnation is a prime example of a devotional practice that arose in seventeenth-century France.[84] St. Vincent spent time with the Oratorians shortly before founding the Congregation of the Mission, and Bérulle served as his spiritual adviser.[85] Many Catholic educators and lay organizations in the United States were connected in some way to the Vincentian tradition, including the Congregation of the Mission itself, but also the Daughters of Charity, the Ladies of Charity, the Sisters of Charity, and the Society of St. Vincent de Paul. Thus, Michel's explication of the liturgy as formation in the theology of the mystical body par excellence held the potential to bridge the gap between the actual practice of the people and what Godfrey Diekmann later called the liturgy: the "only . . . strictly speaking . . . popular devotion" because it applies to the entirety of the Catholic people, across vocation and role.[86] The extent to which the US liturgical movement failed in its endeavor to popularize the liturgy is perhaps connected to the extent to which the movement was unable to facilitate the connection between mystical body theology in private devotions and mystical body theology in liturgical practice.

---

[84] Vincent de Paul, *Common Rules* for the Congregation of the Mission (1658), chapter 10, no. 2, accessed via http://famvin.org/wiki/Common_Rules.

[85] Raymond Deville, "The Seventeenth-Century School of French Spirituality," *Vincentian Heritage Journal* 11, no. 1 (Spring 1990): 19–20.

[86] Godfrey Diekmann, "The Apostolate," *Orate Fratres* 15, no. 1 (1940): 43.

Solidarity Rooted in Christ

Michel returned from Europe with answers to questions that pestered him before he left. He saw the source of contemporary social problems rooted in individualism. In Michel's account, this problem was not solely political and economic. Indeed, ideas, politics, and economics always went together. Michel traced a line of progression leading to contemporary naturalism, the position that admits of no personal God, from the "weakened conception of God" in Deism, which was preceded by the extrinsic, vengeful God of Puritanism and Calvinism.[87] These ideas had a social impact.

The seeds planted by Beauduin reached full flowering after Michel returned from mandatory light pastoral duty on the Chippewa reservation in northern Minnesota. By 1930 Michel's breakneck work schedule had exhausted him. More than one of his colleagues remarked that he appeared never to take a break, so Abbot Alcuin mandated one. It was, however, a Benedictine "break" involving organizing schools, religious education classes, balancing the books, supervising a large farm, and taking a census, all in the first seven months.[88] Yet, Michel was made well enough to return to Saint John's permanently in September 1933, after which his writing about social questions and problems increased dramatically. It seems that the complex of the onset of the Great Depression (1929), the publication of *Quadragesimo Anno* (1931), and his experience of the poverty and hardship faced by the Chippewa catalyzed the incipient conceptual link between liturgy and the social question that he had imbibed from Beauduin.

Michel acknowledges this need for the US liturgical movement to emphasize the interconnectedness of the entire Christian life (or culture), particularly in terms of social reform, in an article published shortly after his return to Saint John's. Characteristically, he did so by a colorful, stirring call that ends the article:

All zealous workers in the liturgical movement must visualize their task with the all-embracing sympathy and the inclusiveness

---

[87] Virgil Michel, *Philosophy of Human Conduct* (Minneapolis: Burgess Publishing Company, 1936), 85.

[88] Marx, *Virgil Michel*, 164.

that was Christ's—else their efforts will be greatly frustrated or entirely doomed to failure. What would have happened if the early Christians, one and all, had gone literally to the Thebaid? What, if they had done so figuratively by keeping their religion strictly to themselves, if they had kept it out of all contact with the cultural environment in which they found themselves, had kept it confined within the walls of the churches in which they worshiped?[89]

How interesting for the Benedictine monk to worry about the implications for the church and for the world if all fifth-century Christians had gone as ascetics to the Theban desert! Since we know relatively little about Michel's time on the reservation, scholars are left to speculate about its impact on Michel's mind, heart, and spirit.[90] While Marx calls Michel's time among the Chippewa an "interesting interlude" in Michel's life, it was clearly not an exotic wilderness retreat but a deep encounter with God's suffering people, one determinative for the course his apostolate would take in its final years. As such, this period for Michel is not unlike Beauduin's time as labor chaplain to the Aumôniers. Both were exercises in solidarity that catalyzed theological commitments to the liturgical-social implications of the theology of the mystical body. This period for Michel obviously requires further study. At this point, however, we can note that Michel's ministry among those who have an obviously fractured relationship with the broader constructed American identity seems to have led him to emphasize the ways in which social reform might aid other marginalized groups in order to bring us all into greater unity. He did not, of course, return to Saint John's recommending that everyone take a holiday to a reservation or that the Chippewa represent the natural blood unity on which a supernatural unity can and should be built.

From early in his career, Michel had emphasized the vast consequences of a deep-seated individualism. The Great Depression was not simply an economic matter, as some would claim, but rather "the logical result of

[89] "The Liturgical Movement and the Future," *America* 54, no. 1 (1935): 6. On this point, see also Howard Duff, "Virgil Michel's Approach to the American Liturgical Movement through His Writings in *Orate Fratres* (1926–1939)" (MA thesis, Villanova University, 2016).

[90] For one example of a scholarly approach to the question, see Michael M. Pomedli, "Ojibwa Influences on Virgil Michel," *Worship* 70, no. 6 (1996): 531–42.

the general philosophy of life that has guided human affairs for some centuries."[91] Its onset only confirmed the failures of individualism. "It takes but a moment's glance," he wrote, "to see that both the totalitarian State and the amorphous mass-rabble aggregate that individualism has made of democracy are quite out of harmony with the Christian concept of society as reflected in the mystical body of Christ."[92] The concept of society reflected in the mystical body is one grounded in solidarity. It draws attention to relationships that are not immediately obvious but nevertheless bind us.

From a very different historical and social location, but with a related set of concerns, contemporary Latino theologian Roberto Goizueta shares with Michel a critical reading of the atomization of modern society. Michel's big-picture analysis of the gradual extrinsicization of God from the world accompanies the gradual individualization of the human person. According to Goizueta, the individualism of the "Protestant principle" (Paul Tillich's term) and the individualism of liberal economics are both fed by the individualism of liberal, Enlightenment politics. This mutually informing threesome results in what he calls the "Western cult of the individual" in which individuals come to understand themselves as separated and isolated from both contemporaries (i.e., communities) and ancestors (i.e., tradition). Relationships, then, are ancillary to the human person and largely chosen rather than assumed. Those that are assumed, Goizueta argues, must themselves be freely chosen before they can exert any claim on the individual. It follows, then, that all relationships are at all times renegotiable.[93]

Of course, the answer to a virulent individualism is not a facile collectivism, as Michel points out. The issue is anthropological, and so more complex. In the anthropology of Michel's mystical body theology, persons find their individuality by grasping their place in the body of Christ. Each person is another Christ and all are bound together in the mystical body. The liturgy, "the life of the Church," as Michel would call it, *makes* the

---

[91] Michel, "The Liturgy and Catholic Life," 129.

[92] Virgil Michel, "Natural and Supernatural Society I: The Sacramental Principle as Guide," *Orate Fratres* 10, no. 6 (18 April 1936): 246.

[93] Roberto Goizueta, "United States Hispanic Theology and the Challenge of Pluralism," in *Frontiers of Hispanic Theology in the United States*, ed. Allan Figueroa Deck (Maryknoll, NY: Orbis Books, 1992), 5.

mystical body of Christ. Thus the societal vision that flows out of mystical body theology is built on the interdependence of solidarity. The dominant Modern idea holds the individual as the basic building block of society. A vision rooted in the mystical body of Christ emphasizes the human person as "intrinsically social by nature and definition"[94] and points to that primordial web of relationships in which and out of which individuals come to understand their very identity as individuals.

As he indicates, Michel saw all problems as ultimately theological problems, a vision that aligns with his Benedictine heritage. Throughout his Rule, St. Benedict consistently exhorts monks to guard against evil and seek Christ in everything that they do, even what may at first appear to be merely mundane. The Rule devotes much attention to the seemingly little things that monks encounter, from how to sleep to how enthusiastically one should laugh.[95] If every decision, even a seemingly inconsequential one, is a decision for or against God, it follows that social and political ills of all kinds have theological roots. And the root causes of the Great Depression are individualistic—a profound failure to recognize and live a communal, cooperative life. Therefore, the solution is the mystical body of Christ:

> In every member joining the mystical body, the redemption of Christ becomes active, essentially in the same way, yet with individual differences. It is in the totality of this fellowship of souls in Christ, that the redemptive work of Christ finds its full realization. For that reason the true Christ-life is realized in the common fellowship as such. The individual realizes it in himself by joining the corporate life of the fellowship, despite the fact that the individual member always retains his own personality and his own personal responsibility.[96]

Michel's vision of the mystical body of Christ addresses the problem of individualism without absorbing the individual in the manner of various

---

[94] Ibid. See also Goizueta, "The Symbolic Realism of U.S. Latino/a Popular Catholicism," *Theological Studies* 65, no. 2 (June 2004): 258.

[95] Benedict of Nursia, *The Holy Rule of St. Benedict*, trans. Rev. Boniface Verheyen (1949), accessed via http://www.ccel.org/ccel/benedict/rule.txt. See, for example, Prologue and chaps. 1, 4, 7, 12, 33, 52, 53.

[96] Michel, *Our Life in Christ*, 36.

collectivisms. In entering into the mystical body of Christ, one becomes "'another Christ,' carrying the divine life in himself."[97] Here, again, we see the influence of the French spirituality school, which emphasized the Christian life as incorporation into Christ; the Christian becomes *alter Christus*. Michel emphasized that it was not only the ordained but each of the faithful who is made into another Christ.

We gain a window into Michel's social thought, especially its reception, by listening to Sen. Eugene McCarthy's biographer. "According to his teachers," Dominic Sandbrook writes, "McCarthy was particularly interested in the problems of the day and was 'very much under the influence of Virgil Michel's ideas.'" Sandbrook continues, "Fr. Virgil was probably the strongest single influence on his political thought." McCarthy graduated from Saint John's in 1935 and returned there to teach economics and education from 1940 to 1943. He became known by his students at Saint John's for his emphasis on Catholic social teaching, especially compassion for the poor and oppressed, referencing Day and the Catholic Worker repeatedly. Later, McCarthy described what was happening at Saint John's in the 1930s: "a sophisticated, an historically advanced application of the Benedictine commitment to worship and work, not as separable, but as the essence of the creative or re-creative role of man." Michel's vision brought these principles firmly to the ground: "The social consequences of his teaching are clear. If we participate in the liturgy according to this teaching, we take on full responsibility for our fellow men disregarding national boundaries, differences of race, or of culture."[98] The French stream of mystical body theology had given Michel a theological apparatus to develop the implications of Benedictine life.

Michel tried to inculcate appreciation of these implications even in his young students. Upon his death, Michel left a manuscript of a textbook for grade-schoolers that was published posthumously in 1939. Part 1 of the text is titled "Source of the Life in Christ." After chapters on God, original sin, and redemption, chapter 4 covers "The New Creation." Chapter 4 is also where Michel discusses the mystical body of Christ—it is the immediate implication of redemption in Christ. It is only after that, in chapter 5,

[97] Ibid., 37.
[98] Dominic Sandbrook, *Eugene McCarthy: The Rise and Fall of Postwar American Liberalism* (New York: Alfred A. Knopf, 2004), 13.

that Michel discusses the church as such.[99] While in some sense theological reflection always begins in the middle of a complex mystery, such organization is no accident for the scholastic-minded Michel, who was often telling colleagues to think in a more organized fashion. Thus, the mystical body of Christ is the effect of the incarnation–paschal mystery and theologically prior to ecclesiology. The church is clearly central to Christ's redemptive work, but reflection on the mystical body is wider than reflection on the church. For Michel, this does not mean that the church is an expendable add-on. Rather, the opposite: it is the clearest place where we encounter and learn about the mystical body.

That deeper cognizance of the mystical body of Christ—the fundamental form of our salvation—cemented in liturgical practice leads to various insights about social difficulties. Two years before his death, in the pages of *Orate Fratres*, Michel celebrated "the casual statement of a social worker" who proclaimed, "The only remedy against race prejudice . . . is to get the children to understand what their membership in the mystical body really means." He acknowledged the myriad differences among humans and elaborated on her claim:

> How can all these natural and unnatural differences be weathered by man . . . ? Only by a common consciousness of a bond far deeper than all these which binds all men in a common fellowship, a bond that not only surmounts nature but elevates it supernaturally. . . . Such a bond is the mystical body of Christ, not merely as a supernatural fellowship, but as a supernatural source of divine energy and life for each individual member of it.

In order to supplant the individualistic and nationalistic tendencies rampant in Europe and taking some root in the United States, Christians must strive to "attain and spread consciousness of the wonderful doctrine of the mystical body of Christ as a truth to be lived and at the same time a source of spiritual inspiration and of supernatural strength for living faithful to that truth." [100] The solidarity of the mystical body led Michel to work with de Hueck Doherty to facilitate Saint John's University's reception of African American students by way of her Friendship House

---

[99] Michel, *Our Life in Christ.*
[100] Virgil Michel, "The Mystical Body," *Orate Fratres* 10 (1936): 419–21.

in Harlem.[101] One cannot help but notice the contrast on this point with Adam's approach to mystical body theology. For Adam, the realization of supernatural unity in the mystical body required a fundamental natural, racial unity. For Michel, the supernatural character of the mystical body breaks open tribalism. The unity of the mystical body is far deeper than any other natural cause for unity that we might identify. In terms of a theology of grace, we might say that Michel allows for greater disruption in the order of redemption than does Adam.

Michel wearied of hearing many of his fellow Americans, even his fellow Catholics, denounce communism repeatedly without addressing, as had Popes Leo XIII and Pius XI in their social encyclicals, the dangers posed by industrial capitalism. Exasperation leaps off the page when he writes, "If I mention the blindness ever of spiritual leaders to the immensely important trend of events, I am not referring to a disregard of the menace of communism . . . nor primarily to the menace of fascism . . . but rather to the more insidious menace that modern capitalism or bourgeois civilization has constituted for all spiritual values."[102] It was unfettered capitalism (i.e., economic individualistic ideology) that led to the rubble of the Great Depression after all.

As Michel inspired McCarthy, he also engaged various radical movements. His support of organized labor led some to think him more on their side than perhaps he ultimately was. One Catholic communist wrote a letter to Michel expressing a "hurt protest" after Michel had argued in a *Commonweal* article that those on the side of labor were just as capable of individualism as the capitalists.[103] And, as always, Michel attacked individualism with great vim. Like G. K. Chesterton, Hilaire Belloc, and many Catholics of his day, Michel considered himself a distributist in economic matters, a position based on the vision outlined in *Rerum Novarum* and, later, *Quadragesimo Anno*. Yet, he was surprised at the places he found these principles articulated. In a 1935 letter to Marvin Lowes of

[101] Dawn Gibeau, "Fr. Virgil, St. John's Monks Spread Idea that Liturgy Creates Community," *National Catholic Reporter* 30, no. 13 (10 December 1993): 13.

[102] Virgil Michel, Foreword to Emmanuel Mounier, *A Personalist Manifesto*, trans. the monks of Saint John's Abbey (New York: Longmans, Green Co., 1938), xii.

[103] Robert O. Carleton to Michel, Brooklyn, 28 May 1938, SJAA, Series Z, Box 23, Folder 7.

the *American Review,* Michel refers to Lowes's desire to have a Catholic priest critique C. H. Douglas's 1924 book, *Social Credit,* which espouses a distributist vision. Michel says that he approached Douglas's work "as a scoffer and left as an admirer." He was met with "great surprise . . . to find out to what high degree Douglas's *Social Credit* is such a remarkable plan for effecting the distributist system." [104]

In a letter to a New York Franciscan suspicious of the Catholic Worker, Michel vigorously defends Day's budding social movement: "As far as I know there is no more successful antagonist against Communism in this country than the Catholic Worker." [105] Michel thought that any rejection of communism had to be careful not to abandon the plight of the worker. Further in 1937, Michel—tongue-in-cheek—lays out a program for the fight against communism. He notes the fervor with which many American Catholics have been calling for a "good old American fight" against the Reds. Michel's own eight-point campaign plan of Christian warfare includes preaching the mystical body and universal brotherhood of all as well as the social teaching of the church from the pulpit, pooling extra resources for the needy, and opening all Catholic institutions as housing for the homeless. Of course Michel means to illustrate how Catholic opposition to communism does not include opposition to shared resources. This much, he would say, could be clearly ascertained from the liturgy, which is why the most important point in his battle plan is that each "soldier" begin the day with Mass.

Like his mentor Beauduin, Michel's thinking about the mystical body led him to embrace movements and take positions that emphasized solidarity. Contemporary theologian Meghan J. Clark reflects on solidarity as it has been developed in Catholic Social Teaching:

> Unlike interdependence, development, or increasing social complexity, solidarity develops as a theoretical way to understand many different aspects of the human person and the human reality. Not simply a reflection on the status quo, the call to solidarity is a

[104] Michel, Collegeville, to Marvin M. Lowes, New York, 16 January 1935, SJAA, Series Z, Box 25, Folder 7.

[105] Michel to Adalbert Callahan, OFM, Collegeville, 6 February 1936, SJAA, Series Z, Box 23, Folder 7.

normative theological reflection on the way human persons and human communities were created and intended to develop and flourish. To say that solidarity is an integral part of the very creation of human persons is furthermore to say that this intended solidarity is the way human communities *ought* to exist.[106]

Mystical body theology for Michel draws us in to what Clark calls "the way human persons and human communities were created and intended to flourish," but because of the very nature of the image, it does so in a christological key. Human beings are all members or potential members of the mystical body; thus they all have a real relationship to Christ the head. When Michel gestures toward a form of society indicated by the mystical body of Christ, he suggests that it is one that avoids the twin dangers of excessive individualism and collectivism. Clark calls these two errors the vices associated with the virtue of solidarity. Excessive individualism is the vice of deficiency and collectivism is the vice of excess. The virtue (as Pope John Paul II deemed solidarity) is the prudent exercise of the golden mean, steering a course between these two vices.[107] Michel thought that the liturgy helped Christians to steer that course and his own life represents tireless efforts to cultivate this virtue, which requires not only individual character development but also cooperation and collaboration with others.

Conclusions

Michel was not, strictly speaking, a theologian. In fact, none of the group that made up what Paul Hanly Furfey referred to as the "new social Catholicism"[108] was. Among Americans such as Michel, Day, Furfey, de Hueck Doherty, John LaFarge, Daniel Lord, and others, the mystical

---

[106] Meghan J. Clark, *The Vision of Catholic Social Thought: The Virtue of Solidarity and the Praxis of Human Rights* (Minneapolis: Fortress Press, 2014), 20.

[107] Ibid., 114–20. For an example of Pope John Paul II's discussion of solidarity as a virtue, see *Sollicitudo Rei Socialis* (1987), no. 40.

[108] On "the new social Catholicism," see Joseph P. Chinnici and Angelyn Dries, eds., *Prayer and Practice in the American Catholic Community* (Maryknoll, NY: Orbis Books, 2000), 156–59. Chinnici and Dries published Furfey's letter to Norman McKenna on which Furfey copied Michel, among others. Among the salient principles

body of Christ was not simply an ecclesiological image or category but rather a descriptor of how life in Christ should be lived. Ostensibly, this is because the new social Catholicism was not driven by theologians—who were at the time largely neoscholastic thinkers—but by intelligent Catholics with a social sense. There appears no sharp division between theology and spirituality among the social Catholics because their theological concerns were always resolutely practical. Since their theological writing was not considered theology per se, they wrote and reflected with a freedom afforded by their circumstance. As we have seen, in the post-*Pascendi* era, theology was construed as a very narrow enterprise, undertaken by Roman-trained neoscholastics who wrote treatises that either were or read very much like manuals. It was a very circumscribed task that often commented on Thomas's commentators. Michel was very critical of this tradition, though he remained a scholastic. While as early as the 1920s and 1930s *ressourcement* theology had its beginnings in Europe, in the United States, scholars thinking theologically were formally situated in other fields, writing for different audiences.[109] Yet they made no less of a contribution.

Following his mentor, Beauduin, Michel's mystical body theology was not limited to ecclesiological treatises and even pushed beyond an ecclesiological category or model. Clearly, for Michel, the mystical body of Christ described the church but blossomed forth into a way of conceiving the whole of the Christ-life, which was always corporate in its orientation and broad in its application. Michel's pragmatic personalist vision fired a more practical theology of the mystical body grounded in the liturgy of the church. The mystical body of Christ was key to living the Christian life—for everyone—it wasn't simply the domain of theologians. It was a main theme in several retreats that he gave. It was the starting point for young people to think about the implications of God's saving work in Christ. It had implications for the structure of society, for asceticism, for the family, for education, for art and architecture.

that appear to tie together new social Catholics, Furfey includes the conviction that "we must live the doctrine of the Mystical Body of Christ."

[109] See Portier, *Divided Friends*, 326ff. Portier identifies three specific post-*Pascendi* avenues for theological thinking in the United States: (1) The National Catholic War Council and the Social Sciences, (2) Catholic Medievalism, and (3) History.

CHAPTER 3

Receded Body

Mystical Body of Christ after Mid-Century

At the conclusion of the last chapter, mystical body theology was, even beyond the 1920s, roaring. But by 1970, treatises dedicated to the mystical body of Christ had virtually disappeared from Catholic discourse. What had been a pervasive theological norm for Michel, and for the French stream to which he was indebted, became an ecclesiological building block, an image or model among many in composing an adequate ecclesiology.

Even in terms of ecclesiology, many thought that, following the 1943 magisterial endorsement of mystical body theology by Pope Pius XII, this would be a dominant ecclesial image at Vatican II. Drawing largely on the work of de Lubac, among others, the council foregrounded the fundamental mystery of the church as well as its sacramental character in the first chapter of *Lumen Gentium*. These decisions were undoubtedly rooted in the mystical body revival. Yet, while "mystical body" peppered the preparatory schemas, it only flashed in the conciliar documents themselves. There are many, many elements at play, especially at the council, in this shift of theological sensibility. This chapter aims to highlight and contextualize several of the factors leading to mystical body theology's ebb: the effects of World War II, the rise of Catholic critical biblical scholarship, and, finally, the consolidation of Roman-stream mystical body theology in the working documents of the Second Vatican Council.

The Catholic Library Association's *Catholic Periodical Index* tells the story. In the very first volume, covering 1930 to 1933, the heading "Mystical Body" simply refers readers to the subject "Catholic Church." There, one finds about a dozen entries pertaining directly to the theme of the mystical body of Christ, including articles by Fr. Vincent McNabb, several from *Orate Fratres*, as well as a few reviews of a book on the theme written by Abbé Joseph Anger and translated by the Paulist editor of the *Catholic World*, John J. Burke. The next volume, which spans the five years from 1934 to 1938, lists seventy-three entries under the heading "Mystical Body of Christ," including a cross-reference to "Priesthood, Universal."

The cross-reference indicates precisely the cutting-edge nature of the theology of the mystical body during this period. The question of the priesthood of believers, having dominated the Protestant Reformation, was not a mainstream topic of Catholic theological conversation in the 1930s. Reviving it was, however, a key component of Michel's program for liturgical renewal. Indeed, the heading shows three articles, one in *Orate Fratres* itself and another in *Catholic School Journal* by Gerald Ellard, associate editor of *Orate Fratres*. The third is part of a series on the history and implications of *alter Christus* theology in the *Ecclesiastical Review*. The patristic truism, *Christianus alter Christus* or "the Christian is another Christ" was also thematic to Michel's apostolate, especially its pedagogical arm.[1] Joseph Bluett, in his bibliography of mystical body theology in French, English, and Latin periodicals, describes 1937 as "the crest of the acceleration" of mystical body studies.[2] Especially at its zenith, mystical body theology in the English-speaking world was connected to, and itself opening up, new avenues in Catholic theological reflection.

With its fourteenth volume in 1967–1968, *The Catholic Periodical Index* merged with *The Guide to Catholic Literature*, creating *The Catholic Periodical and Literature Index* (CPLI). In addition to the 123 fully indexed periodicals, there were now several thousand books included on the register. By this point, however, mystical body of Christ theology had

---

[1] For its most famous locus, see St. Cyprian of Carthage, *De dominica oratione*, trans. Robert Ernest Wallis, in *Ante-Nicene Fathers*, vol. 5, ed. Alexander Roberts, James Donaldson, and A. Cleveland Coxe (Buffalo, NY: Christian Literature Publishing Co., 1886), no. 9, where Cyprian reflects on divine filiation. Michel often used the phrase and found it supportive of his mystical body theology, even as Mersch found Cyprian's work to render a mere "moral union" (Mersch, *The Whole Christ*, 383). As noted in the last chapter, Michel derived this theology from Bérulle through Marmion and Beauduin.

[2] Joseph Bluett, "The Mystical Body: A Bibliography, 1890–1940," *Theological Studies* 3 (1942): 262.

slowed to a trickle. This volume showed three citations under "Mystical Body of Christ" and the next four volumes, cataloging materials through 1976, contained a total of six citations (only two in English), with no subject heading at all for "mystical body of Christ" in volume eighteen (1975–1976). "Mystical body of Christ" had disappeared from the CPLI.

At the Second Vatican Council

Clearly, something had changed over those forty years. Initial inclinations would lead us to suggest the Second Vatican Council as the primary impetus for change. The council's well-known prioritization of the image "People of God" as the title of chapter 2 in *Lumen Gentium* served as a signal of change from Pius XII's *Mystici Corporis Christi*. The phrase "mystical body [of Christ]" does appear several times throughout the conciliar documents, often when the bishops wish to indicate the church present across space and time,[3] but it is no longer the most noble, most sublime, and most divine expression for the church of Christ, as Pius had deemed it.[4] Chapter 1 explored, to some extent, the genesis and wider context of *Mystici Corporis*, but in order to understand what happened on the floor of the council and to appreciate the influence that *Mystici* had on those in attendance it is necessary to understand some of the encyclical's ramifications.

Mystici had shifted the ecclesiological conversation on the continent in several ways. First, it encouraged nascent Catholic ecumenical activity. As James Livingston notes, the encyclical stands in a line of "an increasingly positive attitude toward the salvation of non-Christians" by

---

[3] A noncomprehensive list of mystical body mentions in the documents of the Second Vatican Council includes *Sacrosantum Concilium*, no. 7 (with reference to worship offered by Head and members in the liturgy), 99 (regarding Liturgy of the Hours); *Lumen Gentium*, nos. 7, 8 (notably here mystical body of Christ is paired with "the society structured with hierarchical organs" as two ends of the one pole that makes the one church), 23 (twice), 26 (mystical body without prepositional phrase), 50, 54 (mystical body without prepositional phrase); *Gaudium et Spes*, no. 50; *Ad Gentes*, no. 7; *Christus Dominus*, no. 33; *Perfectae Caritatis*, no. 7; *Apostolicam Actuositatem*, nos. 2 (mystical body without prepositional phrase), 3 (the apostolic charge comes to the laity directly from Christ the Head into whose Mystical Body they are incorporated in baptism).

[4] *Mystici Corporis*, no. 13.

an emphasis on invincible ignorance. He favorably quotes a scholar who says that Pius widens the understanding of implicit membership in the church to implicit relationship with God.[5] As noted in chapter 1, however, the encyclical's discussion of those outside the physical boundaries of the Roman Catholic Church is not limited only to those who are in the state of invincible ignorance. As ecumenically minded theologians reflected on the encyclical with their Protestant conversation partners, the questions raised by *Mystici* about membership in the church were brought to direct discussion.

Second, the encyclical describes the Roman Catholic Church as the mystical body of Christ.[6] In light of what has just been said in the preceding paragraph, this point is somewhat paradoxical. Pius firmly planted the center of gravity of the mystical body of Christ in the Roman Catholic Church, but the encyclical affirmed, in ways that previous magisterial statements had not, the relationship to the mystical body of those outside its visible bounds. In 1943, about two months after *Mystici*'s promulgation, Father Richard (soon to be Cardinal Archbishop) Cushing of Boston had urged a fellow priest to refrain from going on record with a hardline stance against Catholic cooperation with other religions, arguing that "it would antagonize those outside the fold at the very same time when the world needs . . . collaboration among those who call themselves Christians."[7] As archbishop, Cushing oversaw in his archdiocese the 1953 excommunication of Jesuit Leonard Feeney following upon just such a public hardline stance on *extra ecclesiam nulla salus*.[8] It is important to

---

[5] James Livingston et al., *Modern Christian Thought: The Twentieth Century*, 2nd ed., vol. 2 (Minneapolis: Fortress Press, 2006), 475. Livingston draws on Miikka Ruokanen, *The Catholic Doctrine of Non-Christian Religions* (Leiden: Brill, 1992), esp. 18–19.

[6] *Mystici Corporis*, no. 13.

[7] Richard J. Cushing to Bishop Francis McIntyre, 21 August 1943, quoted in John T. McGreevy, *Catholicism and American Freedom: A History* (New York: Norton, 2003), 205.

[8] Literally, "outside the church there is no salvation." At the St. Benedict Center at Harvard, Feeney took this doctrine from the tradition and emphasized the visible bounds of the Roman Catholic Church as "church." On Feeney and the wider context of the affair, see Patrick W. Carey, "Avery Dulles, St. Benedict's Center, and No Salvation Outside the Church, 1940–1953," *Catholic Historical Review* 93 (2007): 553–75. For a longer study from another angle, see George B. Pepper, *The Boston*

recall that Pope Pius XII supported Feeney's excommunication. In fact, the letter from the Holy Office to Cardinal Cushing regarding the matter makes reference to *Mystici Corporis* in defending the church's openness to the salvation of those united to it by an implicit desire.[9] This letter would later be quoted in *Lumen Gentium*.[10]

Augustin Bea, Pope Pius's confessor and future first president of the Secretariat for Promoting Christian Unity, was not present for the drafting of *Mystici Corporis* but, according to Jerome Vereb, did influence much more heavily the postwar encyclical *Mediator Dei* (1947), which can be read as answering some of those questions about church membership raised by *Mystici*.[11] In the latter encyclical, Pius writes: "By the waters of Baptism, as by common right, Christians are made members of the Mystical Body of Christ the Priest, and by the 'character' which is imprinted on their souls, they are appointed to give worship to God. Thus they participate, according to their condition, in the priesthood of Christ."[12] The move toward further recognition of the relationship of non-Catholic Christians begun in *Mystici* reached a further articulation in *Mediator*. Of course, the expressed topic of the latter letter was the liturgy of the church, which Pius described as "public worship . . . rendered by the Mystical Body of Christ in the entirety of its Head and members" and followed up with several important liturgical reforms.[13]

Heresy Case in View of the Secularization of Religion: A Case Study in the Sociology of Religion (Lewiston, NY: E. Mellen Press, 1988).

[9] The letter from the Holy Office to Cushing, dated 8 August 1949, rejected Feeney's position that grave sin was not required for a person's consignment to hell and further that anyone outside the visible bounds of the Roman Catholic Church was outside the reach of salvation. The letter is itself a kind of commentary on *Mystici Corporis*. Marchetti-Selvaggiani and Ottaviani of the Holy Office refer to the encyclical multiple times throughout their letter. They interpret the encyclical rather narrowly, but they nevertheless reject Feeney's hardline stance. Their letter was published, with an accompanying English translation, in *The American Ecclesiastical Review* after Cushing was instructed by Rome to make the letter public. See F. Cardinal Marchetti-Selvaggiani, Vatican City to Archbishop Richard J. Cushing, Boston, MA, 8 August 1949 in *The American Ecclesiastical Review* 127 (1952): 307-15.

[10] *Lumen Gentium*, no. 16, supplementary note 19.

[11] On Bea's work in this regard, see Vereb, *Because He Was a German!*, 131-43.

[12] Pius XII, *Mediator Dei*, no. 88.

[13] *Mediator Dei*, no. 20.

The fact remains that the conception of the mystical body of Christ narrowed after *Mystici*. And from the viewpoint of Pope Pius's 1950 encyclical *Humani Generis*, *Mystici* had clearly identified the Roman Catholic Church and the mystical body of Christ as one and the same. *Humani Generis*, ghostwritten by Tromp, had splashed cold water on the hot and crackling *ressourcement* movement.[14] There is another, often missed, implication of *Mystici* for Catholic theology. The encyclical also delimited mystical body theology to ecclesiology. That is to say, after *Mystici*, ecclesiology was the indubitable proper sphere of inquiry for studies concerning the mystical body of Christ. This is an important point because it sets the framework for its consideration at the council and also narrows the view of postconciliar commentators on the development of mystical body theology, by whom it is often considered as a model of the Church, or in some similar conceptual framework. As we have seen, however, in the decades before *Mystici*, especially for the French stream and for Michel, mystical body was not limited to ecclesiology but functioned more as a fundamental theological norm from which a variety of insights flowed.

Not only was mystical body theology narrowed to ecclesiology after *Mystici*, but ecclesiology was magisterially narrowed to mystical body theology. This is the third point, a key to understanding the place of mys-

---

[14] Pius XII, *Humani Generis*, no. 27. In Latin, *corpus Christi mysticum et Ecclesiam Catholicam Romanam unum idemque esse*. On Tromp's role in *Humani Generis*, see Teuffenbach, *Aus Liebe und Treue zur Kirche*, 40. Teuffenbach's archival research has demonstrated that Tromp played a key role in that encyclical as well; she writes, *Aufgrund der Archivforschung kann inzwischen auch mit großer Sicherheit gesagt werden, daß Tromp Endredaktor der Enzyklika 'Humani Generis' war* (ibid.). Michael Kerlin has noted the obvious impact of Garrigou-Lagrange's theological work, if not his direct hand, on the content of *Humani Generis*: "For years, Garrigou-Lagrange had advised pontifical congregations and had maintained an official role with the Holy Office of the Inquisition. What is more, as one who had regular conversations with Pius XII, he was surely privy to the worries of the pope and the curialists, and probably did his share to make them worry about matters philosophical and theological. When *Humani Generis* appeared, it was hard to miss his influence. . . . No one has ever found a 'smoking gun' proving that Garrigou-Lagrange shared in ghostwriting *Humani Generis* or has ever fixed his exact contribution. But . . . it is plain that he had a major role in its gestation" (Michael Kerlin, "Reginald Garrigou-Lagrange: Defending the Faith from *Pascendi dominici gregis* to *Humani Generis*," *U.S. Catholic Historian* 25, no. 1 [2007]: 110–11).

tical body theology at Vatican II. The encyclical laid down a new formal starting point for ecclesiology from the magisterium. While Pius X and Pius XI had made passing reference to the mystical body of Christ in some of their letters, mostly in conjunction with Catholic Action exhortations, there had never been a magisterial document of *Mystici*'s scope that had reflected on the church itself. As such, *Mystici Corporis* made mystical body theology the *de facto* starting point for the discussions on the nature of the church at Vatican II.

The composition of the theological preparatory commission charged with writing schemas for the bishops' initial consideration ensured that the mystical body theology dominant in the schema *De Ecclesia* would be of the Roman stream. Tromp—the commission's secretary—who had served as Pope Pius's chief collaborator for *Mystici* was also heavily involved in preparing the initial schema on the church. At the council itself, Yves Congar summed up Tromp's approach to the schema, discussions concerning it, and related questions: "He brings everything under his one thesis: *Ecclesia catholica est sola Ecclesia; est Corpus Christi mysticum*."[15] Thus, the theology of the mystical body articulated in the schema did not sound the same liturgical, ecumenical, quasi-porous, and sacramental tones as had that of Beauduin, Mersch, and Michel.

The first chapter of the schema—a joint effort of Tromp and Ugo Lattanzi—explicated the mystical body of Christ in two paragraphs, with an emphasis on its visibility and the various roles within it, and ended with a final two paragraphs that assert the identity between the visible society and the mystical body, Roman Catholicism and the church of Christ.[16] A cadre of especially French and Belgian *periti*, including Gérard Philips, Congar, de Lubac, and Joseph Lécuyer, were intent on broadening this conception of the mystical body of Christ, as applied to the church.

When the schema was, in fact, presented on the floor of the council, Achille Cardinal Liénart began the discussion with his now famous critique of the draft for insinuating that the whole of the mystical body was

---

[15] Congar, *My Journal of the Council*, 66. English translation: "The Catholic Church is the only Church; it is the Mystical Body of Christ."

[16] Joseph Komonchak, "The Struggle for the Council during the Preparation of Vatican II (1960–1962)," in *History of Vatican II*, ed. Giuseppe Alberigo and Joseph Komonchak, vol. 1 (Maryknoll, NY: Orbis Books, 1996), 288.

contained in the Roman Catholic Church, which began a series of calls from bishops for an entirely new working document on the church.[17] Liénart knew the French stream. Following him, Bernard Cardinal Alfrink described well the Roman (and the schema's) approach to the mystical body when he noted that while he appreciated defining the church as the body of Christ, the draft placed too much emphasis on the image's external sense and does not adequately engage the relationship of others to the mystical body.[18] Joseph Cardinal Frings, one of the most outspoken German prelates against the Shoah in the early 1940s, added to the chorus a few days later, describing the mystical body theology in the schema as "very sociological."[19]

It was Philips, the Leuven theologian and great conciliator, who eventually proposed the new working text in a 1962 committee meeting. It began by emphasizing—from the start—the church as mystery and only then moving to a chapter on the church as hierarchical. In so doing, Philips and his collaborators separated the two elements that the Roman school of mystical body theology had cemented together: the christological and fundamentally mysterious quality of the church, which had been an ingredient in other strains of mystical body theology, and the hierarchical structure of the church, which flowed from that mystery but which was not the dispenser or sole arbiter of it. In his commentary on *Lumen Gentium*, Philips emphasized the thoroughly christological character of the constitution in its final form: "The Constitution on the Church adopts from the very beginning the Christocentric perspective, a perspective which is insistently affirmed throughout the development. The Church is profoundly convinced of it: The light of the Gentiles radiates not from her but from her divine Founder: yet, the Church well knows,

---

[17] *Acta synodalia Sacrosancti Concilii Oecumenici Vaticani II*, vol. 1, no. 4 (Vatican City: Vatican Polyglot Press, 1970), 126-27. Cf. Congar, *My Journal of the Council*, 224. See also Gaillardetz, *The Church in the Making*, 9-13, 43-45, 69. Gaillardetz follows the line of interpretation that the Mystical Body theology of *Mystici Corporis* was a precursor to Vatican II, with an important christological emphasis that endured but that suffered from an overly narrow "absolute identification of the mystical body of Christ with the Roman Catholic Church" (69). Further, the encyclical lacked an articulation of the more sacramental character, the spiritual dynamism of the church; the pope "limited his reflections to the visibility and institutional integrity of the church" (43).

[18] Congar, *My Journal of the Council*, 225. Cf. *Acta synodalia* 1/4, 134-36.

[19] Congar, *My Journal of the Council*, 232. Cf. *Acta synodalia* 1/4, 218-20.

that being reflected on her countenance, this irradiation reaches the whole of humanity."[20] Philips thus maintained the christological emphasis of the mystical body movement while distancing it from the strong juridical emphases of many in the Roman school.

In emphasizing the christological, the draft that reached the council floor in 1963 had been aided by a reference to the church as sacrament. That emphasis came largely from the German contingent, led by theologian Otto Semmelroth. On the floor, Frings called for a more extensive treatment in *De Ecclesia* on the church as sacrament, and, in turn, Dennis Doyle observes, "Even more extensively than the 1963 draft, the final 1964 *Lumen Gentium* reflects the use of the concept of the Church as sacrament as a major integrating theme and structuring element."[21] Doyle emphasizes the introduction, and further elaboration, of the idea of the church as sacrament as a major moment in the debates on the church. He demonstrates how the idea was indebted to Semmelroth and that Semmelroth, like Philips, "maintained an explicitly christological focus,"[22] yet Philips, like the French, maintained a more qualified endorsement of the church as sacrament.[23]

As the debate continued, the suggestion arose that the third chapter, on the people of God, be placed before the second, on the hierarchy. This move was lauded by many, including Polish bishop Karol Wojtyla, the future Pope John Paul II, who nevertheless argued on the council floor

[20] Gérard Philips, *L'Église et son mystère au IIe Concile du Vatican: Histoire, texte, et commentaire de la constitution "Lumen gentium,"* vol. 1 (Paris: Desclée, 1967), 71. See Georges Cardinal Cottier, "The Perception of the Church as 'Reflected Light' That Unites the Fathers of the First Millennium and Vatican Council II," *Thirty Days in the Church and in the World* 29, no. 7/8 (2011): 36–40. I have followed Cottier's translation.

[21] Doyle, "Otto Semmelroth, SJ, and the Ecclesiology of the 'Church as Sacrament' at Vatican II," 203. See also Congar, *My Journal of the Council*, 322.

[22] Dennis M. Doyle, "Otto Semmelroth and the Advance of Church as Sacrament at Vatican II," *Theological Studies* 76, no. 1 (2015): 84. Doyle's research supports the notion that the Roman stream of mystical body theology had eviscerated the theology of its deeply sacramental character.

[23] Ibid. See also Joseph Ratzinger, *Principles of Catholic Theology: Building Stones for a Fundamental Theology* (San Francisco: Ignatius Press, 1987; German orig., 1982), 44–45. Ratzinger notes the figurative quality of the designation "sacrament" as it is first employed in *Lumen Gentium*. Further, he finds the Belgian draft "more cautious in its approach" than the German one.

that among the shortcomings of "people of God" theology was a failure to emphasize that the church was indeed a "perfect society" in the sense that it had all the means necessary for attaining the supernatural end.[24] Wojtyla's insistence that *societas perfecta* not be lost makes sense in light of his wartime experience in Poland. Wojtyla saw the need for a strong church structure that could function in parallel fashion to the state. Further, the uncertainty that mystical body theology brought in the midst of the war lent itself to usurpation by and sympathy with the Nazi Party. The effect of *Lumen Gentium*'s people of God chapter has been well documented. It situated the hierarchy within the broader framework of a church made up of everyone—laity and clergy together.

According to Joseph Komonchak, after this major shift, but also in consideration of other revisions to *De Ecclesia*, Tromp appears to have clandestinely removed "dogmatic" from the title of the schema *De Ecclesia* because, Tromp said, "The initial intention was to write a dogmatic constitution, but now other elements have been mixed in. So the value has changed."[25] Much was at stake here. The first chapter had taken to a description of the church as a mystery. For Tromp, Alfredo Cardinal Ottaviani, and others formed in the Roman school, this was a satisfactory mode of reflection for spiritual or pastoral discourse but not for a document deemed dogmatic. Dogmatic discourse was didactic, propositional, and apologetic. Spiritual discourse was reflective, discursive, and open-ended. Roman theologians countenanced spirituality but would never place it on a par with dogmatic theology.

---

[24] *Acta synodalia* 2/3, 154–56. Wojtyla's theology of perfect society was more nuanced than Bellarmine's, which had been developed by neoscholastics and reacted against by many mystical body proponents in the twentieth century. The Bellarmanian notion included the sense of "perfect" as essentially complete but applied it to both the natural and supernatural realms. As perfect, the church did not depend on the state for its existence. Therefore, "perfect society" asserted the freedom of the church from princes and kings who sought to control it. By the late nineteenth century, this phrase had lost much of its theological energy. Here, Wojtyla is expressly concerned about the means of salvation enjoyed by the church. This was a question considered by the council in discussions concerning ecumenism. That is, to what extent does the Catholic Church hold all of the means necessary for salvation? And what then of other Christian communions? Wojtyla wanted to ensure that the council asserted that the Catholic Church had the full complement of those means.

[25] Sebastian Tromp, "Relatio Secretarii," 26, quoted in Joseph Komonchak, "Toward an Ecclesiology of Communion," in *The History of Vatican II*, 4:41.

Garrigou-Lagrange embodied this duality. Garrigou's career in theology was dedicated to the neoscholastic enterprise of commenting on Thomas's commentators and thus advising the Holy Office. Nevertheless, he also published in the distinct, considerably less objective, field of spirituality (or mystical theology). He wrote a monograph on St. John of the Cross and presumably assigned his future student—Wojtyla—to do the same at the Angelicum, though the adviser was ultimately critical of the student's effort. Garrigou's book on St. John of the Cross argued that St. John's more mystical theology was completely in line with Thomistic thinking. According to his biographer, "Catholic spirituality deals with God's gracious gift of himself through his Holy Spirit; it is concerned with the human person as potential and actual recipient of utter Gratuity. When all is said and done, Catholic spirituality is about the profound living of the Gospel of Jesus Christ—recognizing with Garrigou that 'no religion that is profoundly lived is without an interior life, with that intimate and frequent conversation which we have not only with ourselves but with God.' "[26] Notably, Garrigou's early essay on the mystical body of Christ was published in a journal for spirituality.[27]

Without the designation dogmatic, according to Tromp, the schema on the church "does not enjoy the same value as the dogmatic schemas of Vatican I."[28] Tromp's desperate tactics help to throw light on the distinctions among streams of mystical body theology. The Roman stream differed from the French not only in doctrinal emphases and technical matters but also in sensibility. The contrast is summed up by Mersch's critique of scholastic mystical body theology: they exchange richness for clarity.[29]

---

[26] See Richard Peddicord, *The Sacred Monster of Thomism: An Introduction to the Life and Legacy of Reginald Garrigou-Lagrange, O.P.* (South Bend, IN: St. Augustine's Press, 2005), 180. The internal quotation is from Reginald Garrigou-Lagrange, *The Three Ages of the Interior Life*, trans. M. Timothea Doyle, vol. 1 (St. Louis: Herder, 1947), 8.

[27] See Reginald Garrigou-Lagrange, "L'Église, corps mystique du Christ," *La Vie Spirituelle* 18 (1928): 6–23. Garrigou-Lagrange held a status in Catholic theology that led François Mauriac to call him *le monstre sacré* (Peddicord, *The Sacred Monster*, 2). Presumably, Mauriac used the phrase in its idiomatic sense of one who is well known and eccentric but untouchable and beyond reproach.

[28] Tromp, "Relatio Secretarii," 26, quoted in Komonchak, "Toward an Ecclesiology of Communion," in *The History of Vatican II*, 4:41.

[29] Mersch, *The Whole Christ*, 452.

The short discussion of the mystical body of Christ that does find its way into chapter 1 of *Lumen Gentium* bears the influence of the German and French streams much more so than the Roman stream, traces of which are found in chapter 3 on the hierarchical character of the church. Rather than beginning with St. Paul's experience on the road to Damascus, as did St. Augustine,[30] the constitution's treatment of the mystical body begins with Paul's discussion of our new creation in the death of Christ and his gift of the Spirit (Gal 6:15 and 2 Cor 5:17) and proceeds to the other *loci classici* of the doctrine: 1 Corinthians and Romans. At this point, according to Christopher O'Donnell:

> We are then left with four main suggestions as to the origin of Paul's concept of Body of Christ: first, the Greek social metaphor [developed from Aesop's fable by Menenius Agrippa], which he has already transcended in 1 Cor [by reflecting on the deep relationship between Christians and Christ in vv. 12 and 27]; second, his reflection on the Eucharist; third, Jewish reflections on Adam, including the whole human race, a point which, however, is difficult to establish; fourth, and more probably, his doctrine of the Christian being "in Christ" (*en Christô*). In these texts, and in Rom 12:5, also cited in LG 7, the vision of Paul does not seem to go beyond that of the local community.[31]

Lumen Gentium continues, however, to the deutero-Pauline epistles, drawing on the slightly different vision of those texts, which broaden the sense of the body of Christ. Again to quote O'Donnell, "Now the Church is not the local community but the whole Church." Christ is its head, and the notion of fullness (*plêrôma*) of the Body of Christ is introduced (see Col 2:9; Eph 1:22-23; 3:19; 4:12-13).[32] It is in these Ephesians texts that the sense of the body of Christ becomes more fully cosmic and so, too, *Lumen Gentium's* brief consideration of the mystical body of Christ moves from the more personal, to the immediate community, to its more cosmic dimensions.

---

[30] Stanislaus J. Grabowski, "St. Augustine and the Doctrine of the Mystical Body of Christ," *Theological Studies* 7, no. 1 (1946): 78-79.

[31] Christopher O'Donnell, "Body of Christ," in *Ecclesia: A Theological Encyclopedia of the Church* (Collegeville, MN: Liturgical Press, 1996), 63.

[32] Ibid.

Susan Wood suggests further that the deutero-Pauline texts offer a corrective to the temptation to over-identify Christ and the church with mystical body theology and that *Lumen Gentium* uses these texts to such an effect:

> This distinction between Christ and the church makes it impossible to identify the church as a prolongation of the Incarnation in such a way that the uniqueness and particularity of the historical Jesus Christ is lost, a danger faced by strict adherence to the body of Christ model. This distinction also assures that the church always remains subordinate to its head, Christ, and does not claim for itself what belongs uniquely to Christ. Vatican II's *Lumen gentium*, qualifies and nuances the relationship between the church and the body of Christ, in article 7.[33]

These texts, she points out, name Christ as the head of the mystical body, distinct from its members, the church, and set up the council's well-known characterization of the church as subsisting in (*subsistit in*) the Catholic Church.

Earlier, I demonstrated that the vagueness of mystical body theology tends to be grounded in some firmer reality; it needs an anchor, lest it drift off into the Docetic sea of false mysticism. Pelz's book served as a case in point and *Mystici Corporis* explicitly highlighted the risk. Since the Roman stream of mystical body theology had taken to anchoring the theology firmly in the structure of the Roman Catholic Church, the question remains whether Philips's efforts leave mystical body theology with an "open ground." Because Philips and company shifted the center of gravity of *Lumen Gentium*, mystical body theology did not carry the weight in the document that it once did. Various proposals have been put forward by theologians concerning the theological leitmotif of the constitution and of the documents themselves, including the pilgrim people of God and, especially more recently, communion. Tempered by the variety of theological themes in the context of the conciliar documents, as well as the variety of images in chapter 1 of *Lumen Gentium*, mystical body

---

[33] Susan Wood, "Continuity and Development in Roman Catholic Ecclesiology," *Ecclesiology* 7 (2011): 152.

theology does not hold the same danger, nor does it hold the weight, that Pius had once given it.[34]

On one reading, the council's achievement (beginning with Philips's initiative) is the pinnacle of the mystical body recovery. From this perspective, the mystical body movement did its work. The dominant "other" challenged by mystical body theology in the twentieth century was church as *societas perfecta*. Pope Pius had linked mystical body theology to a perfect society ecclesiology in his encyclical. Joining the mystical body movement with the juridicism inherent in the perfect society ecclesiology, however, left theologians and many bishops less than satisfied.[35] But by mid-century, perfect society had been widely dethroned, opening the door for other images of the church to enter theological discourse. On this reading, the prominence given to people of God at the council need not be seen as a rejection of mystical body theology but rather as a sublation of it in which its goals were achieved. The christological center and emphasis on mystery in the first chapter illustrate the point. Despite the stringent critiques of mystical body theology by those who espoused a people of God ecclesiology prior to the council, they were reconciled at the council.

Dulles suggested that mystical body of Christ and people of God were virtually equivalent ecclesiological descriptors, especially in their democratic tendencies; he considers both under his mystical communion model.[36] The key difference for Dulles is that people of God allows for more

[34] This is perhaps related to other difficulties that have been noted since the council. Godfrey Diekmann, Virgil Michel's successor as editor of *Orate Fratres*, suggested in an interview that the council did not unlock the full potential of the mystical body movement that his forebear was committed to popularizing, especially the link between liturgy and ethics that it secured. See Seamus Paul Finn, "Michel's Contribution to Linking Liturgical and Social Apostolates in the American Catholic Church: A 50 Year Perspective" (PhD diss., Boston University, 1991), 191–92. Finn conducted this interview with Diekmann on 27 June 1990.

[35] Richard McBrien notes: "*Lumen Gentium* portrays the Church according to many different biblical images, not just as the Mystical Body of Christ, which had been interpreted in the past in a highly juridical manner. If there is, for the constitution, a single dominant biblical image of the Church, it is indeed that of people of God, to which an entire chapter is devoted" ("The Church [*Lumen Gentium*]," in *Contemporary Catholic Theology: A Reader*, ed. Michael A. Hayes and Liam Gearon [New York: Continuum, 1998], 285).

[36] Dulles, *Models of the Church*, 53. Dulles notes in his introduction that in the early development of his ideas there were more than five models. Limiting himself

distance between the church and its divine head.[37] They are united in their opposition to the much more institutional perfect society ecclesiology.

There is indeed a sense in which Dulles is correct that those interested in a more *ressourcement* version of the mystical body were, at the council, united with those who argued for the prominence of the people of God image. As Archbishop Denis Hurley put it, at the council "the Church [found] itself in a 'back-to-the-Bible' campaign" in which a conceptual ecclesiology was replaced with an ecclesiology based on various biblical images. Hurley was not unfamiliar with the French-speaking mystical body recovery, as he recollects about the council: "I was on the progressive side as a consequence of reading the writings of the likes of Karl Rahner, Congar and Chenu, which changed my theological outlook. Mersch's *The Whole Christ* had a particular effect on me regarding the notion of Christ within us."[38] Insofar as mystical body theology was a major component of the push back against the overly conceptual neo-Thomistic framework, it met with success in this shift at the council.

The debate that gave rise to the theology of the people of God, however, began long before the council and was not initially as conciliatory to mystical body of Christ theology as postconciliar interpretations sometimes suggest. The catalyzing effect of trying to overcome a certain position held by a small, powerful number at the council—who happened also to be touting the mystical body of Christ—brought the mystical body and people of God camps closer together.

Fading before Vatican II

It is difficult to overstate what occurred at the council. A closer look at the CPLI gives us clues that the mystical body's waning began even be-

---

to five models may explain the consolidation of people of God and mystical body of Christ into one model.

[37] The echoes of "people of God" with the opening words of the US Constitution were not lost on American Catholics, giving the image a decidedly more liberal democratic cast. See, for example, Bruce Russett, "We the People of God: How Democratic Should the Church Be?," *Commonweal* 130, no. 15 (2003): 27–30; Sidney Callahan, "We, the People—of God: The Church Needs a Constitution," *Commonweal* 124, no. 9 (1997): 6–7.

[38] Archbishop Denis E. Hurley, "Council Reminiscences," Symposium at Heythrop College, Kensington, London, 12 October 2002, *The Downside Review* 422 (2003): 56.

fore the council. Volume 4 (1943–1948) offers only seventeen entries over these six years. This is, of course, during the years immediately following *Mystici Corporis*. Pius XII's letter made mystical body theology the default ecclesiological position of the magisterium; however, theological work tells another story. The tide was already flowing in another direction. In volume 5 (1948–1950), there are fifteen entries over three years, but the shift is evident. Of the few articles listed in this last volume, many are catechetical, elaborating established doctrine. Many are from *American Ecclesiastical Review*, a monthly publication known far less at this time for its edgy positions than Michel's *Orate Fratres* or Beauduin's *Irénikon*. *Eastern Churches Quarterly* alone is pushing the theological envelope with reflections on the mystical body and ecumenism.[39]

Gregory Baum, writing about the nature of lay participation in doctrinal development, senses that mystical body theology has been fully integrated into Catholic life, teaching, and practice as the council gets underway.[40] Baum surmises that, thanks to the hard work of pastors and theologians, the heavy lifting of the mystical body recovery has been accomplished. His argument is bolstered by the fact that the *vota*, or statements of the bishops of what they would like to consider at the council, indicated a desire among many—especially the bishops outside of the West—for a dogmatic definition of the mystical body of Christ.[41] This would be one way of explaining the shift and eventual drop-off in mystical body literature leading up to the council—all the work had been done already.

With a decline in interest in the early to mid-1940s,[42] it is difficult to argue that mystical body theology had its full momentum going into the

[39] Bernard Leeming, "Doctrine of the Mystical Body and Its Connection with Ecumenical Work," *Eastern Churches Quarterly* 7 (1948): 519–37.

[40] Gregory Baum, "The Laity and the Council," *New Blackfriars* 43, no. 500 (1962): 61.

[41] According to Étienne Fouilloux, there were a number of bishops heading into the council who called for the council to formally declare a dogma. Along with Marian dogmas, which were by far the most commonly suggested, the mystical body of Christ was often mentioned. See Alberigo and Komonchak, *The History of Vatican II*, 1:112, 128.

[42] As mentioned above, Bluett called 1937 "the crest" of mystical body theological study, and J. Eileen Scully, writing about French-language mystical body theology, called 1935 "the summit" in terms of published articles. See Scully, "The Theology,"

council, even if the Roman theologians made it thematic to the schema *De Ecclesia*. Among those curial types, mystical body had reached a consensus, and there was a certain perception of *Roma locuta, causa finita est*. The debate was over.

Nevertheless, there are two other factors—relevant to both Europe and the United States—that challenged and stunted the mystical body recovery earlier in the century. We shall consider each in turn: first, the effect of World War II and, second, the impact of Catholic critical biblical scholarship, which will take us back around to the question of "mystical body of Christ" and "people of God" at Vatican II.

Broken Body after the War: Europe

As has been noted, it was in the Romantic imagination of the nineteenth-century Tübingen school, especially that of Möhler, that a creative recovery of mystical body theology germinated. Several German theologians developed Möhler's work in the early twentieth century such that the most fruitful period of writing about the mystical body coincided with the beginning of the Second World War.

Congruent with the shift in the CPLI, Kevin McNamara notes that following the appearance of *Mystici Corporis* in 1943 there was a noticeable lack of interest in mystical body theology in Germany. McNamara mentions the war as a reason for the loss of enthusiasm. Specifically, McNamara notes that the theology of the mystical body was "ruthlessly exploited by the Nazis."[43] While that may be true, we have seen that there were certain Catholics, on the periphery of the Nazi Party, who were

---

59. Edward Hahnenberg also argues for a decline in the mid-1940s: "In the years after *Mystici Corporis*, enthusiasm for the theology of the mystical body began to fade. The question of membership had thrown doubt on the coherence of the encyclical; meanwhile, disillusionment grew with the model's appeal to an abstract community spirit—following the war, Germans were especially conscious of the dangers of an uncritical embrace of *Volkgeist*. While the post-war period was one of theological vitality, even before Pius XII's encyclical critical studies had begun to appear that questioned mystical body as the comprehensive model of Church" (Hahnenberg, "The Mystical Body of Christ and Communion Ecclesiology: Historical Parallels," 13).

[43] McNamara, "The Ecclesiological Movement in Germany in the Twentieth Century," 352.

willing to help along the link between Nazi race rhetoric and mystical body theology.

Especially in Europe, the specter of Nazi collectivism did indeed cast a pall over mystical body theology or, at the very least, give pause to those who would employ it broadly. Expanding on McNamara's point, Walter Breitenfeld wrote just after the war: "Nazis liked to talk of the 'sacrament of blood,' they tried to replace the conception of the Mystical Body of Christ by a crude materialistic collectivism and used even the language of the Church to this end. They attempted to displace the Communitas Sanctorum by a racial community and a veneration of national heroes."[44] Breitenfeld was a lecturer in social studies at Salzburg's Catholic University who fled from the Gestapo to England in 1939 after helping numerous Austrians escape Nazi persecution.

Notably, some at the council, including Joseph Ratzinger, were also concerned about an embrace of "people of God" (*Volk Gottes* in German) because of the specter of that Nazi propagandist use of *Herrenvolk* ("master race") and *Volksgemeinschaft* ("people's community"), among other racial appropriations of *Volk*. While such associations could be made reflexively, mystical body theology had been much more directly used to support the Nazi agenda during the period of that party's political rise.

Even in the midst of the war, after he too fled Austria for fear of Nazi reprisal, Eric Voegelin argued in *The Review of Politics* that Nazi race rhetoric was a perverted development of mystical body of Christ theology. The political philosopher's critique is both interesting and instructive in itself. Describing the race idea in Nazi Germany, he writes:

> Its main feature is, negatively, a slow fading out of the consciousness of the mystical body of Christ, thereby opening the gates to emotional and intellectual forces which replace the Christian substance without the members of the community even becoming aware of the fact. This transformation has become possible because *the body idea was thinned out to the "mystical" idea*; . . . the mystical body construction is one of two alternatives, the other one being a purely pneumatic construction of the community. When the development accentuates more the pneumatic

---

[44] Walter C. Breitenfeld, "Nazi Liturgy," *New Blackfriars* 27, no. 311 (1946): 46.

aspect, then the way is free for a reconstruction of the spiritual meaning of community along lines diverging from the Christian. By a slight change of accents the evolution of symbols may depart from the Christological interpretation of like-mindedness to other spiritual assumptions. The change is gradual, but one may say that *a decisive step is reached when the* pneuma hagiosynes *of Christ is replaced by reason as the substance which constitutes the unity of mankind.* The 17th- and 18th-century rationalism may still preserve deistic forms, and in that sense an element of transcendentalism; and it may try to avoid a rupture with the church as a social institution, but the ideas of man and community have become essentially secularised. And even though the idea of reason still preserves the universalism inherent in Christianity, it is obvious that once the problem of community is reduced to the problem of finding a spiritual bond, *new symbols may arise which do not cover all mankind but only particular groups as in the case of the national spirit idea, or the idea of the workers' class.* In this sense, the spiritualisation of the body idea prepared the way for an era of spiritual symbols which have no connection with the more primitive type of family symbols, and prepares also the way for new body symbols which may arise independent from the earlier blood symbols.[45]

Typical of Voegelin's approach, he argues that a political theory is connected to secularized theology. His analysis of the tendency of mystical body theology to become disembodied, however, gets at the postwar fearfulness of its potential to be abstract and, therefore, conducive to co-option. Therefore, those who would argue that mystical body theology offered a middle road between individualism and collectivism had a more difficult time doing so after the war. Mannes Koster is deeply concerned about the support that mystical body theology has lent National Socialism in Germany and, thus, critiques it as a stand-alone ecclesiological term. By 1965, doubtless still thinking about the events of decades past, he would worry about the potential correspondence between mystical

---

[45] Eric Voegelin, "The Growth of the Race Idea," *The Review of Politics* 2, no. 3 (1940): 293; emphasis mine. Voegelin's work also, of course, had some influence in the United States, where he took up residence after his expulsion from Vienna.

body theology and a Marxist mystical union.[46] Koster argues that there is an easy slide from talk about the mystical body of Christ to, on the one hand, a Marxist mystical union of people, which is required to precede and ground the mystical body, or, on the other hand, an outright denial of mediation à la Pelz.[47] Koster clearly identifies the two major errors of German mystical body theology. The negative associations with mystical body theology halted its momentum, especially in Germany, but also throughout the rest of the continent.

Broken Body after the War: United States

In the United States, World War II affected the mainstream of mystical body theology in a different manner. As it did in the European context, mystical body theology faded—this much is clear from the CLPI. Farther away from the link forged between mystical body theology and Nazism, "new social Catholics"—who had been the main popularizers of mystical body theology—were undercut by the national united front of wartime politics.[48] William Portier sums up the impact succinctly: "Post-war prosperity and consensus tended to flatten out and re-direct in more conventional directions the energies produced by the economic pressures of the 1930s."[49] Entering the postwar consensus period, critiques of mainstream American individualism had more difficulty gaining traction. Thus, mystical body theology endured in small pockets, primarily among those who directly engaged social strife.

During its heyday, Day had written about the mystical body of Christ:

---

[46] Napiwodzki, "Eine Ekklesiologie im Werden," 47–48, 75.

[47] Ibid., 75n12.

[48] For more about the wider context of united front postwar politics in the United States and its effects on scholarship and public intellectuals, see Peter Novick, *That Noble Dream: The "Objectivity Question" and the American Historical Profession* (Cambridge, UK: Cambridge University Press, 1988), esp. 281–411. See also William C. Beyer, "Creating 'Common Ground' on the Home Front: Race, Class, and Ethnicity in a 1940s Quarterly Magazine," in *The Home-Front War: World War II and American Society*, ed. Kenneth Paul O'Brien and Lynn Hudson Parsons, Contributions in American History 161 (Westport, CT: Greenwood, 1995), 41–61, on the cultural impact of the advent of the journal *Common Ground* in forming a World War II united front.

[49] "'Good Friday in December': World War II in the Editorials of Preservation of the Faith Magazine, 1939–1945," *U.S. Catholic Historian* 27, no. 2 (2009): 43.

The illnesses of injustice, hate, disunion, race hatred, prejudice, class war, selfishness, greed, nationalism, and war weaken this Mystical Body, just as the prayer and sacrifices of countless of the faithful strengthen it. . . .

Because of this dogma of the Mystical Body, Catholics may not allow their souls to be clouded with greed, selfishness and hate. They may not hate Negroes, Jews, Communists. When they are guilty of prejudice, they are injuring the Mystical Body of Christ. It is as though they wielded the scourges in the hands of the soldiers who attacked our Lord. If a man hates his neighbor, he is hating Christ. . . .

All men are brothers. The saint as well as the sinner whom we may not judge as we wish not to be judged. This dogma of the Mystical Body precludes all ideas of class war.

And it is to promulgate this dogma—to bring it to the man in the street, that the Catholic Worker is dedicated.[50]

Day continued to expound on the mystical body of Christ a year later in an article in which she makes her well-documented admiration for Michel and his cause explicit. About the mystical body, she writes, "The Mystical Body of Christ is a union—a unit—and action within the Body is common action. In the Liturgy we have the means to teach Catholics . . . that they ARE members of one body and that 'an injury to one is an injury to all.'"[51] Anne Klejment's helpful analysis of Day's mystical body theology suggests that she challenged the dominant understanding that the mystical body of Christ was coextensive with the Roman Catholic Church. At this time, however, that question was very much in dispute.[52]

---

[50] Dorothy Day, "The Mystical Body of Christ," *Catholic Worker* (October 1934): 3.

[51] Dorothy Day, "Liturgy and Sociology," *Catholic Worker* (December 1935): 4.

[52] Anne Klejment, "The Spirituality of Dorothy Day's Pacifism," *U.S. Catholic Historian* 27, no. 2 (June 2009): 1-24. See, for example, Michel's review of Fulton Sheen, *The Mystical Body of Christ* (1935) in *Orate Fratres* 10 (April 1936): 281-85, in which he skewers Sheen for his lack of clarity on this disputed question. See also, William R. O'Connor, "The Mystical Body of Christ: Reality or Metaphor?," *The Irish Ecclesiastical Record* 46 (1935): 136-53. O'Connor connects the mystical body to the discourse on the sheep and the goats (Matt 25:35-40)—an example of a connection that would be deeply suspect to later historical critics but was powerful and productive for early twentieth-century theologians—and therefore identifies Christ with both

Throughout the war, Day and the *Catholic Worker*, much maligned, maintained their pacifist stance, rooted as it was in mystical body theology.[53] After the war, in defense of her actions on behalf of communists in the period of the Red Scare, Day appeals again to the mystical body of Christ, specifically describing how war undercuts the mystical body:

> And as for our great masses of Catholic people, they will be dragged in, poor though they be, or workers though they be, to use the same means of force and violence, to hate their enemy, to defend the status quo, because there will be no time for fine distinctions then and the Catholic will not be able to apologize for his siding with the duPonts, the Morgans, the Girdlers, war profiteers, the cynical politicians, the literary people, the intellectuals who will use fine and exalted phrases to inspire and integrate the body and soul of the worker in one passion—the desire for sweat, blood and tears, for suffering, and they will use these mysterious cravings of the human heart and once again betray the workers into war. War, the rending of the Mystical Body of Christ, as St. Cyprian called it.[54]

Radical social critiques like Day's, especially those addressing civil unrest, are the context in which a robust, socially engaged mystical body theology endures after the war. Day continued to fight against the deep suspicion of communists that came with the Cold War, all the while furthering the Worker's mission to love the destitute, who, of course, remained in need even as the unemployment rate dropped.[55]

---

members (his disciples) and potential members (the least of these), and the latter in a special way (141–42).

[53] For an analysis of Day, her continuing pacifism, and its fallout, see Sandra Yocum Mize, "'We Are Still Pacifists': Dorothy Day's Pacifism During World War II," in *Dorothy Day and the Catholic Worker Movement: Centenary Essays*, ed. William J. Thorn, Phillip M. Runkel, and Susan Mountin, Marquette Studies in Theology 32 (Milwaukee, WI: Marquette University Press, 2001), 465–73.

[54] Dorothy Day, "Beyond Politics," *Catholic Worker* (November 1949): 2. Day's reference to Cyprian, like Michel's, is interesting in light of Mersch's contrast of the mystical body theology of his own patristic hero, St. Cyril of Alexandria, with St. Cyprian.

[55] See Day, "Beyond Politics"; Dorothy Day, *The Long Loneliness* (San Francisco: Harper, 1952), esp. 233–84. See also Day's defense of the Catholic Worker's opposition to all violence during the Spanish Civil War, in which she describes the Spanish

Mystical body theology also endured in the context of the fight for civil rights. As early as the 1940s, the mystical body of Christ was seen as a powerful image for describing a desegregated church and, more broadly, a desegregated society. For example, R. Bentley Anderson, SJ, describes the Commission on Human Rights (CHR), an interracial group founded in the archdiocese of New Orleans in 1949 to attend black and white parishes as a mixed-race group. Among other such organizations, the CHR drew on mystical body theology to justify their endeavors, stating that all are "one in the mystical body of Christ, regardless of race, color or national origin."[56] It is difficult to imagine substituting "people of God" for "mystical body of Christ" in that line without losing some of its visceral force. Anderson unearths the theology of the mystical body of Christ operative among many interracial groups in New Orleans right up through 1957, the end of his period of study.[57] LaFarge had written extensively of race relations and the mystical body of Christ in the interbellum period and continued to attack racial injustice as contrary to the mystical body after the war, as late as 1960, three years before his death.[58] De Hueck Doherty

---

people, "all of them our brothers in Christ—all of them Temples of the Holy Ghost, all of them members or potential members of the Mystical Body of Christ." Dorothy Day, "Explains CW Stand on Use of Force," *Catholic Worker* (September 1938): 1, 4, 7.

[56] "CHR Statement, 1950," quoted in R. Bentley Anderson, *Black, White, and Catholic: New Orleans Interracialism, 1947–1956* (Nashville, TN: Vanderbilt University Press, 2008), 16–17.

[57] See ibid., 20, 59, 88, 144.

[58] See John LaFarge, *The Catholic View Point on Race Relations* (Garden City, NY: Hanover House, 1960), esp. 68–69. See also the earlier *The Race Question and the Negro* (New York: Longmans, 1943), esp. 105–6, 238. In 1937, LaFarge had written, "Christ preached moreover a unity based not on man's natural life alone but upon the prerogatives of the supernatural life conferred upon mankind by the Redemption, and the prerogatives formed by the personal relationships of all individuals sharing in that supernatural life with His own Divine Person. Through the institution of His Church as a universal, perpetual, supra-national Society, all mankind was offered participation in a unity higher than that which the mere fact of common creation and common anthropological origin afforded. This higher unity is symbolized in the figure of the Mystical Body of Christ. As members of the one Body of which Christ is the Head the children of God enter into a unique relationship not only with one another but with the whole of mankind as well" (see *Interracial Justice: A Study of the Catholic Doctrine of Race Relations* [New York: America Press, 1937], 60). Though it occurred during the heyday of mystical body theology in the 1940s, the integration of St. Louis University

continued her work toward racial reconciliation into the 1950s and wrote about the mystical body of Christ throughout her life, emphasizing its call to oneness. In Doherty's hands, "mystical body of Christ" is a Western expression of *sobornost*, the Russian Orthodox idea of kenotic communion across time and space that fueled ecumenical activity in the East.[59]

African American Catholics who worked for racial reconciliation often appealed, like the CHR, to the theology of the mystical body. In 1950, Helen Caldwell Day, a Catholic convert, founded Blessed Martin House of Hospitality in Memphis, Tennessee, an interracial community that served single working mothers. In her book about the work and example of this interracial Catholic community in the South, Day describes the makeup of the house: "The qualifications for membership were broad. A member might be white or colored, Catholic or non-Catholic, so long as he was interested in the life of the Church as the Mystical Body of Christ and the welfare of the members therein."[60] Like Dorothy Day, Caldwell Day often described the reach of the mystical body as extending beyond the visible bounds of the Roman Catholic Church and was deeply critical of attempts to constrain its unifying purchase, especially in the case of race relations. "We speak of the Church as if it were this building, or this group of people, and not the Mystical Body of Christ," she writes in 1954, "and not only that. After speaking of its unity, we openly divide the Body—as if Christ could be made two—so there is not for us one Church, but two, one 'Catholic' and one 'Colored Catholic.'"[61] As it did for Day, Michel, and others, the doctrine of the mystical body for Caldwell Day—at the same time porous and normative—derived its origin from the Eucharist. The movement, an inclusive circle really, from eucharistic celebration, to the link between loving God and loving others, to personal appropriation, to social critique is clear in a lengthy passage from Caldwell Day's earlier autobiography *Color, Ebony*:

---

is also of note here because of its connections to mystical body theology. See Daniel Van Slyke, "Claude Heithaus, S.J., and the Integration of Saint Louis University: The Mystical Body of Christ and University Politics," in *Theology and Lived Christianity*, ed. David M. Hammond (Mystic, CT: Twenty-Third Publications, 2000), 139–73.

[59] Catherine de Hueck Doherty, *Essential Writings*, selected with an introduction by David Meconi (Maryknoll, NY: Orbis Books, 2009), esp. 67–97, 120–21, 143–44

[60] Helen Caldwell Day, *Not without Tears* (New York: Sheed and Ward, 1954), 11.

[61] Ibid., 57.

When the priest raised Our Lord, that we might adore Him in the Host, I would think that even while we gazed upon Him, we were part of His Mystical Body, members of Him and of each other.

Then I could understand how He could say that the whole of the law lay in the commandments "Love God" and "Love your neighbor." They were really the same commandment, for neither is possible without the other. Love is the keynote of Christianity; with it, everything is possible, without it, nothing.

I could no longer justify hate nor prejudice against any person, for now I knew my neighbor was anyone whom I could love or serve me. There's no one else left.[62]

When in 1952 Day visited her fellow Catholic Worker in Memphis, Helen and Dorothy went to Mass together. So impressed with the community, while struck by the many challenges it faced, Day wrote:

But with a sense of the Mystical Body, the knowledge comes that we can lower or heighten the strength and love in that Body, we can work as Helen does, among the least of God's children. Every act in that little house is an act of love, a gesture of love which reanimates and increases love and builds up this great force of love to overcome hatred and evil in the world. Poverty and pre-carity, self-denial and suffering, surely here is a tremendous use of the spiritual weapons, a letting loose of grace upon the world far more powerful than any atom or hydrogen bomb.[63]

Medical doctor Arthur Falls founded a Catholic Worker house in Chicago and worked tirelessly for civil rights. In the words of Lincoln Rice, "The doctrine of the mystical body of Christ . . . played a key role for Falls in interpreting his own life experiences and in laying a

---

[62] Helen Caldwell Day, *Color, Ebony* (New York: Sheed and Ward, 1951), 112. Quoted in Sandra Yocum Mize, "On the Back Roads: Searching for American Catholic Intellectual Traditions," in *American Catholic Traditions: Resources for Renewal*, ed. Sandra Yocum Mize and William L. Portier, The Annual Publication of the College Theology Society 42 (Maryknoll, NY: Orbis Books, 1996), 20.

[63] Dorothy Day, "On Pilgrimage," *Catholic Worker* (November 1952): 4.

foundation for further action." [64] Especially significant is that Falls contrasted the mystical body of Christ, in which Catholics were united in solidarity, with the mythical body of Christ, his characterization of the failure of especially white Catholics to embrace the doctrine fully and so live concretely united to their brothers and sisters in Christ of all races. He continued his work to prompt fellow Christians to live the true mystical body of Christ right up to, and beyond, the passage of civil rights legislation. Writing reflectively in 1962, he said "that the practical application of . . . the mystical body of Christ either had to be demonstrated or else the whole structure seemed shaky to me." [65]

The connection in the United States between social action and enduring appeals to mystical body theology cements the inherent link between the two. With the dawn of the postwar consensus, those critiques neither were as numerous nor gained as much traction. The return to economic prosperity after the Great Depression softened receptivity to the more radical social proposals of those Catholics who were driving mystical body theology forward. With noted exceptions, the few who continued to discuss the mystical body of Christ in the States were the theologians, who were far less diverse at the time than their counterparts in Europe. They primarily wrote for the *American Ecclesiastical Review* and debated topics such as "The Status of St. Robert Bellarmine's Teaching about the Membership of Occult Heretics in the Catholic Church." [66] As mystical body faded, then, there were, on the one hand, pockets of continued reference to it in the midst of ongoing social struggles and, on the other, a few neoscholastic mentions.

---

[64] Lincoln R. Rice, "Confronting the Heresy of 'The Mythical Body of Christ': The Life of Dr. Arthur Falls," *American Catholic Studies* 123, no. 2 (2012): 61. Rice notes that Falls was responsible for the change in the masthead of the *Catholic Worker*, beginning with issue 7 of volume 1 to include a black worker, instead of two white workers (73). He also notes that Falls was friends with Michel (74).

[65] Arthur Falls, Unpublished Autobiography (August Meier Papers, Schomburg Center for Research in Black Culture, New York Public Library, New York, NY), 158–59. Quoted in Rice, "Confronting the Heresy," 77.

[66] This is the title of an article written by Joseph Clifford Fenton in the *American Ecclesiastical Review* 122 (March 1950): 207–21, a title with potential implications for ecumenical relations, but an article not at all interested in them.

There is some evidence that the connection between social critique and mystical body theology endures among some of the few who have invoked it more recently. M. Shawn Copeland has argued that mystical body of Christ theology can "make explicit the eschatological meaning of Christian solidarity," especially as it pertains to oppressed and despised populations.[67] On the other hand, there are contemporary liturgists who speak of the mystical body in "hushed reverent tones," to borrow Michael Baxter's characterization of these same Catholics' appropriation of Michel, who tend to eviscerate the theology of its sharp, socially critical edge.[68]

(Mystical) Body of Christ: The Rise of Catholic Historical-Critical Biblical Scholarship

The second reason that enthusiasm surrounding mystical body theology began to recede before the council is the advancement of historical-critical methods in Catholic biblical scholarship.

In 1943, the same year in which he promulgated *Mystici Corporis*, Pope Pius XII issued another landmark encyclical, *Divino Afflante Spiritu*.[69] *Divino* spurred on Catholic biblical studies, officially acknowledging a role for the historical-critical method in scriptural scholarship. Luke Timothy Johnson has called it "the symbolic (and real) point of pivot" in the twentieth-century history of Catholic biblical scholarship. "It . . . changed everything."[70] By 1960, critical biblical scholarship among

[67] M. Shawn Copeland, *Enfleshing Freedom: Body, Race, and Being* (Minneapolis: Fortress Press, 2010), esp. 102–4. Copeland, without extensive reference to the development of mystical body theology, suggests a recovery of mystical body theology shorn of the "juridical and hierarchical terms" enshrined in *Mystici Corporis*. She cites Bernard Lonergan as a more favorable theorist.

[68] Baxter, "Reintroducing Virgil Michel," 499–500. For a good example of these liturgists' use of mystical body theology, see Christopher Carstens and Douglas Martis, *Mystical Body, Mystical Voice: Encountering Christ in the Words of the Mass* (Chicago: Liturgy Training Publications, 2011), esp. 26–29.

[69] Pope Pius XII, *Divino Afflante Spiritu: On Promoting Biblical Studies, Commemorating the Fiftieth Anniversary of Providentissimus Deus* (30 September 1943).

[70] Luke Timothy Johnson and William S. Kurz, *The Future of Catholic Biblical Scholarship: A Constructive Conversation* (Grand Rapids, MI: Eerdmans, 2002), 3–4. For a discussion of the impact this change had on Catholic biblical scholarship in the United States, see Jeffrey L. Morrow, "The Fate of Catholic Biblical Interpretation in

Catholics had disseminated to such an extent that simple assertions of mystical body theology's Pauline roots were no longer tolerated. Having been part of the general intellectual furniture, especially in the United States, for decades, the fact that the phrase "mystical body of Christ" does not appear as such in the epistles, and that perhaps St. Paul's "body of Christ" was more restrictive in meaning than the nineteenth- and twentieth-century usage of it, took some time for Catholics to digest. By 1960, criticism had disseminated to the extent that a Catholic commentary on Paul earned this castigation from a reviewer in the journal *Religious Education*: "Surely Paul did not preach the *Mystical* Body of Christ, a much later concept. Rather than following the thought of St. Paul, Father Cox seems to fit Pauline teaching into a framework of modern theology."[71]

With the benefit of critical scholarship, Catholics began to see that the Tübingen school's recovery of the mystical body of Christ imbued it with a meaning it had not had prior. For Möhler the mystical body of Christ was an organic reality that extended throughout time and across space. Scripture scholars now argued that Paul intended no such pervasive meaning in his letters to the Corinthians and Romans. Rather, when Paul instructed early Christians to be the body of Christ, he had in mind only a church in a specific locale. His meaning was narrower, geographically speaking. He does not discuss, for example, the church at Corinth and the church at Rome as bound together in the body of Christ, and he did not understand the inhabitants of heaven making up, along with those on earth, various members of the body.

The critique of mystical body theology's uncritical claim of Pauline support had begun in Europe even before Pius's encyclical. In 1942, Lucien Cerfaux published a philological study of the Pauline epistles in which he argues that people of God is a more foundational ecclesiological image than mystical body for Paul. With undertones of concern about supersessionism, Cerfaux writes: "This notion of a spiritual organism, at which we have arrived by a synthesis of the mystical life in Christ and the unity

---

America," in *Weaving the American Catholic Tapestry: Essays in Honor of William L. Portier*, ed. Derek C. Hatch and Timothy R. Gabrielli (Eugene, OR: Wipf & Stock, 2017), 41–59.

[71] F. Adrian Davis, review of *It Is Paul Who Writes*, by Ronald Knox and Ronald Cox, CM, *Religious Education* 55 (1960): 316.

of the Christian world, does not in any way replace the primitive and basic definition of the Church as the people of God. It may modify it, but nothing more." And further: "The idea of the people of God remains, but it becomes more inward and more spiritual. Instead of being just his people, the Christian community is also the 'body' of Christ, and its unity stems from the life of Christ which flows within it and within each of its members." Therefore, Cerfaux concludes, body of Christ is "something that can be predicated of the Church without affecting the already existing and fundamental idea of the Church, and without necessarily coinciding with its meaning." [72] In Cerfaux's reflections on the melding of these two ecclesiological images, one hears echoes of *Lumen Gentium*'s opening chapter on the mystery of the church, on which he worked at the council. [73] He writes, "All members of the Church possess a heavenly mode of living even now. They are already in heaven. All this happens 'in a mystery,' so that the all-containing glory cannot yet be seen. The Church's secret is that it possesses a heavenly, but hidden, mode of life. It is one of the Church's mysteries that it exists in mystery itself." [74]

Cerfaux was explicitly interested in recovering a sense of the Jewish roots of the church that he thought had been lost—a loss which surely facilitated the Nazi triumph in Germany. In Cerfaux's exegesis of 1 Corinthians, he points out that *sōma* (body) indicates identification with neither the physical body of Christ nor his eucharistic body. Further, it is impossible to think of a "mystical Christ as distinct from Christ as a person," which would give "to the word σῶμα a meaning which it can never admit." He concludes that "it remains for us to translate: 'You are a body, a body which is that of Christ (dependent on him, and in which his life flows).'" [75] Cerfaux rejects readings that apply the more Romantic sense of mystical body theology to Paul's theology. He even rejects any deep sense of the unity across time and space indicated in patristic theology. He maintains, however, the mystical identification of Christ with

---

[72] Lucien Cerfaux, *The Church in the Theology of St. Paul*, trans. Geoffrey Webb and Adrian Walker (New York: Herder, 1959; French orig., 1942), 282, 286, 375.

[73] Alberto Melloni, "The Beginning of the Second Period: The Great Debate on the Church," in *The History of Vatican II*, ed. Giuseppe Alberigo, English version ed. Joseph Komonchak, vol. 3 (Maryknoll, NY: Orbis Books, 2006), 109.

[74] Cerfaux, *The Church in the Theology*, 377.

[75] Ibid., 277.

Christians, a point that fits much more comfortably with a theology of deification than an ecclesiology per se. "Let us say once again that the body, with which this mystical identification is made, is none other than the real and personal body which lived, died, and was glorified, and with which the bread in the Eucharist is identified. Christians are identified in a very real, although still mystical way in the Eucharist and in another way in baptism. Identified with this body, they are one among themselves; they are all 'one' by reference to the body of Christ." [76]

Cerfaux's theology was influential at the council even beyond his own explicit contributions, sometimes to the frustration of his fellow theologians. Describing the Leuven theologians in particular at the council, Congar wrote in his journal, "What Cerfaux has said is a bit above the word of the Gospel." [77] Nevertheless, clearly Cerfaux's explication of the notion of the people of God in the Pauline corpus was a major aid to the final form of *Lumen Gentium*.[78]

The development of historical-critical biblical studies of Paul—like Cerfaux's—corresponded with a lack of confidence in mystical body theology, especially because Paul himself never uses the adjective "mystical." [79] The adjective appears to be an unnecessary accretion. Therefore, body of Christ becomes much more acceptable in Catholic theology than mystical body of Christ. A contributor to *The Furrow* sums it up bluntly in 1953: St. Paul first said that the Church is the Body of Christ. But it is seldom pointed out that he did not say she is the Mystical Body of Christ. "One phrase [the former] is a metaphor, one is not [the latter]." [80] In this he echoed, with some parsing, Koster's sharp critique of Mystical Body of Christ as "merely a metaphor of the instrumentalist institution." [81] Yves

---

[76] Ibid., 277–78.

[77] Congar, *My Journal of the Council*, 508.

[78] Dennis Doyle has demonstrated that people of God served as a galvanizing image for those developing the more sacramental sense of the church in contrast to the mystical body–dominant ecclesiology of Tromp and the preparatory schemas. See Doyle, "Otto Semmelroth and the Advance of Church as Sacrament at Vatican II."

[79] Schüssler Fiorenza, "Vatican II and the Aggiornamento of Roman Catholic Theology," in Livingston et al., *Modern Christian Thought*, 239.

[80] Sean MacCarthy, "Teaching the Mystical Body: A Suggestion," *The Furrow* 4, no. 5 (1953): 269.

[81] Mannes Dominikus Koster, *Ekklesiologie im Werden* (Paderborn: Bonifacius-Druckerei, 1940), quoted in McNamara, "The Ecclesiological Movement in Germany

Congar would later affirm Koster's study of the church in the Pauline epistles as the first crack in the dominance of mystical body theology.[82] What Koster accomplished in the German sphere, Cerfaux brought to the Belgian-French.

The *New Catholic Encyclopedia*, first published in 1967 and revised in 2003, sums up the position of biblical scholarship:

> The Pauline theme of the Body of Christ has . . . primarily a soteriological provenience and meaning. It always involves a reference to the individual Body of Christ, i.e., to him who has borne death upon his own Body on the cross, and who enters into heaven to become of new life in his glorious Body. The mode of this most unique of unions by which the glorious Christ compasses in himself all Christians as his members is something St. Paul is not much concerned with.[83]

Theological development of the image—especially in Augustine and Gregory the Great—had strayed from Paul to emphasize solidarity throughout time and space.

There are two important points to be made about the residual questions surrounding Pauline exegesis and mystical body of Christ theology. First, the explanation above depends, of course, on the critical distinction between the authentic Pauline epistles and pseudepigrapha. As we have seen above in the readings of *Lumen Gentium* 7 by O'Donnell and Wood, the deutero-Pauline letters present a very interesting case for the development of the notion of the body of Christ within the New Testament canon, in which the concept extends beyond the local community. In scholarship on the theology of the apostle Paul, the distinction between authentic writings and later developments is very important indeed. But if, as in the case of mystical body of Christ theology, the focus turns to the development of a theological idea across the tradition, then the more canonical hermeneutic is not only relevant but even imperative.

---

in the Twentieth Century," 350–51. We shall return to the debate concerning mystical body and metaphor in chapter 4 below.

    [82] Yves Congar, *Le Concile de Vatican II: Son église, peuple de Dieu, et corps du Christ*, Théologie Historique 71 (Paris: Editions Beauchesne, 1984), 122–24.

    [83] F. X. Lawler and Dennis M. Doyle, "Mystical Body of Christ," in *The New Catholic Encyclopedia*, 2nd ed., vol. 10 (Farmington Hills, MI: Gale, 2003), 101.

Second, with respect to Paul's own theology of the body of Christ, scholars continue the tug of war between the more Hellenistic Paul and the more Jewish Paul (to oversimplify things a bit). In Pauline studies, the extent to which Paul's notion of the body is indebted to Stoicism, or rather to late Jewish *Merkabah* mysticism, is very much up for debate. Scholars adhering to the predominantly Hellenistic Paul have illustrated that the Greco-Roman sense of the body itself had more cosmic dimensions than its roots in Aesop's fable of the body would indicate. That sense of bodiliness—extending across space and adopted by Agrippa—substantiated Rome's imperial sense of itself: one whole, with many parts extended geographically.[84] Though Agrippa's use of the image of the body is primarily horizontal, it is surely difficult in the Roman imagination to separate anything worldly from its godly connections. Stoics often referred to the earth as the body of Zeus. The Greco-Roman imagination, then, already had an inbuilt cosmic sense of a god's body wrought horizontally.

Among those who emphasize Paul as a practitioner of *Merkabah* mysticism—a tradition rooted in Ezekiel's vision of divine glory, in the form of a human figure on God's chariot throne (*merkabah*)—Paul's discussion of life in Christ and the body of Christ takes on a much richer sense of participation in the very life of God, extended far and wide. Alan Segal foregrounds Paul's mystical encounter with Christ on the road to Damascus and remarks:

> Paul describes his own spiritual experiences in terms appropriate to a Jewish apocalyptic-mystagogue of the first century. He, like Enoch, relates his experiences of heavenly travel, in which he sees the secrets of the universe revealed. He believes his salvation to lie in a body-to-body identification with his heavenly savior, who sits on the divine throne and functions as God's glorious manifestation. He identifies this experience with his conversion, although it apparently characterizes a lifetime of spiritual discipline rather than a single event.[85]

---

[84] Michelle V. Lee, *Paul, the Stoics, and the Body of Christ*, Society for New Testament Studies Monograph Series (Cambridge, UK: Cambridge University Press, 2006), 31–40.

[85] Alan Segal, *Paul the Convert: The Apostolate and Apostasy of Saul the Pharisee* (New Haven, CT: Yale University Press, 1992), 35.

The outcome of these profound experiences for Paul is no less than an understanding of his own deification—a deification that will be brought to fulfillment upon his death. For all of its congruence with Second Temple Jewish mystical texts, Paul's vision is unique in that those texts do not extend to all believers. Segal writes, "Paul understands that he has been transformed into a divine state, which will be fully realized after his death; Paul claims that his vision and transformation is somehow a mystical identification; and Paul claims to have received a calling, his special status as intermediary. Paul specifies the meaning of this calling for all believers, a concept absent the Enochic texts."[86] The extension, then, of Paul's encounter with God to all of the church renders Paul's body of Christ language deeper and more pervasive than a mere moral union.

Segal's work suggests that Paul's choice of body language was already deeply theologically infused from his formation in Jewish mysticism. Not only did Paul conceive of his conversion and new life in Christ in the eschatological terms given him by the Jewish mystical tradition, but that those very terms helped him to describe the here and now, a unique witness of Paul's own mysticism. Paul's conversion experience includes, in the manner of Ezekiel's prophecy, an encounter with the Glory of God. Throughout the Jewish Scriptures God's appearance takes human shape, called *Kavod* or "the Glory of God." Paul saw this experience as materially indistinct from the experiences of the Eleven, and it therefore justified his status as an apostle (see Gal 1 and 1 Cor 15). But it had further ramifications. About Luke's descriptions of Paul's conversion, Segal writes, "This unusual feature of identification between the believer and Christ, closely related to Paul's own conversion, is a fascinating unexplored aspect of Paul's thought. It is the mystery that can be most clearly addressed by the serious study of Jewish apocalypticism and mysticism."[87] Using Paul's conversion experience as paradigm, and his formation in Jewish mysticism that gave him the categories for explaining it, Segal moves to the impact on the *ekklēsia*, "Because believers on earth, by virtue of their conversion, have been transformed into the body of Christ, who is the image of God, the destiny of believers will be the same as the destiny of Christ."[88]

[86] Ibid., 47.
[87] Ibid., 11.
[88] Ibid., 67.

Aside from the complexities brought to Pauline scholarship by attention to Second Temple Jewish mysticism, some social-scientific New Testament scholarship has drawn out greater complexity in Paul's discourse around the body of Christ, which is more amenable to the French stream's mystical body theology. For example, British scholar David G. Horrell has argued that Paul's appeal to the body of Christ is not simply an appropriation of Agrippa's image of the body to emphasize unity but an appeal to solidarity rooted in early Christian sacramental practice.[89] Undertaking primarily a study of Pauline ethics, Horrell notes that, for Paul, union with Christ is the basis for making sense of solidarity, a solidarity that extends beyond the visible confines of the Christian community.[90] While not the organic sense of body theology intended by Möhler and others, Horrell's contribution does widen Paul's theology of the body of Christ, and it does so with careful attention to its baptismal and eucharistic ritual roots.

The debates concerning Pauline scholarship cannot, of course, be solved here. Nevertheless, this brief excursus has demonstrated the complexity involved in pinning down the Pauline notion of the body of Christ. There is a richness and depth to the notion that extends beyond mere metaphor. This is suggested by the place of the famous body of Christ discussion in 1 Corinthians. Catholic biblical scholarship in the wake of *Divino Afflante Spiritu* changed the conversation about the mystical body of Christ. Scholars pointed out that the formulation, in itself, is not directly Pauline and further that the deutero-Pauline epistles develop the body of Christ theology in a distinct way from Paul himself. This work clearly challenged the pervasive theology of the mystical body. Yet, continuing studies of Paul have connected his theology of the body of Christ to a more mystical sense through different avenues (Roman or Jewish) and with different implications.

---

[89] David G. Horrell, *Solidarity and Difference: A Contemporary Reading of Paul's Ethics* (London: T&T Clark, 2005), esp. 99–132.

[90] Ibid. Horrell tends to describe "solidarity" as that which inheres among the diverse Christian community itself and "difference" as the engagement with those outside the Christian community. Horrell's usage of these terms seems related to his conversation partners, Jürgen Habermas and Stanley Hauerwas, whose positions he tends to overdraw to make his own very important points. The notion of solidarity I have been drawing out of mystical body theology encompasses both of these senses— by its nature it pushes beyond the visible boundaries of the church.

Conclusions

Recalling the three distinct streams of mystical body theology—the Roman, the German-Romantic, and the French-speaking socio-liturgical—sheds some light on the divergent perceptions of mystical body theology in the late twentieth and early twenty-first centuries.

Thus, when in 1998 liturgist Nathan Mitchell says, "This image of the body—where some members are inherently inferior to others and all are subordinate to the head—emphasized the rational, juridical, hierarchical, and magisterial qualities of the Church, especially its structures of authority and obedience," he is describing the Roman stream.[91] It is fair to say that the Roman stream's mystical body theology—the one thematic in the schema first presented to the council—was challenged by the *ressourcement* movement and ultimately rejected by the council.

Continuing Möhler's legacy, twentieth-century Tübingen theologians saw in the theology of mystical body a way of describing the organic reality of the Christian people extended throughout space and time. Of course, this is the German stream. As we have seen, Adam and others (such as Eschweiler and Lortz) grounded mystical body theology in German national unity, in horrifying fashion. Adam employed the image to argue against both neoscholastic juridicism and individualistic congregationalism. It was this strain of mystical body theology that created a sour taste after the war. The theological path forward on the floor of the council did not appear to be one on which well-known Catholic Nazis and Nazi sympathizers had tread. Contemporary theologians, such as Anselm Min or Cavanaugh, who suggest that mystical body theology failed in the political realm, are likely thinking of this second stream (and also perhaps the first). It bears repeating that not all German mystical body theology went in this direction. Guardini contributed to the mystical body revival while directly challenging Nazi perversions and, as a result, was dismissed from his post at the University of Berlin in 1939.

Guardini studied at the University of Fribourg and was a major player in the liturgical movement. Not surprisingly, then, he grounded mystical body theology in the liturgy and sacraments of the church. This much

---

[91] Nathan Mitchell, "Liturgy and Ecclesiology," in *Handbook for Liturgical Studies: Fundamental Liturgy*, ed. Anscar J. Chupungco (Collegeville, MN: Liturgical Press, 1998), 113–14.

Guardini shared with the French stream of mystical body theology. Another characteristic of the French stream is that it was not limited to ecclesiology; it was not simply a model of the church. It was more. It pervaded various arms of theology (Christology, theological anthropology, sacramental theology, liturgy, ethics, etc.) and, especially in Michel's view, became a fundamental Christian vision or way of seeing the world. It is this stream of mystical body theology that does not receive full-throated, but only piecemeal, emphasis at the council. At least part of the reason for this is because the majority of bishops and theologians had been soured on the first two. Following the French stream of mystical body theology might have been a way to cement the connection between liturgy and social transformation—a connection that Margaret Kelleher, among others, insists the council missed.[92]

Seeing mystical body theology through the narrow lens of ecclesiology not only obscures the theological work that it did prior to the council but also precludes us from seeing the ways in which its concerns and categories continue, even after its mid-century eclipse. This oversight is connected to a tendency to privilege Pius XII's encyclical for a description of mystical body theology's form and content (and an often limited reading of *Mystici Corporis*, at that). Observing the ebb of mystical body theology without the narrow lens of ecclesiology leads us to search for its theological heritage in places that we would not initially expect. The contemporary French theological project of Chauvet, in which the author works to offer a "fundamental sacramental reinterpretation of the Christian life," is one such place. Chauvet was formed in the Center for Liturgical Studies at the Institut Catholique in Paris, and, like his forbear Beauduin, though in a very different way, he articulates an intimate connection between sacraments and ethics, with a firm emphasis on corporality or bodiliness. It is to Chauvet's context and work, then, that we now turn.

---

[92] Margaret M. Kelleher, "Liturgy and Social Transformation: Exploring the Relationship," *U.S. Catholic Historian* 16, no. 4 (1998): 64. Some examples of conciliar texts where the emphases of the French stream do indeed surface without explicit mention of mystical body include *Sacrosantum Concilium*, no. 27 on the public and social nature of the Mass, and *Gaudium et Spes*, no. 58, a classic text on inculturation.

CHAPTER 4

Vestigial Body I

The Contours of the French Stream

I n Bonaventure's famous *Itinerarium mentis in Deum* (*Itinerary of the Mind to God*), the Franciscan reflects on his founder's vision of Christ under the appearance of a six-winged seraph. Rather than a mere Platonic ascent, Bonaventure's itinerary is Christ-centered and driven by a robust account of creation with each of the three sets of six wings of the seraph representing particular levels of the journey to God. The first level represents the order of material objects and nonhuman earthly sentient beings. On this level, there is no *imago Dei* to be discerned and beheld. Nevertheless, because of their origin in God, these elements of creation bear what the Seraphic Doctor calls *vestigia,* literally, "footprints" (or "imprints") of God in the world. At the first stage of the itinerary, then, one looks to the created world to find vestiges of God. In Bonaventure's construction it appears that this first step along the journey is essential to reaching its next stages.[1]

---

[1] St. Bonaventure, *Itinerarium Mentis ad Deum* in *Doctoris Seraphici S. Bonaventurae Episcopi Cardinalis Opera Omnia*, vol. 5 (Quaracchi: 1891). Available from: http://faculty.uml. edu/rinnis/45.304%20God%20and%20Philosophy/ITINERARIUM .pdf. In chapter 2, Bonaventure explains the centrality of the senses to the itinerary as well as the christological act of seeing God in God's *vestigia*: "So analysis is an act, which, through abstraction and purification, causes the perceivable object, apprehended directly by the senses, to enter into the intellectual power. And in this way the whole world has to enter the human soul through the gates of the senses and according to these three activities. All of these things are imprints [*vestigia*] through which we can look upon our God. For the perceived object is an appearance born at the core and then impressed upon the organ itself, which impression gives rise to the object

In light of Bonaventure's notion of *vestigia*, there is a dual sense in which the title of this chapter and the next—"Vestigial Body"—functions. In one sense, the vestigial body refers to a way that mystical body theology functioned for the French socio-liturgical stream. That is, flowing out of the public worship of the church—centered in Christ—we come to see the world in a particular way, as caught up in the salvific work accomplished in the preaching, healing, suffering, dying, and rising body of Christ. Thus, we become more attuned to God's *vestigia*. Yes, the source of the theology of the mystical body of Christ rests on the second set of wings in Bonaventure's analysis, that is, attending to others as images of Christ, who is the image of the invisible God (Col 1:15). As we have seen with Michel's work particularly, and the French stream broadly, however, the theology proceeds from that biblical insight and that liturgical encounter and then ripples throughout an entire vision of the world.

A second sense involves the history and development of the theology of mystical body itself. The last chapter demonstrated two major points. First, mystical body of Christ theology faded over the couple of decades that spanned the middle part of the twentieth century due to a variety of factors. The second is a further development of a point made about Michel in chapter 2: a narrow focus and understanding of mystical body theology as simply an ecclesiology misses the richness of its resurgence in the twentieth century. In this sense, then, vestigial body refers to the remnants of mystical body theology that we can find after it has receded. With greater attention to mystical body theology's own multivalence, Chauvet's sacramental reinterpretation of the Christian life emerges as an interesting and relevant example.

Before delving into Chauvet's work itself in the next chapter, we need to explore the deeper context and historical trajectory of the Institut

---

with which one is to become acquainted. This clearly suggests that that which is the invisible image of God, the splendor of His glory and the form of His substance—which is universal due to His primary generation, in the same way as an object generates its appearance from its core—is united by the grace of union, as something perceivable to the bodily organs of a rational individual: that union is led back to the Father in the form of a primordial source and its object. Thus, since all things with which one can become acquainted have to generate their own perceived form, and since in them can be seen the eternal generation of the Word as in a mirror, they clearly proclaim the eternal emanation of the Image and the Son from God the Father" (chap. 2, no. 6–7).

Supérieur de Liturgie (ISL) at the Institut Catholique de Paris, where Chauvet took several courses and then taught for more than thirty years, in order to establish the historical framework of Chauvet's development of the French stream, of which Michel's work represents a significant tributary.

The French Stream and the Institut Supérieur de Liturgie

Reflecting on his own formation in the ebb and flow of theology, Chauvet writes, "All theological discourse depends upon the dominant discourse of the era that preceded it, either to argue against it or to reinforce it. It is obvious that mine has been partly constituted as a reaction against the scholastic discourse of my formation at the theological faculty of Angers."[2] As Philippe Bordeyne goes on to explain in his biographical sketch of Chauvet, that faculty was heavily, though not entirely, influenced by the neoscholasticism of the day, in which Chauvet did not find much vibrancy.[3] In fact, he describes that theology as "too ahistorical and too

---

[2] Louis-Marie Chauvet, "Quand la théologie rencontre les sciences humaines," in *La responsabilité des théologiens: mélanges offerts à Joseph Doré*, ed. François Bousquet et al. (Paris: Desclée, 2002), 401. See also Philippe Bordeyne, "Louis-Marie Chauvet: A Short Biography," in *Sacraments: Revelation of the Humanity of God, Engaging the Fundamental Theology of Louis-Marie Chauvet*, ed. Philippe Bordeyne and Bruce T. Morrill (Collegeville, MN: Liturgical Press, 2008), ix.

[3] Neither Bordeyne nor Chauvet mention any specific professors. Mariologist René Laurentin taught at Angers during Chauvet's time there and was a younger member of the faculty. Laurentin's Thomism is more nuanced than many of his era, and Yves Congar often finds Laurentin on his side of arguments at the council. See, for example, Congar, *My Journal of the Council*, 57, 185, 688. Laurentin himself would go on to write four volumes on the council.

My research has been able to turn up only two other Angers theologians during Chauvet's time there: in moral theology was Marie-Joseph Gerlaud and in Scripture, Pierre Michalon. In an interesting confluence, Abbé Joseph Anger's theological synthesis of Aquinas's thought by way of the theology of the mystical body of Christ was prepared as a doctoral dissertation at Angers in 1910. As noted in chapter 3, John J. Burke translated Anger's book in 1931. Abbé Anger, *The Doctrine of the Mystical Body of Christ According to the Principles of St. Thomas*, trans. John J. Burke (New York: Benziger, 1931). Burke himself has been acknowledged as working out a crude intrinsicism via mystical body theology. See Margaret M. Reher, "Cardinal Dougherty and the IHMs: The Church as the 'Juridic/Mystical' Body of Christ," *U.S. Catholic*

formal (in the sense of formal logic)" to enable the students "to genuinely think and live, and thus bring about a real following."[4] Eventually his theological study would lead him to the thought of Martin Heidegger, whose philosophy would serve Chauvet's larger theological project. At least as important as the continental critique of metaphysics that, as we shall see, frames Chauvet's theological writing is his connection with the ISL. His teaching there was always paired with the pastoral, both because of the nature of the ISL itself and because of Chauvet's consistent parish appointments as a priest of the Diocese of Pantoise. If his work is constituted against his early formation in theology, it was stoked by, and remained in line with, his later formation at the ISL.

Two French commentators on Chauvet emphasize these points. Bordeyne, dean of the theology faculty at the Institut Catholique, comments, "Chauvet's theology is difficult to understand if you omit his constant comings and goings between liturgical life, where one receives whomever comes for sacramental preparation and university teaching. Chauvet is the heir to a tradition of reciprocal interaction between pastoral practices and theological research at a high level that gives witness to the strict relations between the National Center of Pastoral Liturgy . . . and the ISL."[5] When offered a professorship at the Institut Catholique on the recommendation of Pierre-Marie Gy, OP, Chauvet hesitated because of his deep love for diocesan parish ministry and eventually negotiated a situation that allowed him to do both from 1973 until his retirement from the Institut Catholique in 2007.

He still continues service as a pastor at Deuil-la-Barre in north Paris. His acceptance of that teaching post years ago coincided with "a turning

---

Historian 14, no. 4 (1996): 53–62. She quotes Burke: "If Christ is the Life of our souls, and there is nothing in all the world that is not Christ, . . . There is no distinction of natural and supernatural. That distinction is theoretical" (54).

[4] Chauvet, "Quand la théologie rencontre les sciences humaines," 401. In French: *Mais, dès ces premières années 60, les étudiants que nous étions éprouvaient le discours théologique communément tenu comme trop anhistorique et trop formel (au sens de la 'logique formelle') pour donner vraiment à penser et à vivre, et donc pour entrainer une véritable adhésion.*

[5] Bordeyne, "Louis-Marie Chauvet," xii. "National Center of Pastoral Liturgy" is, in French, *Centre National de Pastorale Liturgique. Pastorale* is the noun and *liturgique* the adjective.

point in the history of the Institut, a period of transformation aimed at responding to new needs," observes Patrick Prétot, OSB, ISL director from 2001 to 2010. "From its founding and under the direction of Dom Bernard Botte, the ISL had provided an education which combined general courses in the fundamentals of liturgiology and special topics courses in areas of research that were sometimes very specialized."[6] Prétot describes a transition in which professors began to take the pastoral sphere as not simply the arena of application for liturgical theory and sacramental theology but rather as a source for theological work itself. Chauvet, Prétot explains, was a driver of this transition.[7] With this shift, the ISL more fully embraced the idea of its original visionary, Beauduin, who consistently emphasized the parish realm as significant for theological insight.

When in 1967—a time of no small upheaval in church and society— Chauvet had completed his studies at the Catholic University of the West in Angers, he moved on to doctoral study in Paris. Indeed, Prétot alludes to the 1968 student riots as a component of the shift at the ISL.[8] Chauvet studied at the ISL during the early years of his doctoral studies. He took courses with eventual Vatican II *peritus* Gy on sacraments, on the theology of the liturgy, and on the Divine Office.[9] Gy's influence on Chauvet

[6] Patrick Prétot, "Louis-Marie Chauvet à l'insitute superieur de liturgie," *Transversalités* 111 (July–September 2009): 179. In French: *un tournant de l'histoire de l'Institut, une période de transformation, destinée à répondre à de nouveaux besoins. Depuis sa fondation en effet, et sous l'impulsion de Dom Bernard Botte, l'ISL avait fonctionné sur la base d'un enseignement qui conjuguait des cours généraux dispensant les repères fondamentaux de la science liturgique et des cours spéciaux portant sur des domaines de recherche parfois très spécialisés.*

[7] Ibid., 180.

[8] Ibid. These riots had a widespread effect not only in society generally but also among Catholic thinkers of the day. Michel de Certeau, for example, refocused his efforts in support of pluralization and deep engagement with otherness. He celebrated the challenge, represented by the protestors, to those who insisted on their role as dispensers of culture to the masses, while solemnly acknowledging the deep secularization announced by the moment. By contrast, de Lubac was troubled by the May riots. In the words of Brenna Moore, "He saw in the protestors' demystication of old authorities merely a new form of Whiggish triumphalism and naïveté" (Brenna Moore, "How to Awaken the Dead: Michel de Certeau, Henri de Lubac, and the Instabilities between the Past and the Present," *Spiritus* 12 [Fall 2012]: 176–77).

[9] Prétot, "Louis-Marie Chauvet à l'insitute superieur de liturgie," 178. On Gy, see John D. Laurance, Foreword to Pierre-Marie Gy, *The Reception of Vatican II:*

was substantial. That influence is obvious by the themes Chauvet's work shares with Gy's: the unity of liturgy and sacramental theology; liturgical reflection done in light of pastoral experience, criticism of instrumental causality in sacramental theology, and an emphasis on the centrality of the gathered assembly. Further, Chauvet continued to engage Gy's scholarship throughout his own work and contributed to a Festschrift for Gy in 1990.[10] Later, in *Symbol and Sacrament*, Chauvet refers to Gy on two important points that were central to debates around mystical body theology in the French stream: the issue of the relationship between the sacraments and the gathered ecclesial assembly, and the tendency to narrow the emphasis simply to the moment of consecration (rather than viewing the eucharistic prayer as a whole).[11] In the French stream, with its social bent rooted in the liturgy, to neglect the former issue and embrace the latter was indicative of a narrow vision, which failed to perceive the mystical body of Christ.[12]

When Chauvet arrived as a student, Gy had recently (1964) taken charge of the ISL from its founding director, Botte. In his memoir on the French liturgical movement, Botte refers to Gy as a key collaborator in the formation of the ISL.[13] Botte and Gy joined four other liturgical theologians to provide a program in methods of liturgical theology for

---

Liturgical Reforms in the Life of the Church, The Père Marquette Lecture in Theology (Milwaukee, WI: Marquette University Press, 2003).

[10] Louis-Marie Chauvet, "Nova et vetera: quelques leçons tirées de la tradition relative au sacrement de la réconciliation," in *Rituels: Mélanges offerts au Pierre-Marie Gy, OP*, ed. Pierre-Marie Gy, Paul de Clerck, and Eric Palazzo (Paris: Cerf, 1990), 201–35.

[11] Chauvet, *Symbol and Sacrament*, 185, 468–72.

[12] For example, see Beauduin, "Sur le sens des mots 'présence sacramentelle,'" 153. Beauduin emphasizes the role of the assembly in the anamnesis, considering the entire eucharistic celebration as sacrifice: *en principe et en droit, chacun de nous est pleinement solidaire dans la passion, la mort, la résurrection, l'ascension de notre Chef (récitez le Unde et memores); mais il y faut notre consentement jusqu'à notre mort, il y faut notre Amen: et pour recueillir chaque jour tous ces « Amen », le Christ replace présent son Sacrifice sous forme de participation de ses membres: sacrifice liturgique (c'est-à-dire de toute son Église, de tout son corps mystique).* Cf. Virgil Michel, *My Sacrifice and Yours* (Collegeville, MN: Liturgical Press, 1926). This was one of Michel's first popular-level pamphlets published by Liturgical Press and it emphasized similar points. In the next chapter we shall see how Chauvet reinterprets the notion of the Mass as sacrifice, without abandoning the theology.

[13] Botte, *From Silence to Participation*, 65.

seminary professors, which began in 1953 at Mont César.[14] When Botte was nominated by Bouyer of the Institut Catholique to be the first director of the ISL, he accepted because "Père Gy at this time was too young to take upon himself the responsibilities of this position, but he was chosen as assistant-director."[15] Of his work at the ISL with Gy and two others, Botte writes, "I must pay homage to my main collaborators: Père Gy, Abbé Jounel, Père Dalmais: we came to form a perfectly unified team, and I believe we were able to work well together."[16] It is safe to say not only that Botte and Gy worked closely together but also that their collaboration was of a particularly formative kind for Gy. In fact, Gy would later name Botte and Congar as the most important influences on his theology.[17]

A further examination of Chauvet's theological family tree leads through Botte to Beauduin. Before founding the ISL in 1956, Botte collaborated closely with Beauduin at Mont César. He credits Beauduin with beginning the liturgical movement in 1909 by lecturing on active participation in the liturgy.[18] Beauduin's address marked a beginning not necessarily because of its novel ideas but because of its orientation toward the parishes. Beauduin's pastoral sensibilities were always resolutely theological and these concerns came to animate the ISL—an institution Beauduin dreamed of but never saw come to fruition. Botte describes this sensibility, enshrined in *Questions Liturgiques et Paroissales*, the journal Beauduin began:

> A parish priest today would probably say [its pages] aren't practical enough. But you have to understand what Dom Beauduin wanted to do. . . .

---

[14] Ibid., 87.

[15] Ibid., 94–95.

[16] Ibid., 105.

[17] Laurance, "Foreword," 4. Shortly after the council, Gy had collaborated with Congar, Chenu, and others on Congar and Jean-Pierre Jossua, eds., *La liturgie après Vatican II: Bilans, études, prospective*, Unam Sanctum 66 (Paris: Cerf, 1967). Gy's essay in that volume explored the movement created by *Sacrosanctum Concilium* (111–26); Congar's essay explored a theme that Gy himself never tired of emphasizing and researching: the role of the assembly as the acting subject of the liturgy (241–82).

[18] Botte, *From Silence to Participation*, 10.

First notice the adjective "parish" (*paroissiales*). It seems a little dated today and we'd replace it with the word "pastoral." Dom Beauduin insisted greatly on this. Much later I proposed he drop the adjective, but he protested. He didn't want the magazine to become a technical publication reserved for specialists. He really wanted his audience to be the parish clergy, those who were really in touch with the people. It was a question of reestablishing contact between the altar and the nave in order to make the liturgy an act of the living community. . . .

On the other hand, Dom Beauduin didn't intend to give the clergy practical recipes. The priests didn't need that. What was needed was a change of spirit to make them understand that the liturgy is not a simple ritual mechanism but a source of life for them and for their people.

Some people could see the liturgical movement only as an estheticism designed to make the house of God more attractive and draw crowds to it. But this was not Dom Beauduin's intention and his personal contribution to the magazine showed it. Renewed esteem for the liturgy was not a question of pastoral tactics, but theological truth.[19]

Unlike others involved with the liturgical movement, especially in Germany, Beauduin aimed for the parish priest.[20] The thinking was that without a modest liturgical training, priests would be unable to light a fire in the parishes. Pastoral orientation remained a common emphasis of the Benedictine house, Mont César, which Beauduin and Botte shared, even if these two differed on the title of the journal.

In the late 1940s, Louis Bouyer laid out some serious criticisms of the liturgical movement's direction. Abbot Bernard Capelle of Mont César responded with an argument about the perils of narrow rubric-driven seminary formation, which ill-prepares pastors to sort out mere innovation

---

[19] Ibid., 22–23. See also Quitslund, *Beauduin*, esp. 34–35, and Jozef Lamberts, "The Abbey of Mont-César in Louvain: One Hundred Years Young," *Worship* 73, no. 5 (September 1999): 429–30.

[20] On the differences between European liturgical movements in this regard, see Pecklers, *The Unread Vision*, esp. 14.

from true strides toward reform.[21] Capelle's response is an example of the monastery's thorough pastoral orientation; he wanted seminaries to improve in forming discerning priests. Michel had worked in a similar vein in the United States. He wanted to educate parish priests as well as the laity. *Orate Fratres*, for example, aimed not only for the parish priest but also for the people in the pews.[22]

Botte first came to Mont César to attend the inaugural Liturgical Week—a gathering of scholars and pastors hosted by Beauduin—in August 1910 and entered the monastery in 1912. He collaborated with Beauduin until the outbreak of World War I when Botte, a reserve, was called to mobilize in 1914. Shortly after the war Beauduin left for Rome to serve as professor of liturgy at Sant'Anselmo.[23] Beauduin's biographer suggests that there was less and less sympathy for Beauduin's ideas at Mont César, and Botte tells us that Beauduin's departure was primarily precipitated by Dom Odo Lottin, new prefect of studies at Mont César, who "was afraid of the exuberant activity of Dom Beauduin and told him so."[24]

Beauduin jumped at the opportunity to go to Rome because many of the younger Benedictines who entered Mont César during the war did not know him and did not have much sympathy for the movement. Beauduin had been engaged in a variety of wartime activities, including espionage, secret trips to Great Britain, and hiding those in contempt of the occupation.[25] At Mont César he now felt isolated. For Botte, by contrast, with

[21] See Bernard Capelle, "Crise du movement liturgique?," *Questions Liturgiques et Paroissiales* 32 (1951): 209–17. Bouyer's criticism of para-liturgies can be found in his "Où en est le mouvement liturgique?," *La Maison Dieu* 25 (1951): 34–46. The title of this article parallels that of Bouyer's 1948 critique of mystical body theology.

[22] Michel wrote in the inaugural number of the journal, "A liturgical awakening must come through a sympathetic understanding on the part of the general faithful." Virgil Michel, "Foreword," 2–3.

[23] Quitslund, *Beauduin*, 52. Quitslund dates his departure in the fall of 1921. Botte suggests the date is 1923 (Botte, *From Silence to Participation*, 35), but Quitslund seems to be correct.

[24] Botte, *From Silence to Participation*, 35.

[25] On Beauduin's stunning wartime activities, see Louis Bouyer, *Dom Lambert Beauduin*, 83–102, as well as Loonbeek and Mortiau, *Un pionnier*, 57–68. Undercover, Beauduin took on at least three aliases. He was primarily known as Oscar Fraipont, a wine merchant (specializing in sacramental wine), but also at times as Oscar Bronckart and Louis Lambert.

the encouragement of Abbott Capelle, Mont César became a platform for his newfound teaching and writing about the liturgy. In a more personal vein, Botte writes with clear affection for his confrère:

> His good nature, kindness, and cordiality won me over. Forty years later I had my nephew (a young chemical engineer) take me by car to Chevetogne. We saw Dom Lambert together. Then I left my nephew and went to meet another priest. When I came back, they were the best of friends. Afterwards my nephew told me that he had never met anyone so likeable. Dom Beauduin was that way. By the end of a half-hour's conversation you had the impression you were his best friend. I had looked for an epithet that could best characterize him. I didn't find it in the dictionary but in a title of Chesterton: *Supervivant*. He overflowed with life and made it spring up all around him.[26]

Like Beauduin did, Botte would eventually, in the 1950s, direct his energies toward ecumenical endeavors.[27] Beauduin's vision for liturgical renewal included a school for liturgical studies that would serve as the liturgical counterpart to the School for Thomistic Philosophy at Leuven and the École Biblique in Jerusalem—a think tank for liturgical theology, which would support the pastoral engagement that Beauduin thought the heart of his own liturgical apostolate. According to Jozef Lamberts, "This plan, however, he was unable to realize. His dream was only realized in 1956 when the *Insitut Supérieur de Liturgie*, a graduate institute of liturgical studies, was established in Paris as a cooperation of the *Centre de Pastorale Liturgique* of Paris and the abbey of Mont-César. The *Centre de Pastorale Liturgique* itself was founded in 1943 with Dom Beauduin as its advisor."[28] In essence, then, Botte founded and initially directed the institute that Beauduin had first conceived.

Having established Beauduin's essential contributions to the French stream in chapter 1, we can now see a genealogical, if somewhat oblique, connection between Beauduin, some of the other key figures in the French stream, and Chauvet. It bears recalling here that Beauduin read and reread

---

[26] Botte, *From Silence to Participation*, 16.
[27] Lamberts, "The Abbey of Mont-César," 438.
[28] Ibid., 430.

Mersch's *The Whole Christ*. He also remarked that his friend de Lubac's *Catholicisme* was a book he wished he had written himself.[29] While he may have had some disagreements with these two Jesuits, Beauduin nevertheless found them *sympathique* in terms of theological priorities and emphases. Because Michel was so deeply influenced by Beauduin, the liturgical movement he kick-started, and the mystical body theology he elaborated, it makes historical sense to locate Chauvet in the same long stream of mystical body thought as Michel. Much of that connection resides in the development of the ISL. This is not at all to suggest that all of those involved with the establishment and development of the ISL were involved with the mystical body recovery; however, significant figures were. On the whole, there were disagreements among them, certainly, but the theologians that swam in this stream shared an emphasis on, of course, the theology of the mystical body but also on its rootedness in the liturgy and sacraments of the church, the need to engage social movements, and the necessity of taking insights from the tradition to the pews.

Sacramental Body: Henri de Lubac in the French Stream

In terms of intellectual biography, Chauvet's place in the long stream of French-speaking mystical body theology makes sense. These historical links should not, however, lead us to take any continuity between Chauvet and his forbears for granted. It was Chauvet himself, after all, who commented on the discontinuity of his work from his earlier theological formation in Angers. As is clear from even a cursory read of Chauvet's theology, his work is interested in the nature of mediation, deeply dependent on the category of corporality or bodiliness; it elaborates the nature of the intersection between Scripture, sacrament, and ethics; it proceeds from a close reading of the liturgical action of the church. All of these were central emphases of the French stream. Chauvet's explicit discussion of mystical body theology appears in his interpretation and application of de Lubac's thought. In order to understand that appropriation, we shall now turn to de Lubac's contribution to the French stream of mystical body theology, a contribution ultimately supportive of the theology in the title of his wartime controverted book, *Corpus Mysticum*.

---

[29] Quitslund, *Beauduin*, 243.

Real or Metaphor?

Among those who have written about the mystical body of Christ during the heyday of its twentieth-century revival, there is a range of opinions about precisely how we are to understand the rhetorical, and indeed denotative, force of the image. One question particularly brings the problem to light: Is "mystical body of Christ" a metaphor? As early as 1935, William R. O'Connor concluded, "There is in it a reality and a metaphor, and the metaphor is no less necessary than the reality to bring out its content." "Our embodiment in Christ" is "an objectively existing entity," constituted by sanctifying grace, which renders the bond real, even beyond the metaphorical force of the head-body image. The debate continued throughout the twentieth century, with some theologians concerned about conceptual sloppiness in calling it "real" while others worried that "metaphor" talk would undercut the truth of Christ's continued presence in the world.[30]

Likewise in current scholarship, there is some agreement that the descriptor has both metaphorical and real senses. Anselm Min, for example, says that "the church is not literally the body of Christ and is not hypostatically united with Christ, but it is also the Body of Christ in more than a purely metaphorical sense"; further, "the Body of Christ is a great metaphor."[31] Historically, the precise configuration of that "both/and"—or whether and how the word "metaphor" should be used at all—has been

---

[30] O'Connor, "The Mystical Body of Christ: Reality or Metaphor?," 152–53. Here are some examples of the discussion, from various times and contexts: Geoffrey Preston challenges the "metaphoricisation" of the body in *Mystici Corporis* and insists that "Body of Christ" is not metaphorical but the "expressive organ" of Christ. See *Faces of the Church: Meditations on a Mystery and Its Images*, text prepared by Aidan Nichols, with a foreword by Walter Kasper (Grand Rapids, MI: Eerdmans, 1997), 87–92. Louis Bouyer concurs with "Msgr. [Lucien] Cerfaux" who demonstrated that in Romans and 1 Corinthians "'body' is applied to the Church in an obviously metaphorical fashion." See Bouyer, *The Church of God*, 303. Avery Dulles suggests that there is a sense in which "Body of Christ" is metaphorical. See *Models of the Church*, 54.

[31] Anselm Min, "The Church as the Flesh of Christ Crucified: Toward an Incarnational Theology of the Church in the Age of Globalization," in *Religion, Economics, and Culture in Conflict and Conversation*, ed. Maureen O'Connell and Laurie Cassidy, 2010 College Theology Society Annual, vol. 56 (Maryknoll, NY: Orbis Books, 2011), 97.

a matter of dispute. At issue is the fundamental theology question of the presence of Christ in and through the church.

Mannes Koster's aforementioned critique of mystical body of Christ as simply a metaphor supported his defense of "people of God" (*Volk Gottes*) as a superior ecclesiological image because of its realism—it locates the Christian people in the covenant and describes who they actually are. Whereas, Koster claimed, fancying Christians as Christ's arms, legs, etc., is a helpful way of imagining the various roles of the church it is not, of course, actually real. While he had other concerns as well, Koster was critical of those theologians who reduced the mystical body of Christ to a kind of corporate flow chart of the church. In their hands, it became overly horizontal—a mystical body akin to other mystical unions across space, like states and kingdoms. Their emphasis on the church as an extension of the hypostatic union made clear that there are human and divine elements in the church, but the vertical bonds were primarily in-dividual (between believer and Christ) and not social (among believers and Christ). Koster's critique holds some real force when directed at the Roman stream. It is, however, instructive to place it next to O'Connor's article from five years earlier in which he insists that the sacramental life of the church is the key to grasping the reality of the mystical body of Christ vis-à-vis every other mystical body. Thus one might say that the mystical body of Christ is real insofar as the sacraments are efficacious, but that gets us ahead of ourselves just a bit.

British Jesuit, and once Bombay archbishop, Alban Goodier provides an interesting window into some late nineteenth- and early twentieth-century attitudes concerning the mystical body of Christ. "Some of us remember a time," he writes, "when to be enthusiastic about [the mystical body of Christ] was to be thought in dangerous proximity to Modernism. We were warned by our spiritual fathers, and our theological professors, that to treat it as more than a vivid metaphor was not heretical, perhaps, but at least temerarious, and liable to lead to much misunderstanding."[32] Goodier entered the novitiate in 1887 and was ordained in 1903. His post–*Aeterni Patris* neo-Thomist formation reflects a common Thomist concern that mystical body might become more than a *similitudo*. In the *Summa Theologiae*, Thomas Aquinas had reflected on Christ's headship

---

[32] Goodier, "The Mystical Body," 289.

of the church as metaphorical and a likeness: "It must be said that in metaphorical speech we must not expect a likeness in all aspects, for thus it would be not a likeness [*similitudo*], but the truth of the matter." Thomas's language here opens up some questions about the relationship between metaphor and truth, particularly in what senses one can have both at the same time.[33]

De Lubac rejects the idea that mystical body of Christ should be understood primarily as a metaphor, since doing so undercuts the real, though mediated, character of the doctrine. Referring to currents in the late nineteenth century, de Lubac writes,

> The general tendency was to emphasize the *metaphorical* character of the expression [mystical body of Christ], to the point of watering down the *realism* of the doctrine it contained. The biblical image was viewed as fitted only to put across an idea which remained that of a society undoubtedly supernatural in its origin and end, and with equally supernatural means at its disposal, but without mystical unity in the true sense of the words. It seems as if we must diagnose as a symptom of this state of mind—in some cases at least—the open refusal (in the teeth of a solid tradition, both patristic and Thomist) to grant that the Holy Spirit was Himself the Soul of this Body.[34]

In the next chapter, we shall return to de Lubac's claim that a thin pneumatology is a symptom of this problem, but for the moment let us focus on the disease—a watering down of the realism and an emphasis on metaphor. De Lubac wrote this in *Meditations sur l'église* (translated as *Splendor of the Church*) in 1953, in which he employs the phrase "mystical body of Christ" multiple times favorably, to refer either to the church or to the eucharistic liturgical action.[35] In fact, he specifically understands Pius's

---

[33] *Summa Theologiae* 3.8.1.ad 2. My translation. In Latin: *dicendum quod in metaphoricis locutionibus non oportet attendi similitudinem quantum ad omnia, sic enim non esset similitudo, sed rei veritas.* Diffusing the complications significantly, the Fathers of the English Dominican Province translate *rei veritas* as "identity" rather than the more literal "truth of the thing."

[34] De Lubac, *The Splendor of the Church*, 95.

[35] See ibid., 102–3, 127–34, 239, 334.

Mystici Corporis as having undercut any tendency to assume "a closed circuit of doctrine that puts an end to discussion and reflection alike and discourages the raising of new questions."[36] His later comments enable us to read his earlier *Corpus Mysticum* as a direct historical challenge to this disease.[37] For de Lubac the burden of *Corpus Mysticum* (at least as he understood it in his later years) was not to contrast the *corpus mysticum* (or mystical body) of the Eucharist with the *corpus verum* (or true body) of the church. Rather, the treatise meant to challenge the abstracting tendencies of at least two strains of mystical body theology—first, those that supported various uses of mystical to apply to any connection of persons across space (e.g., the nation as the mystical body of the king) and, second, those that abstracted the adjective's point of reference from the liturgy, specifically the Eucharist.[38]

[36] Ibid., 28.

[37] Henri de Lubac, *Corpus Mysticum*. Reading the earlier *Corpus Mysticum* through the later *Splendor of the Church* is warranted because in that later period de Lubac himself referred to *Corpus Mysticum* as naïve and further because his usage of mystical body of Christ for both the Eucharist and for the church in the later work indicates that his intention in *Corpus Mysticum* was not to eradicate mystical body theology, only to refine it. Pius XII's encyclical had not yet been published when de Lubac wrote *Corpus Mysticum* (1938–1939). A second, revised edition, on which the English edition is based, appeared in 1949. It is understandable that after *Humani Generis* (August 1950), which he feared implicated him, and the theological silence imposed on him by his superiors two months earlier, that he would be very careful with his words for that reason in 1953. Nevertheless, de Lubac's integral—and not simply peripheral—use of the phrase in later work supports the argument that de Lubac did not intend to wipe out mystical body of Christ from theological discourse with *Corpus Mysticum*. Viewed through the lens of the variegated streams of mystical body theology, it would make more sense in terms of de Lubac's ecclesiological work, his wider corpus, and his own context that de Lubac offered a challenge to the Roman, and perhaps even German, streams of mystical body theology, which were more disconnected from the liturgy and sacraments of the church, and at the same time generally more given to the sociological designation, mystical body.

[38] The extent to which his efforts both had and had not been broadly received is obvious from this 1953 narrative: "In the absence of the chaplain of a certain pious organisation, on a recent occasion, the senior member gave the talk. Speaking on the Mystical Body he showed a thorough familiarity with the encyclical and other treatises. Before concluding he let fall a bombshell, to the effect that in Holy Communion we received the Mystical Body. This, of course, is an extreme example, but it does seem to show, since the person who made the blunder was not unintelligent, that it is not

This was not merely a theoretical concern for de Lubac. As has been demonstrated by several scholars, de Lubac's fierce resistance to the Vichy regime in the early 1940s and its shadow Nazi control after 1942 was supported by his theological endeavors.[39] Given the theological and political dynamics of the day, one could see de Lubac's resistance to the Nazi regime and challenge to neoscholastic theology as of a piece. Komonchak writes:

> One of the Jesuit superiors in Rome who was critical of [de Lubac's] theological views in 1946 had been quite critical of his opposition to Vichy. Garrigou-Lagrange, who was one of the first and most vigorous critics of *"la nouvelle théologie,"* had long supported the Action française, and his defense of Vichy had reached the point of accusing anyone who supported de Gaulle of mortal sin. Garrigou was also very close to Léon Bérard, who had served as the Vichy ambassador to the Holy See and had sent back a notorious dispatch in which he not only stated that the Vatican had no major objections to the Vichy anti-Jewish legislation but defended it by citations from St. Thomas, which de Lubac believes were contributed by "Thomists," either in Rome or in France. Many of the theologians who would be lumped together as leaders of *"la nouvelle théologie"* had been active participants in the Christian resistance to Nazism and to Vichy.[40]

Though all of his references to Karl Adam's work are positive,[41] one can see how de Lubac's exasperation with Vichy accommodationists—decrying their "'naïvely supernatural' language"[42]—could also be applied to Adam's defense of Nazi racial politics with mystical body theology. It is likely that

---

enough to preach sentences about the doctrine, even if culled from the encyclical, but that a more analytical exposition is needed" (MacCarthy, "Teaching the Mystical Body," 269–70). MacCarthy goes on to suggest that the image of body should be set aside for some time in order to emphasize "the Church as divinely instituted society" (271).

[39] See David Grumett, *De Lubac: A Guide for the Perplexed* (New York: T&T Clark, 2007), esp. 28–45.

[40] Komonchak, "Theology and Culture at Mid-Century," 601–2.

[41] See, for examples, de Lubac, *Splendor*, 28, 50, 99, 255; de Lubac, *Catholicism: Christ and the Common Destiny of Man*, trans. Elizabeth Englund (San Francisco: Ignatius Press, 1988), 17, 321.

[42] Grumett, *De Lubac*, 39.

de Lubac, concerned with matters at home, did not encounter some of the more horrifying implications of Adam's mystical body theology. De Lubac might retroactively remind us that insofar as Adam's mystical body theology is separated from a thick account of the Eucharist, it is subject to the critique presented in *Corpus Mysticum*.

Corpus Mysticum and Mediation

It was that 1938–1939 work (published in the 1944 Vichy context, with a 1941 imprimatur, and revised for a 1949 second edition) that illustrated the linguistic shift of *corpus mysticum* from a descriptor of the Eucharist to a descriptor of the church, especially in the late twelfth century, after the eucharistic controversy surrounding Berengar of Tours during the previous century.[43] The major argument of *Corpus Mysticum* is that in discussion of the threefold body of Christ—historical/glorified, eucharistic, and ecclesial—the action of Christ comes to be more and more circumscribed as the second two become less and less closely identified. As mentioned, the relevant context for de Lubac here is the Berengarian controversy. In response to Berengar's spiritualist theology of eucharistic presence, polemicists overemphasize the link between the first two referents of Christ's body (historical/glorified and eucharistic) in a hyper-realistic response. De Lubac writes: "It could be said that the ultra-orthodox party fell into the trap that had been set for them by the heretic [Berengar], or again that they allied with him in mutilating that traditional teaching: one group holding to symbolism, the other to the 'truth.' Against *mystically, not truly*, was set, in no less exclusive a sense, *truly, not mystically*. Perhaps orthodoxy was safeguarded, but on the other hand, doctrine was certainly impoverished."[44] Neither Berengar nor his opponents were able to imagine a real presence of Christ that was not

---

[43] William T. Cavanaugh, who makes extensive use of de Lubac's *Corpus Mysticum*, has pointed out the dangers of mystical body theology as they were received in 1970s–1980s Chile. We explored his reading of *Mystici Corporis* in chapter 1. Cavanaugh claims that the espousal of mystical body theology stood in opposition to the real (*corpus verum*) and thus led Chilean bishops and other officials to give Catholics' bodies over to state control while professing cure of souls.

[44] De Lubac, *Corpus Mysticum*, 223.

physicalist. Berengar rejected it, and his opponents Lanfranc and eventually Humbert accepted it.[45]

De Lubac describes this methodological problem as one of rationalistic presuppositions: "If I were to seek to characterize this doctrine [Berengar's] not so much by the arguments in which it ended, as by the spirit that animated it and by the methodology it used, it would be better to say that it presented itself as a form of rationalism and dialectic," instead of as symbol pure and simple.[46] In the chapter of *Corpus Mysticum* provocatively titled "From Symbolism to Dialectic" de Lubac argues that the richness of the patristic vision of *corpus mysticum* thinned after Berengar and into the scholastic period such that "even among those who still considered it of great importance, symbolism became something artificial and unnecessary" and with it, "the essential link that bonded the Eucharistic rite to the unity of the Church . . . disappeared." Moving forward, "long-established custom kept [the language of symbols] in place, but their 'power of evocation' had worn out," that is, "the symbolism became extrinsic: from now on it could be ignored without damaging the integrity of the sacrament."[47]

That is to say, the problem that de Lubac exposes in *Corpus Mysticum* is a problem of *mediation*. Symbolic is not the difficulty. The mediated bodies of Christ—the eucharistic and ecclesial—belong together. They cannot be separated from the Christ they mediate. It is not simply a flip-flop of the terms "mystical" and "true" that occurs with Berengar but rather a new division between mystical, sacramental, and true that had not really existed before the twelfth century. In essence, then, the

---

[45] See Gary Macy, *The Theologies of the Eucharist in the Early Scholastic Period* (Oxford, UK: Clarendon Press, 1984), 18–72. The oath that Berengar was made to recite at the Council of Rome in 1059 was drafted by Humbert and included the assertion that the bones of Christ were "crushed by the teeth of the faithful" in consuming the Eucharist. The trope of Berengar carried on well into the scholastic era. In a likely reference to the Cathars, who often used the Berengarian oath to mock Catholics as cannibals, St. Thomas refers to the heirs of Berengarius in *Summa Theologiae* III.75.1.res. Such a reference is not foreign to Thomas's order, the Dominicans, which came into existence to fight the Cathar heresy.

[46] De Lubac, *Corpus Mysticum*, 225.

[47] Ibid., 244–46. The internal quotation is, significantly, from Mersch, *Le corps mystique du Christ*, 2nd ed., 2:422–23.

threefold body becomes merely a twofold body.[48] Into the eighteenth century, a good many theologians, de Lubac avers, "developed an idea of [the church] that was less and less realist, *because* less and less mystical."[49] Remembering Goodier's point that to be enthusiastic about mystical body theology was to be suspected of Modernism, it is difficult not to see in de Lubac's clarification on these points a challenge to his own theological context in which modernists were associated with symbol and their neo-scholastic opponents championed dialectic.[50]

De Lubac points out that the adjective mystical (*mysticum*) depends on the noun mystery, Greek *mystērion*, which is translated into Latin by either *mysterium* or *sacramentum*. The nuances of these two terms are many and their usage, de Lubac tells us, is not consistent. In generalizing, one is able to say that "a mystery [*mysterium*] . . . is more of an action than a thing," thus "while the *sacramentum* is 'confected', carried, deposed, kept, divided, broken, distributed, received, absorbed, eaten and drunk, the *mysterium* itself is 'done', worked, celebrated, offered, completed, interrupted, re-started, frequented. By the first [*sacramentum*] we are nourished, purified, fortified, vivified; we assist, serve, and officiate at the second [*mysterium*]. It is the accomplishment of the mystery which produces the sacrament."[51]

De Lubac's description of the nature of *mysterium* could be applied to his project as a whole as it concerns the relationship between the eucharistic species and the ecclesial body that it constitutes. He insists that "it focuses [neither on the sign nor the hidden reality but] on both at the same time: on their mutual relationship, union and implications, on the way in which one passes into the other, or is penetrated by the other." Thus, "we are presented here . . . with something unclear and fluid. It conveys a dynamism and synthesis."[52] Reflecting on the nature of mystical body theology in the twentieth century, one can detect precisely this impact of the modifier "mystical" on the various incarnations of the theology. It was

[48] De Lubac, *Corpus Mysticum*, 106, 166.

[49] Ibid., 259; emphasis mine.

[50] See Pope Pius X, *Pascendi Dominici Gregis*, esp. no. 19.

[51] De Lubac, *Corpus Mysticum*, 49–50. With respect to the final sentence, de Lubac credits St. Athanasius.

[52] Ibid., 51.

this fluidity that led to the need for mystical body theology to be grounded in more concrete, embodied realities. De Lubac helps to make clearer Mersch's insistence, echoed by Michel, that the doctrine of the mystical body of Christ necessarily retains a certain vagueness.[53]

In *Splendor*, de Lubac also indicates another tendency that he wished to stem in his historical study of the term "mystical body." Once separated from the Eucharist, there is an increasing use of the term "mystical body" (devoid of its christological prepositional phrase) as a merely sociological designation, as in a group of people bound across space. Thus, he tells us, some say "the Church is a mystical body whose head is the Pope." Of course, the church is a group of people bound across space, but such an expression alone is inadequate, for it ignores that the members of the church are the members of Christ.[54] This would sever the first (historical/glorified) from the third (ecclesial) bodies of Christ. De Lubac is careful not to suggest swinging the pendulum to the other side. That is, to rule out any sociological analyses of the church that can aid us in understanding the accidentals. This type of analysis can be very valuable. Yet, "if we talk of a 'sociological Church,' we only accentuate a dichotomy already suspect"; rather, such discourse should proceed with due caution so as not to behave "like the son who insults his mother."[55]

De Lubac highlights, in this later work, particular insights from *Corpus Mysticum*. In the earlier book he uncovered various uses in the fifteenth and sixteenth centuries of simply the body of the Church (sans any reference to Christ or, less important, the word *mysticum* in any form), commenting that "speaking of the body of the Church could therefore be nothing more than a slightly more descriptive way of talking about the 'body of Christians,' as the Romans used to speak of the 'body of the Greeks,' of the 'body of Jews.'"[56] Thus, disconnected from its eucharistic

---

[53] Mersch, *The Whole Christ*, 452.

[54] De Lubac, *The Splendor of the Church*, 128–30. The example de Lubac cites is Jacques Almain, *De Potestate Ecclesiastica et Laica Contra Ockham*, from the early sixteenth century.

[55] De Lubac, *The Splendor of the Church*, 100–101.

[56] De Lubac, *Corpus Mysticum*, 85. De Lubac cites pages in the 1936 and 1937 volumes of the *Journal of Theological Studies* to this point. A bit of investigation demonstrates that both of these are brief notes indicating that the Greek *soma* was indeed used in pre–New Testament literature to refer to a collection of people or a

referent, *corpus* comes to mean simply a people collected under a particular moniker. Extending further into the sixteenth century and into modernity (in figures such as Suarez and Immanuel Kant), de Lubac exposes a notion of mystical body that is entirely horizontal.[57] For Kant, particularly, that horizontal notion is made up of those "reasonable beings formed by the free submission of each one to the rule of moral laws."[58] This general application of mystical body to class structure and to various national and international groups continues to develop throughout modernity.[59]

Wrested free from the Eucharist and then even from its reference to Christ, mystical body became a sociological term. By contrast, Wood comments, de Lubac's use of the body image intends ontological, not sociological, purchase.[60] The context, both early modernity and later de Lubac's own, is not unimportant here. As the church in the modern era loses the authority it had in Christendom—albeit an authority that was always jockeying with that of kings and princes—the christological character of mystical body of Christ is likewise shorn off, returning the phrase to a meaning more akin to the usage of Augustus or Agrippa, though with a distinctly modern voluntaristic quality. The deadly dichotomy between the eucharistic body and the ecclesial body rendered the church susceptible to intense privatization and it was ill-equipped to respond theologically to the challenge of modernity on a broad scale, except by accepting its rationalistic playing field. The voluntarism of the age (Kant's "free submission of each one") had now been substituted for St. Thomas's vision of members and potential members of the mystical body of Christ. Thus, the christological character of a phrase that, in its origin, had been tied so closely to the Eucharist, is now relegated merely to the eucharistic elements of the altar. The true Christ is found (only?) there.

---

society. The first claims to disprove a widely accepted notion that the Pauline usage was unique, the second elaborates several other examples. The full citations are T. W. Manson, "A Parallel to a N.T. Use of σῶμα," *Journal of Theological Studies* 37, no. 148 (October 1936): 385, and G. C. Richards, "Parallels to a N.T. Use of σῶμα," *Journal of Theological Studies* 38, no. 150 (April 1937): 165.

[57] De Lubac, *Corpus Mysticum*, 118.

[58] Ibid. De Lubac cites Immanuel Kant's *Transcendental Methodology* here.

[59] De Lubac, *Corpus Mysticum*, 249ff.

[60] Wood, *Spiritual Exegesis*, 87.

Paradox and Individualism in the French Context

De Lubac's *Corpus Mysticum* was primarily aimed at neoscholastic theologians of his day who accepted the rationalist ground of modern discourse as the basis for their reinterpretation of scholastic theology. Those theologians, many of whom were associated with the Roman stream, understood mystical body of Christ in a structural/social manner to refer to the ecclesial body and then supported/developed an individualistic eucharistic piety that revered the consecrated host, with little, if any, ecclesial-social connection.[61] In such a configuration there is merely an

[61] Lawrence Paul Hemming helpfully highlights the critique of rationalism embedded in *Corpus Mysticum*. Hemming points out de Lubac's concern that rational dialectic overwhelms prayer, especially the liturgical kind. He challenges Catherine Pickstock and Michel de Certeau, who, he charges, establish a new "deadly dichotomy" between the historical/glorified body, on the one hand, and the eucharistic/ecclesial bodies, on the other. Hemming's goal of underscoring the sense in which de Lubac's text takes aim at rationalism is, however, partially blunted by his nearly dismissing the way in which the text also goes after individualism. In de Lubac's own context these two were conjoined; rationalist and individualist tendencies characterized Enlightenment intellectuals as well as the neoscholastics that opposed them. The challenge to individualism, beginning with de Lubac's *Catholicisme: Les aspects sociaux du dogme* (Paris: Cerf, 1938), was central to his own theological project and also runs through *Corpus Mysticum*. What does not (and here is where Hemming is correct) is the necessary indictment of eucharistic devotion that some have linked to that challenge. To follow this latter course seems to begin with one observation made by de Lubac at the end of the book (*Corpus Mysticum*, 259) and to make it into the aim of the entire work. See Lawrence Paul Hemming, "Henri de Lubac: Reading *Corpus Mysticum*," *New Blackfriars* 90, no. 1029 (September 2009): 519–34, esp. 528. Joseph Komonchak makes a point that highlights both of the major critiques embedded in *Corpus Mysticum*—individualism and rationalism—in "Theology and Culture at Mid-Century," 589–93.

Further, Hemming's critique of de Certeau is overwrought. The latter clearly challenges two attempts to reduce the ternary character of the Body of Christ to a binary during the Reformation. See Michel de Certeau, *The Mystic Fable: The Sixteenth and Seventeenth Centuries* (Chicago: University of Chicago Press, 1992; French orig., 1982), 82–90. Hemming's claim that "de Lubac understood the real shift to be the triumph of rationalism, exemplified by Berengar's thought, emerging to assert itself as the basis and ground of theological thinking, eclipsing the grounding character of the liturgy as the source of meaning in theology" (519) is striking in its amenability to de Certeau's project. In fact, de Certeau explains how that process continues when *la mystique* becomes a discipline unto itself instead of an adjective modifying embodied

extrinsic relationship between individual, church, and sacrament. That is, the sacraments are moments for individuals to be filled with grace, and then, guaranteed by the structure of the church, its pope, etc., these individuals are bound together in mystical union. In forming that union, church structure holds primacy over the Eucharist. This conclusion is borne out by the fact that de Lubac himself refers to the church as the Mystical Body of Christ several times in *Meditations*,[62] including an explanation of *Corpus Mysticum* itself: "The Eucharist, in its turn, realizes the church, in the strict sense of the words. . . . And thus the social body of the Church, that *corpus christianorum*, united round its visible pastors for the Lord's Supper, really does become the Mystical Body of Christ; it is really Christ who assimilates it to Himself, so that the Church is then truly the 'Corpus Christi *effecta*.'"[63] De Lubac is faithful to his familiar emphasis on paradox in *Corpus Mysticum*—the mystical body of Christ

---

practices that make the Body of Christ present in the world. He argues that in the late seventeenth century, mystics (like physics or optics) becomes a discrete genre, and so represents a detachment from confidence in sacramental structures and the ecclesial role of contemplation. Mysticism became its own system. The institutional structures that support such a move are informed by the rationalism of the early modern era. Thus de Certeau writes, "The history of the thirteenth to the fifteenth centuries might have as its general identifying characteristic the specialization of the elite classes and the marginalization of a majority of the population with respect to the codes of a world that until then had functioned as a network of relations." Modernity begins, then, as early as the thirteenth century, as a hyper-specialization of discourse. "This problematic gave rise, among the mystics, to the invention of a different body, born of and for the discourse intending to produce reform—an alien body against which the institution of medicine would eventually win out in imposing a scientific body" (see *The Mystic Fable* 85, also 110–12). Of course, the difference between Hemming and de Certeau (and also between de Certeau and de Lubac) is a difference in emphasis on the more subversive aspects of mystical prayer practices for de Certeau instead of on liturgical practices. See de Certeau's complex and fascinating account of the possession of Jeanne des Anges, with its layers of ecclesial-monarchical tensions and mystical prayer, in *The Possession at Loudun*, trans. Michael B. Smith (Chicago: University of Chicago Press, 2000). Nevertheless, de Certeau understands, and even thematizes, de Lubac's critique of rationalism in *Corpus Mysticum*.

[62] de Lubac, *The Splendor of the Church*, 102–3, 127–34, 152–53, 239, 334.

[63] Ibid., 152–53.

is a precarious interplay of the three bodies of Christ, on which emphasis waxes and wanes. The key is to avoid the deadly break.[64]

Situated in the French stream, it is not surprising that, as Raymond Moloney has argued, the main purpose of *Corpus Mysticum* was to defend the social nature of Catholicism and support Catholic work on behalf of social causes.[65] In the ebb and flow of theology, de Lubac was not troubled by "Christomonism" but, like his North American counterparts, was more concerned with creeping individualism.[66] The sociological definition of the church—as merely an organization like other organizations—was the real threat as de Lubac conceived it. He was troubled that those who were fighting for a deeper social identity—workers' organizations, for example—often laid individualism at the foot of the Catholic Church. In response, de Lubac wanted to illustrate that the church, in its very essence, is social. Like Beauduin before him, de Lubac's concerns were about social reform. As Moloney puts it: "Apostolically he wished to provide various Catholic social movements of the day with a theology of the corporate which would ground their activities in the sources of the faith. Doctrinally he wished not only to open up Christians to their social responsibilities but also to the basis of those responsibilities in the spiritual interdependence which binds the members of Christ's body into one." Perhaps de Lubac's greatest achievement on the social question, at least one that has been neglected since, is

> grounding . . . social involvement in a mystical vision and in a
> level of spiritual belonging and mutual responsibility revealed

---

[64] Wood, *Spiritual Exegesis*, 82–85. Susan Wood argues that de Lubac's notion of the relationship between the church and the mystical body of Christ developed from *Splendor of the Church* to his *Church: Paradox and Mystery*, trans. James R. Dunne (New York: Ecclesia Press, 1969; French orig., 1967). In the later work, he writes, "We shall not reduce the Mystical Body of Christ to equivalence with the forms of the Roman Church, nor will we water down the Church until it becomes a 'body' conceived in entirely 'mystical' fashion" (20). Wood remarks that de Lubac is ultimately unclear on the relationship between the church and the mystical body of Christ or, rather, he is neck deep in the paradox of the mystery of the church.

[65] Raymond Moloney, "Henri de Lubac on Church and Eucharist," *Irish Theological Quarterly* 70, no. 4 (December 2005): 331–42, esp. 334.

[66] Wood concludes that some statements in de Lubac's corpus can be considered "Christomonistic" but that they are balanced by others (*Spiritual Exegesis*, 89).

only by the doctrine of the body of Christ. This is the level on which we are all members of one another and mediators to one another of the life of God shared with us. This is the life which the Eucharist is to nourish, and this is the level of community which is the foundation of all our involvement in society.[67]

De Lubac's *Corpus Mysticum* fits into the context of the renewal of mystical body theology shepherded by the liturgical movement and the *nouvelle théologie*. In fact, Mersch had written, "The Eucharist is not simply the sacrament of the Real Presence, but it also has a necessary connection with ecclesiastical unity."[68] Mersch had not worked out the nuances that de Lubac's position evinces, but clearly they were not working at cross-purposes.

In de Lubac's earlier *Catholicism*, he noted, "The informed reader will notice that we owe much to Fr. Mersch."[69] Toward the end of *Corpus Mysticum*, de Lubac, diagnosing the needs of his own era and of the liturgical movement, offers a proposal: "It seems it would therefore be of great interest, we might even say pressing urgency, given the present state of what remains of 'Christendom', to return to the sacramental origins of the 'mystical body' in order to steep ourselves in it." We need to see in the eucharistic celebration the unity of the three bodies of Christ. "Such an assessment seems to impose itself all the more because without it the very strength of the corporate aspirations which can currently be felt at the heart of the Church, and which are in particular driving the liturgical movement, cannot be without peril."[70] His work, then, aims at supporting and bolstering the connections between sacraments and social questions while it challenges the Roman stream, as well as the German-Romantic stream insofar as the latter disconnected the mystical body from the Eucharist.[71]

---

[67] Moloney, "Henri de Lubac," 342.

[68] Mersch, *The Whole Christ*, 426. As we have seen, Mersch himself is also rather frustrated with the limits of neoscholastic theology.

[69] De Lubac, *Catholicism*, 17n7.

[70] De Lubac, *Corpus Mysticum*, 260.

[71] In *Models of the Church*, Avery Dulles considers de Lubac's ecclesiology primarily under his Sacrament model. This makes sense especially because the title of chapter 6 of *Splendor of the Church* is "Sacrament of Christ." And, of course, Dulles does not

Conclusions

We began this chapter by promising a return to the contemporary, tracing out the vestiges of early twentieth-century mystical body theology in Chauvet's project. While a careful reading of Chauvet's work itself awaits us in the next chapter, we have set the stage for reading that work well by understanding both Chauvet's historical connections to the French stream and de Lubac's contribution to mystical body theology.

Chauvet's relationship with the ISL played a key role in his theological development, especially after he rejected the neoscholastic categories and method of his own education. Genealogically we can now see how Chauvet's theology is influenced not only by the philosophical contributions of Heidegger and Maurice Merleau-Ponty, but also by elements of the French stream of mystical body theology, that same stream in which Michel swam.

The second part of the chapter demonstrated a couple of important aspects of de Lubac's approach to mystical body theology. First, de Lubac was a booster, rather than a knocker, of French-stream mystical body revival. Rather than challenging the legitimacy of mystical body theology, he picked up and developed the deeply sacramental emphasis embedded in the French stream and carried it a bit further. Second, his main purposes in writing about the mystical body of Christ were to counter the creeping modern individualism and rationalism in Catholic theology, which unnecessarily dismembered the theological mystery bound up in Christ's body. In so doing, we seem to have veered off course, leaving Chauvet in the

---

claim that models are mutually exclusive. It is best, however, to understand de Lubac's project, especially in his earlier work, but continuing in his later work, as an attempt to bring together that model with what Dulles calls the Mystical Communion model. Under that latter model, Dulles includes both People of God and (Mystical) Body of Christ. Dennis Doyle helpfully points out that these two images represent different emphases in Catholic theology, in *Communion Ecclesiology: Vision and Versions* (Maryknoll, NY: Orbis Books, 2000), 18. Mannes Koster's critique and others like it make clear the tensions existed even before Vatican II. Karl Adam's response to Koster draws out the tensions Doyle highlights. See Karl Adam, "Ekklesiologie im Werden? Kritische Bemerkungen zu M. D. Koster's Kritik an den ekklesiologischen Versuchen der Gegenwart," *Theologische Quartalschrift* 122 (1941), 145–66. It is notable that one of Adam's major concerns is that the quest for the definitive definition of the church's essence taken by Koster is wrongheaded and doomed to failure.

dust. Yet, contextualizing and clarifying de Lubac's approach to mystical body theology is important for understanding the vestiges in Chauvet's corpus. As we shall see, de Lubac's *Corpus Mysticum* is a key ingredient in Chauvet's development of the theological thrust of the French stream.

CHAPTER 5

Vestigial Body 2

Chauvet and the (Mystical) Body

I n order to spot specific vestiges of the French stream in contemporary theology, we now turn to Chauvet's theology of corporality, his
engagement with the French philosophical milieu of the 1970s and
1980s, and his reading of de Lubac's *Corpus Mysticum*. In doing so, it will
be become clear how Chauvet brings the emphases of the French stream
forward in a theological vision that, akin to that of the major figures in
that stream, is broad in scope, emphasizes the body thematically, and
aims to link the liturgical and ethical components of Christian identity.

"In the Sacraments" with Chauvet

Returning to patristic insights, de Lubac finds that various eucharistic
descriptors—such as "truth in mystery" or "image of the sacrament"—in
their construction, opened up to the whole of Christian existence. That is,
they could well be descriptors of what it means to see and live the Christian life. After citing St. Ambrose, St. Augustine, St. Gregory Nazianzen,
and St. Gregory the Great, de Lubac concludes:

> As long as this world lasts, we are still living *"in the sacraments."*
> . . . And in the providential diversity of their forms, without it
> ever being possible to separate their "spiritual" and the "bodily"
> aspects [*sic*], are not all the means of salvation at the same time,

according to whether we see them from within or from outside,
and in relation to a sterile past or to a good anticipated, an image,
that is to say simultaneously both figure and truth?[1]

Chauvet's project could be described precisely as working out the implications of what it means for us to live "in the sacraments." His is a theology that launches from, as de Lubac insists, a profound sense that life at least on this side of the eschaton is life in "both figure and truth."

One of the marks of the French stream is that it extended beyond ecclesiological reflection to ascertain a Christic vision of the world. Nevertheless, the liturgy was the starting point from which one could encounter and learn to discern the mystical body of Christ. In fact, we can recall that Michel used "the sacramental principle," "the Christ-life," and "mystical body of Christ" interchangeably.[2] Thus, Chauvet's theological project can be understood, at least in one sense, as a further conceptualization of these aims of the French stream.

At the beginning of his magnum opus, *Symbol and Sacrament*, Chauvet describes that book as a "*sacramental reinterpretation* [*relecture* in French] . . . of what it means *to lead a Christian life. A foundational theology of sacramentality.*"[3] Chauvet expresses two major motivations for this work: a desire, in France, for the constitutive marks (or principal pillars) of Christian identity and the inadequacy of scholastic sacramental thinking. With respect to the first, Chauvet addresses a pastoral desire—among "interested laypersons of all ages"—in 1980s France for an account of the sacramental in relation to the particularity of Christian identity.[4]

---

[1] De Lubac, *Corpus Mysticum*, 197.

[2] See chapter 2. This tendency runs throughout Michel's work, but is most apparent in "Natural and Supernatural Society," 243–47; see also Michel et al., *Our Life in Christ*.

[3] Chauvet, *Symbol and Sacrament*, 1. All italics are Chauvet's unless otherwise noted.

[4] Such concerns are, of course, not limited to France and, in fact, have become more pressing over the past decade or two. As American Catholic institutions see the dwindling of religious orders that founded them paired with a less obvious need to serve the Catholic subcultural community who created them, identity questions rise to the surface.

He identifies Scripture, sacrament, and ethics as the three marks proper to Christian identity and explores the relationship among them throughout the rest of the book. One of Chauvet's major concerns is that this theological effort does not dissolve "the distinct sacraments into the blur of a 'general sacramentality.'"[5] Thus, the liturgical rites themselves serve as the foundation of his sacramental reinterpretation of the Christian life. As noted in the previous chapter, Chauvet's road through the ISL formed him in the long line of French-speaking participants in the liturgical movement in the early twentieth century, including Beauduin, who inspired the founding of the ISL. Indeed, Prétot argues that Chauvet can be properly understood only when placed in the line of the liturgical movement that preceded him. Prétot emphasizes, in particular, the key point that liturgical action shapes not only the individual who receives a sacrament but the entire assembly celebrating the sacrament and rippling outward to the whole body of Christ.[6]

Like his early twentieth-century forbears, Chauvet gives a fundamental primacy to liturgy and sacraments, specifically the rites, understood as the symbolic order of the church. In those rites, Christians come to be Christian, analogous to (and even coterminous with) humans becoming subjects in the symbolic order of their culture. Prétot points out that the liturgical grounding of Chauvet's project "is sometimes ignored by those who rely on the thought of Chauvet, separating it from its fundamental liturgical field at the risk of creating another form of scholasticism in which the category 'symbol' would play a role that in the past was assigned to hylomorphism (substance-changing)."[7] Rather, what we learn from the sacraments is that we receive who we are from what goes before us. They are places of rich mediation. Chauvet writes, "The sacramental rites, as

---

[5] Chauvet, *Symbol and Sacrament*, 1.

[6] Patrick Prétot, "The Sacraments as 'Celebrations of the Church': Liturgy's Impact on Sacramental Theology," in Bordeyne and Morrill, *Sacraments*, 25–42. Prétot discusses Odo Casel in particular, whose work on the recovery of mystery was influential on liturgical reformers in the early twentieth century. Casel's notion of mystery was grounded in the liturgy of the church. Others in the liturgical movement, particularly those in the United States driven by the vision of Michel, emphasized the mysterious union that flows from and back to the liturgy—a kind of Christoform solidarity that holds potential for social regeneration.

[7] Prétot, "The Sacraments as 'Celebrations of the Church,'" 26.

places in the wholly human—the too human—where grace is bestowed on the significant materiality of gestures, postures, objects, and words which make them up, while not the *only* representation, are still *the most eminent representation of this pro-cession of the divine God within God's re-cession at the heart of what is most human."* [8] *Corporéité* is the term that Chauvet uses to describe our unavoidable location in tradition, language, and culture. If we are to experience God, there is no other way than in mediated fashion, in our corporality, at the risk of the body.

Taking heed of Prétot's warning, it remains obvious by the title of Chauvet's masterwork, *Symbol and Sacrament*, that the categories of language and symbol, rather than of sign and cause, help him to develop the implications of celebrating the sacraments. There is a clear challenge to classic scholastic sacramental categories. While Chauvet's critique extends to thirteenth-century sacramental theology, his present context and comments cited above about his formation at Angers would lead us to conclude that his more immediate opponents are those teachers of the neoscholastic persuasion.[9]

Thus, a few decades after de Lubac's *Corpus Mysticum*, Chauvet carries on the French theological challenge to neoscholasticism that Beauduin, Mersch, and de Lubac, among others, had sustained during the early to mid-twentieth century. Armed with Heidegger, who was also formed in a

---

[8] Chauvet, *Symbol and Sacrament*, 373.

[9] There are several vociferous defenses of scholastic language, and that of St. Thomas in particular, from Chauvet's critique. See, for example, Frederick Christian Bauerschmidt, " 'The Body of Christ Is Made from Bread': Transubstantiation and the Grammar of Creation," *International Journal of Systematic Theology* 18, no. 1 (January 2016): 30–46, and Bernhard Blankenhorn, "The Instrumental Causality of the Sacraments: Thomas Aquinas and Louis-Marie Chauvet," *Nova et Vetera* 4, no. 2 (2006): 255–94. On the level of bare concepts, these pieces demonstrate that scholastic sacramental theological categories hold more richness than Chauvet gives them credit for. The contextual analysis here demonstrates, however, that Chauvet is not working merely in bare concepts. As he himself points out, his project is a challenge to the theological formation he received. Both Bauerschmidt and Blankenhorn indicate that Chauvet qualifies his critique of Thomas in *Symbol and Sacrament*. While Chauvet decides to pursue a theological project with postmodern philosophy as handmaiden, and not a rereading of St. Thomas, it seems to me that those qualifications are further evidence of his main concern: neoscholastic theological thinking in the early to mid-twentieth century.

neoscholastic seminary,[10] and French poststructuralism, Chauvet takes a step further and critiques these scholastic sacramental categories as fundamentally onto-theo-logical and, therefore, unable to take embodiment seriously. It is Heidegger who proclaims the history of metaphysics as onto-theo-logic.[11] Heidegger charges Western philosophical thought with undertaking an endless search for the ground of reality. In so doing, Western metaphysics has, according to Heidegger, reflected on Being (with a capital "B") in order to find what is most basic or foundational to beings, understood as various instantiations of Being. It is a short step, then, to call this ground, Being with a capital "B," God. This is the onto (Being)-theo (God)-logical character of classical Western metaphysics. Western thinking is therefore inattentive to the third element always present in the schema of Being and beings—the ontological difference—the difference between Being and beings that nevertheless always connects them. The ontological difference is more primordial than Being precisely because it makes any such distinction between Being and beings possible. Having made such a thoroughgoing critique of the history of metaphysics as onto-theological, Heidegger understands the philosophical task as perhaps better suited to godless thinking (i.e., non-metaphysical thinking). For Heidegger, true theological thinking is something other than philosophy, perhaps something poetic, that would discourse not about the *causa sui* (the cause in itself, Being), in front of which one can neither sing nor dance, but about what he called the "divine God."[12]

In sacramental theology, the onto-theo-logical problem of a lack of attention to the difference between God and us manifests itself as the reification of grace. Inattention to the depth of mediation required for the divine-human relationship ultimately reduces grace to a product, an item acquired or, in the words of Garrigou-Lagrange, "poured into the heart."[13]

---

[10] See William Portier, "*Ancilla Invita:* Heidegger, the Theologians, and God," *Sciences Religieuses* 14, no. 2 (Spring 1985): 161–80.

[11] For the *locus classicus* of this critique, see Martin Heidegger, "The Onto-Theo-Logical Constitution of Metaphysics," in *Identity and Difference*, trans. Joan Stambaugh (New York: Harper and Row, 1969), 42–76.

[12] See Heidegger, *The Piety of Thinking, Essays by Martin Heidegger*, trans. James G. Hart and John C. Maraldo (Bloomington: Indiana University Press, 1976), 1–60.

[13] Garrigou-Lagrange, *Reality*, 298. He explicitly situates "grace . . . in the mode of production" (300).

In this mode, humans can only stand externally to God, as receivers of some object. Relationships among people and between people and God are conceived in the "technical model of cause and effect."[14]

A fundamental recognition that we rest "in the sacraments" in this life is a starting point for what Chauvet describes as primarily a theological account of Christian identity. It is clear here that, for Chauvet, glaring, unmediated presence results in nihilism of one form or another. This nihilism claims to round on mystery in all-too-quick fashion. It thus succumbs to the temptation of immediacy, of wanting God utterly present here and now before me, of refusing to assent to the loss of divine-like projections, an assent that Chauvet calls faith.[15] Since reality is necessarily mediated by symbols, we never encounter reality without some absence of it. "To consent to this presence of absence is to consent to *never being able to leave mediation behind*—mediation of the symbolic order that always-already precedes human beings and allows them to become human because they start from a world already humanized before them and passed on to them as a universe of meaning."[16]

A recognition of thoroughgoing mediation opens up space for talk about *reality* that does not bracket the ontological and simply avert to the symbolic order as complete surface play. Rather, Chauvet's emphasis on mediation affirms the reality of embodied human experience. The various phenomena that human beings experience (thoughts, dreams, cars, other people, emotions) lead to the phenomenological appreciation of a particular range of what can be considered real. What may be real for humans—love, for example—is not real to trees. Symbols are contrary to the productionist/causal language that dominates onto-theology and the discourse of signs. Symbols make reality present, but do so *as symbols*, that is, with a mark of absence. "This, for sure, does not weaken the reality of . . . [eucharistic] presence, but qualifies it for what it is: *human* presence."[17]

---

[14] Chauvet, *Symbol and Sacrament*, 22–24.

[15] Ibid., 62–63.

[16] Ibid., 98.

[17] Louis-Marie Chauvet, "The Broken Bread as Theological Figure of Eucharistic Presence," in *Sacramental Presence in a Postmodern Context*, ed. Lieven Boeve and Lambert Leijssen (Louvain, BE: Peeters Publishing, 2001), 258.

Chauvet's warrants are deeply scriptural. He finds in God's gift of manna in the desert the paradigmatic example of grace, which is a non-thing. Manna's very name is a question, *man hu?* (what is this?); it is present but curiously absent; it nourishes but "conform[s] to every taste" (Wis 16:20, NABRE); it is given utterly free of charge, eludes empirical verifiability, and is therefore outside the realm of value.[18] He argues that, because of the manna story, any discussion of sacrament, which necessarily involves grace (the paradigmatic non-value), requires non-productionist discourse. The nature of grace—as the word for God's ongoing relationship with humans—requires another approach, a "*discourse from which the believing subject is inseparable*,"[19] a theology at the risk of the body, as the subtitle of his shorter book has it.[20] Chauvet argues for a more symbolic, and therefore relational, understanding of grace in which we are caught up in God's gift exchange with humanity.

Corporality in Chauvet's Reinterpretation

Across the mystical body renewal, questions had been raised concerning the relationship between the mystical body of Christ and the church. The Colossians hymn extols Christ as "the head of the body, the church," but in Corinthians and Romans, Paul is less explicit concerning the relationship between the church and the body of Christ (Col 1:18; 1 Cor 12:12-27; Rom 12:4-5). We saw how Tromp was more emphatic about identifying the Roman Catholic Church and the mystical

---

[18] Chauvet, *Symbol and Sacrament*, 44–45, 222–23. On manna, see Exodus 16 and Wisdom 16.

[19] Chauvet, *Symbol and Sacrament*, 43.

[20] Louis-Marie Chauvet, *The Sacraments: The Word of God at the Mercy of the Body*, trans. Madeleine Beaumont (Collegeville, MN: Liturgical Press, 2001). *La parole de Dieu au risque du corps* is the subtitle of Chauvet's *The Sacraments* in the original French. The English translation, *The Word of God at the Mercy of the Body*, seems inadequate to express the scandalous character of the incarnation and, in turn, of both the sacraments and the act of faith. The book distills Chauvet's argument in *Symbol and Sacrament* with some explicit and practical pastoral applications. Though not directed explicitly at a particular set of social issues, it is nevertheless not insignificant that Chauvet decided to publish this work with the publishing house of the *Jeunesse Ouvrière Chrétienne*, the Young Christian Workers' movement, rather than the more academic Éditions du Cerf.

body of Christ, whereas Mersch understood the relationship as more porous. Michel bristled at Fulton Sheen's claim that the pope is the head of the mystical body because it belied the claim that "the Mystical Body is bigger than the Church on earth."[21] Such questions also come to the fore in Chauvet's account of the body/corporality, particularly when he moves to discuss Christian identity.

Corporality, in the context of Chauvet's work, works directly in opposition to the temptation to construe the ontological difference between God and creation as negative, as obstructing a supposed more direct relationship.[22] Chauvet's symbolic turn aims at rendering it more positive. This symbolic approach also includes a positive reading of absence. He emphasizes a basic phenomenological truth: since all encounters with God, at least in this life, are mediated, there can be no such thing as a raw encounter with presence, so any encounter with God is also an encounter with God's absence. Theologically speaking, this is not bad news but rather the good news of the incarnation. The Eucharist, as mediation par excellence, makes this most clear. Chauvet writes:

> As a symbol, the Eucharist *radicalizes the absence* of the Risen One: why would I celebrate it if I were able to be in immediate possession of him? To celebrate the Eucharist is precisely—contrary to all illuminisms of the Gnostic sort—to consent to this absence; or, rather, to learn little by little to consent to this absence. . . . Putting to death in us the mortal dream of an immediate presence of Christ—mortal, for such a presence can only be suffocating— the eucharistic symbol opens up an emptiness, a *space where God can come to be* in the very heart of our corporeity, *without*

---

[21] Virgil Michel, Review of Fulton Sheen, *The Mystical Body of Christ*, 282. Michel's position is further explained by what appear to be notes he took on Bernard Roland-Gossetin's *La doctrine politique de Saint Thomas d'Aquin* (Paris: Marcel Rivière, 1928), in which he highlighted the latter's discussion of the mystical body in St. Thomas, from which "only damned souls are excluded." Michel, "Political Principles of St. Thomas" (unpublished manuscript, SJAA, Series Z, Box 33, Folder 8.6).

[22] See Glenn P. Ambrose, "Eucharist as a Means for 'Overcoming' Onto-Theology? The Sacramental Theology of Louis-Marie Chauvet" (PhD diss., Graduate Theological Union, 2001), 161–63. Cf. Chauvet, *Symbol and Sacrament*, 92–95.

> *destroying us* or diminishing our autonomy and our responsibility as humans.[23]

To profess faith in God is simultaneously to profess a renunciation of an unmediated encounter with God. It is, therefore, to profess a more or less explicit assent to a particular body, a particular symbolic order that has borne a particular confession of who God is. Chauvet thus describes faith as "*'sacramental' in its constitution*, and not simply by derivation," for it is impossible to conceive of faith outside of the body.[24]

There is a thematic concern throughout Chauvet's work with Gnosticism, or the eclipse of the body in exchange for purely intellectual or decontextualized knowledge. The folly of the cross, Chauvet argues, is that we always-already stand in a relationship of mediation. Jesus of Nazareth, the body of God in humanity, was situated in a time and place. Those who pledge allegiance to him owe him a human body in this time and place. Therefore, the body of God in humanity also has a reality in the church, Christ's primary mediator. The sacraments are "the most distinctive representations" of the church and continually and constantly "force us to confront *mediation . . .* by way of the senses." The link between the body and the soul runs so deep that it cannot be any other way for us. "And so we find ourselves in the end sent back to the *body* as the point where God writes God's self in us."[25] And there we will find God. "Faith in the crucified God dares to affirm that in spite of everything, 'God is appearing' in humanity, that the 'body of Christ' occurs there, according to Paul's expression."[26]

Just as there is no pure, primitive Christianity to which one can appeal, because of the necessity of mediation, so too there is no core Christian identity. To take on Christian identity is a complex and difficult task

---

[23] Louis-Marie Chauvet, "L'Église fait L'Eucharistie; L'Eucharistie fait l'Église: Essai de lecture symbolique," *Revue Catéchèse* 71 (1978): 182. See Brunk, *Liturgy and Life*, 73. I have followed Brunk's translation. He chooses to translate the French term *corporéité* as the more direct English "corporeity," whereas Beaumont chooses "corporality," and some others a combination of the two: "corporeality." I do not see a substantial enough difference among these English terms to find one or another more compelling.

[24] Chauvet, *Symbol and Sacrament*, 155.

[25] Ibid., 82–83.

[26] Ibid., 491.

fraught with paradox. On the one hand, to be Christian is to be part of the church and thus to enter into a defined group. The trap is to recoil into that particularity, to become insular. On the other hand, to make a confession of Christ as Lord is also to open oneself to the universal, the entire kingdom of God.

The temptation here is that the church so bursts open that it can no longer serve as sacrament of the kingdom. The paradox is that the church is never more itself, never more faithful to its particular marks, than when it opens to the universal, to the kingdom, which grows in the world through the particular.[27] Therefore, Christian identity betrays itself if it is not, in some sense, open-ended. Any attempt to narrow that identity to a mere sign or to a thing that is self-selected and easily achieved are rendered wrongheaded by Chauvet's account. Here, Chauvet has arrived at a phenomenological way of holding and developing the insight articulated by St. Thomas that membership of the mystical body must be considered in terms of both act and potentiality.[28] That is, Christian identity too is at the mercy of the body.

Chauvet finds this corporality at the center of the Eucharist. Because one is not participating in one's own actions or expressing one's own religious feelings in the church's ritual, even if one's deepest convictions seem to be floating away and the very idea that perhaps there is no God runs through one's body, the Eucharist remains. Indeed, "what else remains for them but their bodies taking in hand what the Church takes up—a little bread and wine—and saying what the Church says—'my body given for you'—taking and saying these as the gestures and words of him whom the Church confesses as its Lord?"[29] The bodily and deeply symbolic act of chewing on the body of Christ, this rumination on the supreme folly of the cross, counteracts our temptation to make faith merely human wisdom.[30]

---

[27] Ibid., 181.

[28] *Summa Theologiae* III.8.3.res.

[29] Chauvet, *Symbol and Sacrament*, 375–76.

[30] Ibid., 225. Chauvet recalls the seemingly bizarre scriptural accounts of Ezekiel and the visionary of Revelation literally "chewing the Book" which, after chewing, is "as sweet as honey." Translating Scripture to ethics in the Eucharist, Christians chew the Body of Christ. This chewing aids reception of God's Word: "Precisely because it counteracts such a weakening of faith, the symbolic experience of the chewing,

The specificity of the eucharistic sacrifice—it is Jesus Christ, Word made flesh, on which we chew—precludes any generalized, vacuous ethic. Christians favor ethical action, not because that is the essence of all religion, but rather because in Christian action Christ is once again made known to his people.[31] In the eucharistic celebration the paschal mystery is anamnesized, and we are placed in touch, if only through a dark glass, with the culmination of Christ's redemptive work in the eschaton. Yet, God wants to be alive here and now, to assume flesh in the world. The Eucharist impels Christians toward concrete ethical action, that is, being Christ, loving as Christ loved, for the sake of the world.

Indeed, ethics is one element of the tripartite structure of Christian identity for Chauvet. This tripod follows a model gained from Chauvet's major anthropological dialogue partner, Marcel Mauss (1872–1950).[32] The nephew of David Émile Durkheim, Mauss's anthropological work took him to archaic societies in which he discovered and studied gift economies in operation. In the cultures that Mauss studies, Chauvet explains, symbolic exchange is a "total social fact" in that it is operative across social strata and in all manner of exchange from smiles to wives to goods.[33] One cannot turn down hospitality, food, jewels, etc.; on reception of the gift, one is obliged to offer a return gift, not to the giver, but to a third party. This manner of exchange, given the oxymoronic name "obligatory generosity," is not the *quid pro quo* of the market because the primary interest in the gifting cycle is not object driven but relational: "*to be recognized as a subject,* not to lose face, not to fall from one's

---

the rumination, and the ingestion of the Eucharistic bread as the body of the Lord is irreplaceable for us."

[31] Ibid., 264.

[32] Mauss's achievements are many, but his "Essai sur le don" in *Sociologie et anthropologie* (Paris: Presses Universitaires France, 1950), 143–279, elaborates his study of "gift" as important for Chauvet's work. Chauvet also draws on historian Georges Duby, particularly Duby's *Guerriers et paysans, vii–xiie siècle. Premier essor de l'économie européenne* (Paris: Gallimard, 1973), for this key anthropological insight.

[33] Chauvet, *The Sacraments,* 117–18. On the challenges of ascertaining this anthropological insight in the context of global capitalism, see my own "Chauvet in Space: Louis-Marie Chauvet's Sacramental Account of Christian Identity and the Challenges of a Global Consumer Culture," in O'Connell and Cassidy, *Religion, Economics, and Culture in Conflict and Conversation,* 134–56.

social rank, and consequently to compete for prestige."[34] From the order of production, in which equivalence reigns (lend/borrow, buy/sell, give/take), the extravagant gift exchange appears silly.[35] Impoverished people gift others with kingly extravagance because the symbolic order demands it of them in order to be recognized as subjects.

Mauss's insight is not simply an historical one but also an anthropological one: it tells us something about how human beings work, how they become subjects, and how they live within the symbolic order. The structure of symbolic exchange, on which the relational character of human existence operates, is ternary (gift-reception-return gift), whereas market exchange is binary (product-value). Gift giving includes a moment of reception in which the gift is received *as gift* and not as anything else. This moment is irrelevant in market exchange because it involves merely the exchange of things. In symbolic exchange, subjects exchange each other through the object. The gift works as symbol.[36] Chauvet points out, though, that "gift" as we commonly use it does not inherently communicate the same reality found by Mauss in his anthropological investigations. In our context, gifts are more varied and diffuse. Sometimes they are merely the exchange of things. Nevertheless, presents can and do work in the symbolic order, even though they also can be co-opted by the logic of the market. Game shows, wedding registries, and blind Christmas ornament exchanges are some examples of gift exchange that easily slither into the order of production. Yet, without some exchange of gratuitous self-gift—time, attention, an object carefully selected, a meal lovingly prepared—human relationships are stuck in the order of production.[37]

Ethics, in Chauvet's structure of Christian identity, sits in the place of return-gift. In addition to Scripture (gift) and sacraments (reception), ethics involves the necessary, obligatory generosity that flows out of liturgical participation. The mark of Scripture in Chauvet's model "encompasses everything that concerns the *understanding of the faith*," from catechesis

---

[34] Chauvet, *Symbol and Sacrament*, 101–2. Both Mauss and Chauvet point to the inadequacy of our language to name this gift that obligates in turn and that cannot be refused. Hence, the oxymoron.

[35] Ibid., 102–3.

[36] Ibid., 107.

[37] See Chauvet, *The Sacraments*, 120.

to theology, because all of these comment on Scripture.[38] The sacraments in their rituality "tell us that to become a believer is to learn to consent, without resentment, to the corporality of the faith."[39] Therefore, the move in the sacraments is from knowledge of the faith to its recognition, its being seen *as faith*, as gift shot through with absence. Ethics is the result. This final pole includes "every kind of *action* Christians perform in the world" as testimony to Christ—both moral and social.[40] Chauvet is interested in theologizing the continuity-in-tension of worship and ethics, that one flows from the other ("worship divides, service unites" is unrealistically naïve), but also that the classic tension between the temple and prophets endures. Thus, in the Eucharist, the Word of Scripture passes to the corporeal of ethical praxis. In this, Chauvet again marks his place in the extended French stream and its link between liturgy and the social. "Without the return-gift of an *ethical* practice by which the subject 'verifies' what it has received in the sacrament," he explains, "Christian identity would be stillborn."[41]

Further, Chauvet thematically emphasizes that the eucharistic prayers consistently use the pronoun "we."[42] Christian identities are necessarily formed within the ecclesial "we." Here, there are echoes of Michel's strong and intimate link between the celebration of the liturgy and the mystical body of Christ. This "we" is continually made present during the anamnesis: *we* do this in memory of Christ. As such, the gift of salvation is brought into the present from the past, but this only happens as a "we." Anamnesis is necessarily a corporeal act. It drives us into Christ's saving

---

[38] Chauvet, *Symbol and Sacrament*, 178.

[39] Ibid., 153.

[40] Ibid., 179.

[41] Ibid., 281.

[42] Chauvet, "L'Église fait l'eucharistie," 172. Chauvet writes, *On notera d'abord que tout, dans l'eucharistie, se dit en «nous». Ce «nous» désigne l'assemblée concrète qui, réunie le dimanche, «jour du Seigneur», apparaît chez Paul comme le signe fondamental de la Résurrection, parce qu'elle constitue le corps «sacramentel» visible du Seigneur vivant en ce monde (1 Co 10 à 12), le temple nouveau de sa présence dans l'Esprit au milieu des hommes (2 Co 6/16-18 ; Ep 2/20-22). C'est ce «nous» commun qui, comme nouveau le peuple sacerdotal (1 Pi 2/4-10) fait (l')eucharistie, et pas seulement le prêtre comme le laisse entendre encore le langage courant, reflet d'une pratique et d'une théologie des ministères victimes d'une véritable inflation des «pouvoirs sacerdotaux».*

action, placing us closer to that event than we were a few hours before. We receive the task, again and again, of rebuilding a deep sense of memory, even one that, in sacrament, brings the past to the present. Identity as "brothers-and-sisters-for-others in Christ" cannot grow in isolation but is *necessarily* bound up with the body of believers, indeed, one extended through time.[43]

Chauvet's Intellectual Milieu and the Body

We have examined some of the basic contours of Chauvet's sacramental reinterpretation of the Christian life. Before moving to Chauvet's important reading of de Lubac's *Corpus Mysticum*, we pause to consider the intellectual context of France in the 1980s in order to understand Chauvet's engagement with major philosophical voices. This is important for at least two reasons. First, if Chauvet is indeed working out of the long stream of French mystical body theology, he is doing so in extensive dialogue with philosophical work on the body. Therefore, understanding his notion of corporality necessitates some understanding of his dialogue partners.

Second, Chauvet's notion of the symbolic order is language derived from Jacques Lacan. Chauvet sums up the implications of the symbolic order thus: "Any word which seeks to be expressed in a kind of transparent purity is an illusion; no word escapes the necessity of a laborious inscription in a body, a history, a language, a system of signs, a discursive network. Such is the law. The law of mediation. The law of the body." Bodiliness, and therefore mediation, is of the essence of human subjectivity. Bodies locate us in a particular symbolic order; therefore, Chauvet calls the body the "arch-symbol of the whole symbolic order."[44] Human beings are bodies; there is no primordial, Cartesian "I" that exists before the body.[45] "Corporality," he explains, is the concept that "seeks to express

---

[43] See Chauvet, *Symbol and Sacrament*, 269–72.

[44] Ibid., 151.

[45] Ibid., 148–49. Chauvet explains, however, that we can rightly entertain the body as universally human and engrained in our descriptions. God is invariably discussed in terms of height or depth. Our most profound experiences run through the body; thus, the body is primordial. We are broken by a loss; we devour books and are consumed by thoughts. Chauvet insists that these are not secondary phenomena that shape a

this symbolic order which holds that the human being does not have a body, but is a body."[46] Further,

> [This] I-body exists only as woven, inhabited, spoken, by a *triple body* of culture, tradition, and nature. This is what is implied by the concept of *corporality:* one's own physical body certainly, but *as the place where* the triple body—social, ancestral, and cosmic—which makes up the subject is symbolically joined, in an original manner for each one of us according to the different forms of our desires.[47]

Notice that Chauvet mentions the physical body when he speaks of individualization. We are individuated by the unique complex of influences on us but also by the makeup of our physical bodies and the diverse ways that they interact with the world: tones of voice, length of legs, structure of muscles, etc.[48] Further, Chauvet significantly mentions "forms of our desires." This phrase clues us in to an openness, an excess that shapes the compilation of the subject. Such a phrase could merely communicate, in Lacanian fashion, the wayward resurgence of deviated sexual drive,

---

more primordial, inner scheme or relating to reality but are, rather, "constitutive of the internal structure of the human being."

[46] Ibid., 149.

[47] Ibid., 150.

[48] Drawing on Merleau-Ponty, a significant source for Chauvet, Anthony J. Godzieba emphasizes the contingency of bodies as well as a certain distance between "I" and "body." Godzieba writes: "The body at times outruns our intentions and, to some degree, has a life of its own. I am my body, and yet I am also not my body. Think about the sinus headache you wake up with and the recalcitrant body which you have to drag out of bed by sheer force of will" ("Bodies and Persons, Resurrected and Postmodern: Towards a Relational Eschatology," in *Theology and Conversation: Towards a Relational Theology*, ed. Jacques Haers and Peter De Mey [Louvain, BE: University Press, 2003], 219). Coming from a French perspective, it is not surprising that Chauvet leans heavily on the social character of human existence. Glenn Ambrose diagnoses "a tension between the French understanding of a socially situated self and a dominant American spirit that celebrates and deeply desires the autonomy of the individual" (Glenn Ambrose, "Psychoanalysis, Social Psychology and the Sacramental Theology of Louis-Marie Chauvet" [paper presented at the annual meeting of the College Theology Society, Portland, OR, 3–6 June 2010]; copy courtesy of author).

but, as we shall explore below, Chauvet's theological project cannot be reduced to a narrow Lacanian-Freudian imaginary.[49] Chauvet's sense of desire indicates some individuation, but as a Catholic theologian it is not surprising that for Chauvet, desire tends toward or opens up a space for God. It is telling that Chauvet explicitly asks the following question about Heidegger's critique of metaphysics: "Is it possible to situate a theology in the perspective of this thinking without 'recovering' it and, finally, without betraying it in its most essential aspect?"[50] Chauvet of course answers in the affirmative. His question applies too to his appeal to Lacan's linguistic model.

Of course, the notions of corporality and the symbolic order have implications for Chauvet's theology. The sacraments are bodily events and this is no coincidence. Since "the body is the primordial and arch-symbolic form of mediation, as well as the basis for all subjective identification," the sacraments "engage precisely the bodies of believers, as the exemplary symbolic representations of the corporality of the faith."[51] Inscribed on the body by another body in representation of the Body universal, the sacraments are, in this way, pedagogical. They remind us that Christian faith is corporeal and militate against any gnostic-like misconception of communication as pure and direct. The rites, then, are the relevant symbolic order of the church.

Lacan's French reception of Freud has been heavily critiqued as hemming up the human subject within the structure of language such that the subject is veritably obliterated.[52] In Lacan's world, the body bears no excess. While the perils of such a move for Catholic theology are numerous and obvious, in terms of the present study, eradication of the subject would succumb to some of the most dismaying hazards of mystical

---

[49] On the complex nature of "desire" in Lacan, see Lorenzo Chiesa, *Subjectivity and Otherness: A Philosophical Reading of Lacan* (Cambridge, MA: MIT Press, 2007), esp. 141–56.

[50] Chauvet, *Symbol and Sacrament*, 63.

[51] Ibid., 111.

[52] See, for example, Antoine Vergote, "Lacan's Project of Retrieving Freud's Theory of the Subject," in *Phenomenology and Lacanian Psychoanalysis*, ed. Richard Rojcewicz, The Eighth Annual Symposium of the Simon Silverman Phenomenology Center (Pittsburg, PA: Duquesne University, 1992), 29–51.

body theology.[53] Chauvet is steeped in reflection on language, but he approaches language from a predominantly phenomenological tradition. Notice in Chauvet's description of the triple body an openness to excess that is not typical of Lacan's work—bodies are formed in the symbolic order, but ultimately according to our own unique desires. The critique of the Cartesian ego is typical of the phenomenological tradition as well. As Chauvet scholar Glenn Ambrose has ably demonstrated, Lacan's thought is not as central to Chauvet's project as that of phenomenologists Merleau-Ponty and Heidegger and, therefore, the ego is not for Chauvet a mere epiphenomenon of the linguistic order. Rather, his emphasis on embodiment makes room for acting subjects and, further, gestures toward an openness, a reserve from which and through which being can be disclosed.

Chauvet understands his sacramental theology as one that engages contemporary culture.[54] In *Symbol and Sacrament*, this is not the rough ground of popular religion, material culture, or globalization but the intellectual culture of France of his time.[55] Chauvet stands in the long stream of French mystical body theology, but his application of those theological emphases on the body (as well as on the link between sacraments and social questions) engages the changed (postmodern) context of his own milieu. Prétot notes the particular significance, in terms of Chauvet's later work, of courses Chauvet took on "Faith and Sacrament" with Chenu and on "Liturgical Symbols and Demythologization" with Antoine Vergote.[56] Vergote has been deeply critical of Lacan's psychoanalysis from a

---

[53] We have seen, on the one hand, Karl Pelz's obliteration of the human subject vis-à-vis the divine and, on the other, Karl Adam's encapsulation of legitimate subjectivity by Nazi racial collectivism.

[54] He makes this methodology explicit in a course description from the ISL in 1989: *On proposera simultanément un discours sacramentaire qui tienne compte de la culture contemporaine.* Prétot, "Louis-Marie Chauvet à l'Insitut Supérieur de Liturgie," 182.

[55] We can cite the genesis of his work—questions about identity in France—as responding to culture and perhaps his use of the work of Mauss and Duby on gift economy as anthropological analyses that challenge (as does Mauss explicitly) consumer culture. See Chauvet, *Symbol and Sacrement*, esp. 101–18. Chauvet takes up consumer culture explicitly in his earlier *Du symbolique au symbol: Essai sur les sacrements* (Paris: Cerf, 1979). On this question, see Timothy Brunk, "Consumer Culture and the Body: Chauvet's Perspective," *Worship* 82, no. 4 (July 2008): 290–310.

[56] Prétot, "Louis-Marie Chauvet à l'Insitute Superieur de Liturgie," 178.

phenomenological perspective.[57] It is likely not only because of Chauvet's explicit uses of Vergote's work, but because of Vergote's deeply phenomenological influence on Chauvet that Prétot cites him as particularly significant in Chauvet's formation.

In his discussion of corporality and the body in *Symbol and Sacrament*, Chauvet has recourse to several philosophers. In addition to Lacan and Heidegger, who drives Chauvet's critique of scholasticism, he also engages Merleau-Ponty and Emmanuel Levinas. Ambrose helpfully refers to the French context in which Chauvet was writing. For better or worse, Ambrose argues, Lacan's work was the academic lingua franca of 1980s France. He writes:

> Freudian psychoanalytic practice or "therapy" that sought a "cure" in the form of a healthy ego that was adapted to society, was viewed with great suspicion in France. . . . The French resistance to Freud's thought up until the fifties is in part explained by the apparent reluctance of psychoanalysts to be involved in social critique. This lack of social critique led French Marxists and other intellectuals on the left to conclude that psychoanalysis was simply a bourgeois tool for maintaining the status quo.[58]

It was Lacan's interpretation of Freud that turned French intellectuals on to Freud. And they engaged the Lacanian Freud with much gusto. According to Eugene Webb, as a result of the 1960s, the French looked to Lacan's psychoanalysis to solve problems that philosophy, politics, and political science no longer seemed capable of solving.[59]

Ultimately, Chauvet uses Lacan to make a much more phenomenological point. For example, Ambrose points out Chauvet's commentary on the Lacanian point that the subject emerges only in the "enunciation

---

[57] Antoine Vergote, "Lacan's Project of Retrieving Freud's Theory of the Subject"; idem, "The Body as Understood in Contemporary Thought and Biblical Categories," *Philosophy Today* 35 (1991): 93–105.

[58] Glenn Ambrose, "Psychoanalysis, Social Psychology, and the Sacramental Theology of Louis-Marie Chauvet."

[59] Eugene Webb, *The Self Between: From Freud to the New Social Psychology of France* (Seattle: University of Washington Press, 1993), esp. 3–25.

that denounces itself." Heidegger would agree, but for different reasons.[60] According to Heidegger, "It is Being *itself* that withdraws; that is what he wishes to indicate in crossing out the word Being."[61] Chauvet also comments that Levinas makes this same point, but in a different context.[62] This is a clue not that Chauvet would like the phenomenological tradition to be read as eradicating the subject but rather that his appeal to Lacan is less about Lacan and more about Chauvet's audience. In his elaboration of the symbolic order, Chauvet picks up Lacan's famous example of the "stage of the mirror" whereby a child is fascinated with her image reflected in a mirror. The image is an illusory ideal, a "specular I," which is not the real subject because it posits a unified whole, where the infant is a fragmented mass. As Ambrose puts it:

> It can only be viewed negatively and exclusively by Lacan as a narcissistic fantasy and source of alienation because it is a denial of the real state of affairs. All subsequent ego formation in the development of the child follows this initial pattern according to Lacan. Later the "social I" founded on the desire of the other is as bound to the imaginary order and as alienating as the "specular I." The only way to break from this imaginary order of the "specular I" or ego is to acquiesce to the "Law" or the symbolic order.[63]

By contrast, Chauvet takes Lacan's insight as a fundamental posture of humility, but not as eradicating the subject or submitting it completely to the symbolic order. Chauvet recognizes the linguistic reading of reality as only one point of view, not as Lacan would have it, an all-encompassing structure, *linguisterie*. Ambrose concludes, "That the 'I' exists only in the event of speaking does not mean it is purely linguistic reality. Besides being embodied in the subtle body of language and culture, the insight that structuralism is especially adapted to shed light on, the 'I' is always embodied in an individuated living body."[64] That is, it is subject to the exigencies of living bodies.

---

[60] Glenn Ambrose, *The Theology of Louis-Marie Chauvet: Overcoming Onto-Theology with the Sacramental Tradition* (Burlington, VT: Ashgate, 2012), 87–91.

[61] Chauvet, *Symbol and Sacrament*, 49.

[62] Ibid.

[63] Ambrose, *The Theology of Louis-Marie Chauvet*, 76.

[64] Ibid., 78.

Ambrose emphasizes the triple-body of Chauvet's discourse as, in itself, circumventing the temptation presented by Lacan's reading of the symbolic order. To drive the point home that Chauvet is more indebted to phenomenological categories than psychoanalytic ones, Ambrose argues for the significance of Merleau-Ponty's work for understanding Chauvet's notion of the body. He explains that we can understand Chauvet's linguistic account very much in the context of a body-based phenomenology "if we understand the linguistic 'It' and Merleau-Ponty's phenomenological notion of the 'Flesh' to refer to the multiple dimensions of human existence."[65] By "flesh," Merleau-Ponty intends something like the common fabric between "I" and "You," what it is that we share.

> These dimensions are among other things the blood and bones of our living bodies and the real values and dreams of our cultures. In other words, Merleau-Ponty's "Flesh" refers to the whole *world* of human beings and not just a purely physical substrate. Likewise, the symbolic order and "It" of Chauvet's linguistic viewpoint refers both to a cosmic and symbolic world, and not just some purely linguistic reality.[66]

For Chauvet, then, there is excess bound up in the subject. To hem in the subject to the symbolic order or reduce the subject to simply an epiphenomenon of language is to do violence to it.

> Contrary to a strictly structuralist view that would hypostatize a purely linguistic reality, the threefold structure as situated in Chauvet's thought serves as an argument against a sharp dichotomy between consciousness and body as well as between the individual and the social. Human existence is construed as being fundamentally rooted in a particular kind of body-consciousness and intersubjectivity. Furthermore, by placing Merleau-Ponty's phenomenology side by side with this insight of linguistic structuralism, we can perhaps entertain the idea that the I-You-It linguistic structure, rather than imposing a split between human being and nature, may

---

[65] Ambrose, "Eucharist as a Means for 'Overcoming' Onto-Theology?," 159.
[66] Ibid.

in fact reflect the reality of a *real* differentiation in the created order. In other words, I-You-It has an ontological dimension.[67]

There is a parallel between Chauvet's distance from Lacanian erasure of the subject and Michel's distance from Bérulle's self-annihilation. For both, the liturgy of the church constitutes subjectivity, an "enobling of self," to use Michel's phrase.

In Chauvet's work, the structuralist psychoanalytic insight concerning the symbolic order and its pervasiveness is tempered by a phenomenological account of the body that takes greater account of contingency, fragility, and agency. Chauvet's "triple-body" of culture, tradition, and nature allows for a subject that does not always respond to the linguistic default. Whereas Lacan was deeply suspicious of any attempt to grasp the whole, to perceive the entire truth, Chauvet is able to see that human tendency as not utterly negative—indeed it is, at bottom, a desire to see God's face. As Ambrose explains: "Chauvet sees revealed in psychoanalytic discourse not so much a lack, but rather an *open space* that calls for philosophical and theological questioning. The very openness of this space, which can never be filled, calls for an attitude of humility and proper *responsiveness* to God's word."[68] Nevertheless for Chauvet, the consent to the loss or the acceptance of mediation is a necessary condition of our human reality.

It is essential here to remember that Chauvet approaches philosophical discourse as an *ancilla* to his larger theological purpose. This is no small point. In contrast to Jean-Françoise Lyotard's famous definition of postmodernity as the "suspicion of all metanarratives," Chauvet is comfortable working out of the metanarrative of the Christian tradition. In contrast to the deep suspicions of the post-structuralists, Chauvet clearly understands the project in *Symbol and Sacrament* as working out a "structure of Christian identity." Central points he elaborates or seeks to understand with the help of philosophical discourse are often fundamentally scriptural points. God's gift of manna to the Israelites is the paradigm for gift, grace. The Lucan resurrection narratives demonstrate how the subject comes to faith in the symbolic order of the church.[69] As

---

[67] Ibid., 60.
[68] Ibid., 148.
[69] Chauvet, *Symbol and Sacrament*, 161–78.

far as Chauvet goes with Heidegger, he sharply critiques the gulf that Heidegger posits between faith and reason as *"two irreducible worlds"* and further notes the difference between the kenotic posture born of Christian exaltation of the crucified Christ and Heidegger's openness to being, even though both postures admit of a similar attitude.[70] "The crucified God is not crossed-out Being. . . . That the face of God shows itself only by erasing itself, that we think of God less in the metaphysical order of the Unknowable than in the symbolic and historical order of the unrecognizable—quite clearly this is the 'folly,' which theologians attempt to express through their discourse."[71] It is, at bottom, the uniqueness of the incarnation culminating in the paschal mystery that, pace Heidegger, makes theological discourse possible.

That discourse proceeds from the cross. The cross rendered Jesus an object (a nonsubject). The cruxifixion was doubtless a rupture, a break in our expectation akin to prophetic activity in ancient Israel. Yet, theological discourse and Christian living proceeds with the entire paschal mystery in view, that is, in the light of the overarching story of the eschatological culmination of the kingdom. Chauvet writes: "Judaism casts into relief the prophetic dimension of events: they open a new future, itself propelled toward a meta-historical eschatology that draws today forward and gives the key for reading the past. The myth about the origins becomes thereby the bearer of the myth of a new genesis of the world and of humanity propelled toward an *eschaton*: it is from the *Omega* that we read the *Alpha*."[72]

Chauvet and Corpus Mysticum

We have introduced some key aspects of Chauvet's project and clarified the role of body in his sacramental reinterpretation, especially as it relates to his intellectual context. Now we turn to the brief passages in his major work where Chauvet considers mystical body theology explicitly. Chauvet engages de Lubac's *Corpus Mysticum* and receives it as a defense of patristic theology, which generally said that Christ is present truly in the Eucharist *because* he is present in sacrament (in mystery, in figure,

---

[70] Ibid., 58–65.
[71] Ibid., 74–75.
[72] Ibid., 229–30.

in symbol), whereas following Berengar, scholastic theology emphasized that Christ is truly present, *although* that presence is sacramental.[73] Chauvet's critique of the shift that de Lubac describes is primarily about the metaphysical scholastic categories that support the "deadly break." The problem is what Chauvet calls the temptation of immediacy, a lack of recognition that our encounter with the real is only through mediation; the real cannot be "presupposed as something 'behind' the sacramental." Chauvet carefully rejects a particular kind of mystical body theology, one that is "without any relation to the Eucharistic mystery,"[74] and puts a fine point on de Lubac's historical study: "The reality of Christ comes to us in no other way than through its expressive mediation and . . . we can talk about it only *because and insofar as* it is sacramental ('in sacrament,' 'in symbol,' 'in memorial')."[75]

As Chauvet traces the scholastic reaction to Berengar, following de Lubac but also Congar, he moves from the rationalism of Berengar to the rationalism of the scholastics. Later in *Symbol and Sacrament*, Chauvet quotes Berengar: "It is the mark of a great heart to use dialectics in all things. For to use dialectics is to use reason so that those who do not do so, although made in the image of God according to God's reason, show contempt for their own dignity and are not able to be renewed from day to day according to the image of God."[76] Only after foregrounding this issue of rationalism does Chauvet move to discuss the import of the caesura dividing the threefold body of Christ, "the deadly dichotomy" between, on the one side, Christ's historical/glorified body and his sacramental (eucharistic) body and, on the other, Christ's ecclesial body.

In the second half of the twelfth century, after Berengar, the church takes the name *"corps mystique" en un sens absolu*, that absolute sense is a result of a disconnect from the Eucharist.[77] The prepositional phrase is key. Chauvet emphasizes de Lubac's point that the over-application of rational dialectic led to the notion of mystical body applied to the church

---

[73] Ibid., 294.

[74] Ibid., 294–95.

[75] Ibid., 296–97.

[76] Ibid., 293. For the Berengar quotation, Chauvet relies on P. Vignaux, *Philosophie au moyen age* (Paris: A. Colin, 1958), 23.

[77] Chauvet, "Le sacrifice de la messe: Représentation et expiation," *Lumière et vie* 146 (1980): 74. Cf. Chauvet, *Symbol and Sacrament*, 294.

in a merely sociological sense. The problem here is, first, rationalism and, next, the disconnection of mystical body from the Eucharist and ultimately from Christ.

Chauvet sees a faulty understanding of the sacrificial character of the Mass in the wake of Berengar: *La messe deviant ainsi, par l'allégorie, un mime de la Passion.*[78] After Berengar, the center of gravity in terms of the question of sacrifice was on the truth of the sacrificial event in the Eucharist *despite* its sacramental character, rather than the patristic emphasis on the truth of the sacrificial event in the Eucharist *because of* its sacramental character.

Chauvet's interpretation of de Lubac and his rereading of the nature of the Mass as sacrifice would see fuller explication by the time that Chauvet wrote *Symbol and Sacrament*. In the book, he repeats much of what he had written about sacrifice in the earlier article but directs his reinterpretation of the sacrificial character of the Christian life in terms of the threefold character of that identity: Scripture, sacrament, and ethics.[79]

Mystical body, then, is linked to an understanding of the Mass as sacrifice, a soteriology and sacramental theology that has received heightened criticism in French circles because of the controversies surrounding the work of René Girard.[80] Chauvet's reading of de Lubac and discussion of the mystical body is closely linked to his reinterpretation of sacrifice, one of the most treacherous but nevertheless "theologically *precious*" terms.[81] Chauvet thinks that a sense of sacrifice cannot be discarded with respect to the Mass and pursues a reading of Christ's life as sacrificial, "exercised *existentially, and not ritually.*"[82] That is, Christ's life, and his eventual death, is sacrificial precisely

---

[78] Chauvet, "Le sacrifice de la messe," 76–77.

[79] Chauvet, *Symbol and Sacrament*, 316.

[80] René Girard, *Violence and the Sacred*, trans. Patrick Gregory (Baltimore: Johns Hopkins University Press, 1979). While Girard offers a reconceptualization of the sacrificial that is in some ways amenable to the Christian vision, Chauvet cites critiques of Girard that sense a certain "Gnostic smell" in his Christology, in which Christ becomes simply the moral exemplar, the key to an anthropology. Chauvet nevertheless finds Girard's approach a useful launching pad for developing his own, more kenotic, reading of the sacrifice of Christ.

[81] Chauvet, *Symbol and Sacrament*, 315–16.

[82] Ibid., 299.

because it is kenotic. Christ fully embraces his human condition and rejects the temptation (notably in the desert after his baptism and on the cross when teased to rescue himself) to "unburden himself of the full human responsibility he had to assume."[83] Thus, Chauvet follows Vergote and, in some respects, Girard in rendering the sacramental notion of sacrifice, an ethical imperative flowing from the Eucharist, "where we eat [and] drink the body and blood of Christ" in order to live likewise kenotically.[84]

Since narrowing the extension of Christ's priestly *munus* to only or-dained ministry is related to the notion of Mass as sacrifice, and connected to a certain festishization of the eucharistic elements apart from the ec-clesial body, Chauvet emphasizes the priesthood of all believers by virtue of their baptism. He is critical of the tendency to speak in cultic terms about ordained ministers as the only priests.[85] The further development of the penitential system whereby Mass funds supported expiation for sin resulted in the multiplication of a group of ordained ministers whose sole occupation was to say Masses for the forgiveness of sin. Thus, one hundred years after Berengar, St. Thomas—in contradistinction to Peter Lombard—heavily emphasizes the celebrant's role *in persona Christi* especially at the moment of consecration, to the near exclusion of his role *in persona Ecclesiae*, thus pushing "to its ultimate consequences the effects of this '*deadly break*' between Christ and the Church born a century before him."[86]

As noted, the fundamental problem for Chauvet is the scholastic re-course to the language of causality. Chauvet draws out another implication of mystical body theology shorn of its eucharistic character. Rather than overidentifying the church with Christ, such that the church's actions are simply Christ's actions, Chauvet points to an extensive narrowing of the mediative role of the church. Thus, the ordained minister is set apart from the church in order to be more closely identified with Christ.

[83] Ibid., 301.

[84] Ibid., 302.

[85] Ibid., 308.

[86] Aquinas, *Summa Theologiae* III.82.7, ad 3; Peter Lombard, *Sentences* IV.13; Chauvet, *Symbol and Sacrament*, 472–73.

By the time Chauvet reaches the end of his treatment of sacrifice in *Symbol and Sacrament*, he has returned to Augustine and Irenaeus to embrace a full theology of the body of Christ or, as he writes, "'the whole Christ' (*Christus totus*), Head and Body," a phraseology of which Mersch was particularly fond. Chauvet further explains:

> It is impossible to say here "Christ" without at the same time say-ing "the Church": the Eucharist is the *sacramental sym-bolization of both*. The Christian sacrifice manifested in the *sacramentum* is not Christ taken in isolation, but the ecclesial *unum corpus* that must live "in him." In this way does his sacrifice become our sacrifice, and his Pasch our own pasch. . . . One thereby rejects any conception of Christ's sacrifice which, under the pretense of "realism," would be carried out at the expense of the truth of the participants' sacrifice in their mutual relations as members of the same body of Christ. The *sacramentum* cannot effect in truth a relation with Christ without simultaneously effecting, in truth also, a relation with others, a relation which seeks to become enfleshed here and now in the practice of reconciliation between human beings.[87]

We have seen how Chauvet's theological project, especially in *Symbol and Sacrament*, takes up the theme of the body, articulates a sacramental reinterpretation of the Christian life, and unites the poles of Christian identity, including Scripture, sacraments, and ethics. All of these themes were present in the French stream of mystical body of Christ theology in the early twentieth century. We saw further how Chauvet has been critical of mystical body theology insofar as it follows the scholastic assumptions characteristic of the twentieth-century Roman stream. In his principal emphases, Chauvet lands closer to de Lubac in his critique of rationalism, individualism, and the "deadly break" among the threefold body of Christ.

Conclusions: At the Risk of the (Mystical) Body

If Chauvet's fundamental theology of the sacramental structure of Christian faith strikes the reader as paradoxical, then that can only

---

[87] Chauvet, *Symbol and Sacrament*, 313.

attest to its success in articulating something of the tragic beauty of the paschal mystery: God's revelation of salvation as the meeting of divine and human desire (the Spirit) in the human (bodily and historical, assured yet struggling, defeated but triumphant) person of Jesus. Any imaginary shortcut to the immediate presence of divine fulfillment is a sliding away from the faith, a misplacing of the hope, a malnourishment of the love that comes to us in the Spirit of the crucified and risen Christ.[88]

In Chauvet's appropriation, the body—both the physical, fleshy reality and the corporate, womblike structure—deserves a place of preeminence in a nonmetaphysical model of thinking about God. It is precisely the located-ness and shaping-ness of bodies that onto-theo-logic ignores. Therefore, Chauvet's emphasis on corporality aims to take seriously the coming-to-be of human subjects. Subjects come to be subjects through symbolic exchange—not market exchange—which is always constituted by bodies, such that any articulation of religious belief, of faith in God will necessarily occur at the risk (*risque*: hazard, danger, peril) of the body.

Critics of mystical body of Christ theology have asserted that it was "Christomonist" in its heavy emphasis on the hypostatic union and its lack of pneumatology.[89] De Lubac describes the same problem as the refusal to acknowledge the Holy Spirit as the soul of the body. Across its streams, continuity with the incarnation had certainly been an important aspect of mystical body theology. Even before Möhler, for Bérulle and the French school, the mystical body of Christ "becomes a sort of system of spirituality" where the Christian life is understood as the prolongation of the incarnation.[90]

Chauvet rereads the Christian life in a thoroughly sacramental/mediative framework. He stresses that the christological key to mediation (the prepositional phrase "of Christ" in terms of mystical body theology) challenges us to take a more thorough account of the paschal mystery as

---

[88] Bruce T. Morrill, "Building on Chauvet's Work: An Overview" in Bordeyne and Morrill, *Sacraments*, xxii–xxiii.

[89] See Wood, *Spiritual Exegesis*, 149.

[90] Mersch, *The Whole Christ*, 538–40.

theologically, especially sacramentally, relevant. This stands in contrast to the scholastic method in which the hypostatic union was so prominent that theirs became a theology in which "everything is already over . . . in the *hypostatic union.*"[91] That is, the union of divine and human natures in Christ was the primary, and perhaps only, relevant matter for sacramental discourse. This christological insight and critique coincides with Chauvet's wider project. After all, a focus on Jesus' suffering, death, and resurrection involves attention to how it went with the body he is.

Among other effects (a narrow view of the resurrection, a shortening of the kenotic relevance of Christ, etc.), Chauvet argues that the sacramental starting point of the hypostatic union leads likewise to an eclipse of the Holy Spirit, "*the 'holy humanity' of Christ takes the place of the Holy Spirit as the agent and efficient cause of Church unity.*"[92] Chauvet proposes instead a starting point in the paschal mystery, which has at least three implications for Chauvet's project and for considering the mystical body of Christ in its light.

First, it specifies the particularity of Jesus of Nazareth, specifically Christ crucified—that "the face of God shows itself only by erasing itself" "in the crushed humanity of this crucified One."[93] The "folly of the cross" is that we always already stand in a relationship of mediation. Jesus of Nazareth, the body of God in humanity, was situated in a time and place. This emphasizes, in symbolic discourse, the failure of separating the mystical from the real. In other words, every real is necessarily mystical.

Second, Chauvet asserts, those who pledge allegiance to him owe him a human body in this time and place. He writes:

> It is impossible to separate the divine kenosis from the one that must be carried out in ourselves: our corporality is charged with becoming the place for this kenosis. In our corporality, the most distant is also the closest, the most divine is also the most human. . . . Thus we are obliged to give to this God the body of humanity that God asks of us. Corporality is God's place. God whose being is to "not be" (see 1 Cor 1:18; Phil 2:5-8), reduced to

---

[91] Chauvet, *Symbol and Sacrament*, 455.
[92] Ibid., 467.
[93] Ibid., 74.

nothing as God has been by humankind, finds God's "sacrament"
in those who have themselves been reduced to "not-others." [94]

This kenotic connection between ecclesial body, sacramental body, and
historical/glorified body is cemented by the Spirit. "It is significant," Chauvet writes, "that the Spirit is the operating agent of the threefold body
of Christ: his historical body, born of Mary, overshadowed by the Spirit
(Luke 1), and spiritualized into a glorious body; his sacramental body
(first epiclesis); and his ecclesial body (second epiclesis)." [95] He explains
further, "The Spirit, neutral, faceless, nameless except for the names drawn
from cosmic symbolism, is the agent of the divine in God's concealment
in Jesus' personal body, in the body of history the Church gives him, and
joining these two bodies, in the symbolic body of the Eucharist in which
the body of Jesus is given only to be veri-fied [lit. "made truth"] in the
Church's body, as our analysis of the Eucharistic Prayer has shown." [96] Thus,
Chauvet finds in an enriched pneumatology the operator for linking what
de Lubac has called the threefold body of Christ. Notably, it is from the
rite that he derives the Spirit's preeminent place.

Here, we see that the necessary mediation of God must occur in
human corporality, but even further there is an ethical component: the
mystical body of Christ makes God present as its members lay down their
lives as did Christ. Chauvet aims at mitigating the deadly dichotomy by
emphasizing that the Holy Spirit brings forth the body of Christ in humanity when, as part of the sacramental gift exchange, human beings "give
flesh" to their confession of Christ's body in the Eucharist by living the
way of the cross. "Where human beings give flesh to their confession of
the Risen One by following him on the way of the cross for the liberation
of their brothers and sisters (and thus for their own as well), there the
body of Christ comes forth. Of this body, the Church is the eschatological
promise in and for the world." [97]

Third, and clearly not least important, is the enriched pneumatology.
It is the Spirit that breathes life into the anamnesis of the paschal mystery:

---

[94] Ibid., 509.
[95] Ibid., 526.
[96] Ibid., 530–31.
[97] Ibid., 529.

"*Spirit*," Chauvet writes, "is the personal name traditionally given to what, *of God*, gives present and future vigor to such a memorial of the past." [98] Chauvet's close reading of Eucharistic Prayer II makes clear that a theology of the mystical body of Christ cannot proceed without the Spirit, especially if it strives to maintain the link between liturgy and ecclesiology. "In the epicleses, the Spirit is always the agent of the incorporation of the risen Christ into the Church and into the elements of the sacraments." [99] Chauvet illustrates from the rites that the same Spirit is called upon in the eucharistic prayer to transform the elements and to transform the church into Christ's body.

Taking seriously the language and ritual actions of the church, Chauvet is able to articulate a pneumatology that supports, rather than replaces or undercuts, a mystical body theology. What results for Chauvet is what we can perhaps call the aesthetics of sanctity. He writes:

> The Spirit is precisely the agent that makes possible the expression of the crucified Word by removing it to another space than that of concept: the space of the conversion of attitudes, the space of the *body*. Hence, the primary mediation of God's revelation in Christianity is no longer only that of the cosmos and seeing or even that of the word of the Law and hearing, but, recapitulating these two . . . that of the body and living. [100]

The body for Chauvet is not a concrete ground of refuge but rather an indication that God is to be found in Christians becoming, with reference to St. Paul, a "living 'letter of Christ.'" [101] By thematizing corporality as the place of God, Chauvet sets the groundwork for a relentless emphasis on mediation, the mediation that was variously lost in some versions of mystical body theology. The eucharistic physicalism—as in gnawing on flesh and crunching on bones—following the Berengarian controversy reduced the celebration of Eucharist to a mere recipe, on the other side of which there was an unmediated Christ. The physicalism and individualistic piety that flowed from it resulted in an empty sociological mystical body

[98] Ibid., 510.
[99] Ibid., 525.
[100] Ibid., 528.
[101] Ibid., 530.

no longer thought to mediate Christ. Thus, we see such a figure as Luigi Sturzo dismiss the imaginary mysticisms of communism, bolshevism, etc., and instead espouse a robust mystical body theology.[102]

By maintaining, as the French stream consistently had, the liturgy as the primary mediation of Christ, Chauvet's reinterpretation guards against the horribly mistaken Romantic application of mystical body theology to the German *Volk*.

The various elements of Chauvet's "turn to the symbolic" work against these dangers of mystical body of Christ theology. Chauvet's connection to the ISL; his thematic emphasis on the body, the liturgy, and the sacraments of the church; and his aim of developing a fundamental theology of sacramentality in *Symbol and Sacrament* demonstrate his project as a surprising locus of the concerns and categories of the French stream of mystical body theology after its recession earlier in the century. This context illuminates his work as not merely a rejection of a theological tradition (i.e., neoscholasticism) but a development of those who had gone before him in and around the ISL. It is of no small consequence that Chauvet was eventually trained by and worked closely with some key figures who were connected with Beauduin and his liturgical-social mystical body theology. In this view, Chauvet's fundamental theology of the sacramental is not "a thoroughly postmodern obfuscation of the Christian mysteries"[103] but rather a renewed investigation of the French stream's theological concerns in a different philosophical milieu. This is done in the vein of Chauvet's fundamental claim about the theological task, "In its role as hermeneutics, theology has the job, not of retrieving an original meaning but, on the contrary, of *producing*, starting especially from the text of the Scriptures, *new texts*, that is, new practices which *foster* the emergence of a new world."[104]

Demonstrating some of the vestiges that are recognizable in Chauvet's work helps us to see that mystical body theology, especially in its French

---

[102] Luigi Sturzo, *Spiritual Problems of Our Times* (New York: Longmans, Green, and Company, 1945), 166. See also chapter 6 of that work, "The Mystical Body and Human Society."

[103] Joseph Martos, *Doors to the Sacred: A Historical Introduction to Sacraments in the Catholic Church*, rev. ed. (Liguori, MO: Triumph Books, 2001), 139.

[104] Chauvet, *Symbol and Sacrament*, 69.

stream, was not merely an ecclesiological stepping-stone as it has been received in many theological quarters. Further, it establishes a ground and precedent for discerning the impact of that stream of mystical body theology in our contemporary milieu.

Conclusion

I t remains to draw together some of the conclusions of this study, which set out to discover some of the reasons for mystical body theology's mixed heritage in contemporary Catholic theology, understand why the theology receded around mid-century after such vitality in the early twentieth century, and explore further the link between figures as chronologically and geographically diverse as Michel and Chauvet.

We have come to see the theology of the mystical body of Christ as variegated into three major streams, each sharing a commonality that largely inheres across a common language and geographical area of work. In this light, Michel's and Chauvet's common emphasis on the theological import of the body should be seen not as two different iterations of Catholic thinking but rather as two different moments in the same stream of thought. These distinctions not only help us to understand Michel and Chauvet more clearly but also help to explain the diversity of responses to mystical body theology in the postconciliar period, from politically vacuous to juridically heavy, because many such criticisms apply only to selected streams, not to all. Further, they help us to understand the general reception of mystical body theology as an ecclesiology per se, including the assumptions and assertions of Pope Pius XII's *Mystici Corporis*, side-by-side with several efforts to broaden the categorization of the term, especially among historians of spirituality or mystical theologians. In order to appreciate its contribution, mystical body of Christ theology cannot be seen simply as an ecclesiological model.

Chauvet and Michel: Body, Absence, and Theology in the French Stream

Chauvet recently retired from teaching and is still active as a parish priest. The major direction of his research and especially the aspects of it that we have emphasized here were formed in the late 1970s and early 1980s. In the words of Lieven Boeve: "It is the awareness of a theological urgency that drives Chauvet to his reconsideration of the sacramental structure of Christian existence. The gap between classical sacramental theology and contemporary culture puts the very plausibility and relevance of the sacraments, and of Christian existence as a whole, under pressure."[1] That plausibility has a pastoral dimension as well. Michel inhabited the monastery, college campus, and eventually the Chippewa reservation. He found a home with the new social Catholics pushing boundaries in the 1930s. Chauvet inhabits parish rectories and deals with the pastoral questions of Paris suburbs. Both thinkers, then, are deeply rooted in the pastoral practice of theology. Michel wrote pamphlets and educational materials for mass consumption. Chauvet counsels couples preparing for marriage and manages a parish budget. And both are concerned about the lived practice of the faith in the contemporary world. Questions concerning social reconstruction in the 1930s gave way to questions about Christian identity in the 1980s.

Nevertheless, placing his work in the French stream of mystical body theology demonstrates that Chauvet's interest in corporality is not merely a function of philosophical interests of the day but rather proceeds from deeper theological commitments. Adopting the categories of Heidegger, Lacan, Levinas, and Merleau-Ponty is a demonstration of St. Peter Damian's famous line: *philosophia ancilla theologiae*, that is, appropriating philosophical categories in service to a deeply theological point. In Chauvet's hands, the widespread emphasis on corporality becomes, theologically speaking, primarily an emphasis on the liturgy with social implications. In other words, Chauvet's reflections on corporality are second-order reflections derived from Scripture and the liturgy. He engages philosophical work on embodiment to support and develop these fundamental theological sources.

---

[1] Lieven Boeve, "Theology in a Postmodern Context and the Hermeneutical Project of Louis-Marie Chauvet," in Bordeyne and Morrill, *Sacraments*, 14.

Developing the concerns of his forebears in the French stream, the liturgy grounds his appeal to the body and its social implications. Thus, the emphasis on the body does not float off into utter identity with God, juridical structure, or nation as we have seen in versions of mystical body theology earlier in the century. Chauvet's is not purely a sacramentalism *in genere*, but rather a christologically rooted and pneumatologically thick fundamental theology. In this there are echoes of Michel's insistence on the sacramental principle that flows out of the liturgy, infusing the Christian life. Chauvet's project can be understood as a fuller, more complex articulation of Michel's point.

Chauvet's theological accomplishment in this regard is related to his relentless emphasis on mediation, sounding a note of absence with respect to the Christian life. Our knowledge of others, our world, ourselves, and our God is necessarily run through our corporality, or mediated. For example, what Chauvet calls the "temptation of immediacy" includes our tendency to control God, including our attempts to define Christian identity too narrowly or to erase faith in the search for knockdown proof.[2] This is not, however, simply the "surface play" of signs. In a novel published two years before *Symbole et Sacrement*, Don DeLillo offers a well-known reflection on our postmodern reveling in the proliferation of images. *White Noise* portrays "the most photographed barn in America," which can no longer actually be observed by onlookers because they are overwhelmed by the camera flashes and pictures of pictures. "No one sees the barn," DeLillo writes. "Once you see the signs about the barn, it becomes impossible to see the barn."[3] The multiplication of renditions obstructs the reality. Left asking "Is the barn even there?" we are reminded by Chauvet that on the other side of that mediation is Christ. If, on the one hand, Chauvet's work guards against the glaring presence of the scholastic account of the sacraments, on the other, it fends off the possibility that they might just be a charade.

The flip side of the coin from DeLillo's barn is Pelz's version of mystical body theology. If DeLillo asks us if perhaps mediation is everything, Pelz obliterates mediation, insisting that each Christian is, simply, Christ. As Pelz's theology demonstrates, mystical can be applied in a more or less

---

[2] See Chauvet, *The Sacraments*, 39.
[3] Don DeLillo, *White Noise* (New York: Viking, 1985), 12–13.

mediated fashion. In other versions of mystical body theology, mystical has pure horizontal purchase. An encounter with the mystical body mediates only a collection of people spread across extended space. The body is *mystical* only because it is spread out. From this conception, there is a short slide to the formulation "mystical body of the church," a literal replacement of "Christ" with "the church." The delicate dance of presence and absence has been lost.

Chauvet's dialectic of presence and absence comes into sharper relief in his foundational appeal to Luke 24.[4] This scriptural text is perhaps the most important in *Symbol and Sacrament*, rivaled only by Exodus 16. For Chauvet, the Emmaus narrative and the surrounding pericopes suggest a paradigm for what it means to become a Christian—"to pass from non-faith to faith."[5] These narratives represent a Lucan reflection, in the post-ascension time of the church, on the temptation to seek out Jesus in his dead (physical) body, which is no longer available. Attempts to verify Jesus with touch prove unsatisfactory, "'Touch me and see; no ghost has flesh and bones as you can see that I have.' . . . They were still incredulous, still astounded" (Luke 24:39, 41). The disciples who had traveled to Emmaus with him, however, recognized him in the breaking of the bread, an obvious allusion to the eucharistic celebration of the church (see Luke 24:30-31). Chauvet concludes:

> In this time of the Church, the Lord is no longer visible. Luke insists on this point: resurrected, Jesus is the "Living One" (see Luke 24:5)—a divine title—he lives in God, as the account of the ascension clearly emphasizes. However, the *Absent One* is present in his "sacrament" which is the Church: the Church rereading the Scriptures with him in mind, the Church repeating his gestures in memory of him, the Church living the sharing between brothers and sisters in his name. It is in these forms of witness by the Church that Jesus takes on a body and allows himself to be

[4] Chauvet, *Symbol and Sacrament*, 161–78. Chauvet pairs this chapter with two other Lucan texts in explicating how it is that Christians come to be Christians: the baptism of the Ethiopian Eunuch (Acts 8:26-40) and Saul/Paul's conversion (Acts 9:1-20). Of course, the last is an important text, more or less formative, for mystical body theologies across the century.

[5] Ibid., 161.

encountered. Such an interpretation is one of the keys for unlock-
ing these three texts: the Church is never mentioned as such, but
it is everywhere present in veiled fashion; if it seems omitted from
the text, it is because it alone constitutes its authentic "pre-text."[6]

These reflections offer a clear indication of how Chauvet injects a healthy
dose of absence into the French stream. To take seriously, with Chauvet,
our sacramental existence is to set aside the danger of identifying Christ
too closely with the individual Christian or with the church. His thoroughgoing recourse to corporality and the "presence of absence" chasten some
of the potential excesses of mystical body theology, tendencies obvious in
Adam's theology and Tromp's theology and incipient in Mersch's theology
(the least expressly liturgical of those in the French stream studied here).
We no longer see Jesus walking about; in order to find the body of Christ,
we are instructed to seek the church. We feel the absence profoundly and
are tempted to seek the living one among the dead, to paraphrase the
angel's question to the women at the tomb (cf. Luke 24:5). And Peter, run-
ning to the tomb, also found not his body but "the wrappings and nothing
more" (Luke 24:12). It is difficult to shake that temptation of immediacy.

This was an absence that from the angle of the social question, Michel's
constructive social engagement presumed: the church has no ability to
decree institutionally an end to societal problems. Michel saw that movements such as the National Catholic Rural Life Conference, the Catholic
Worker, and Friendship House must drive this work in the twentieth
century. Nevertheless, indebted to his scholastic imagination, there is
still a heavy sense of presence that accompanies his mystical body theology. This makes sense. Despite a lack of political power, the church in
the United States of the 1920s and 1930s had a coherence resulting from
its ongoing identification as "other" to American society and its cohesive
subcultural strategies to combat that identification.[7] His formation in the
liturgy taught him to avoid simply identifying the mediated with the real.
Social reconstruction would not bring heaven to earth. Yet the church
had a vision of pursuing social repair that was neither of the state nor

---

[6] Chauvet, *Symbol and Sacrament*, 163.

[7] On the subculture, its eventual dissolution, and the implications, see William L.
Portier, "Here Come the Evangelical Catholics," *Communio* 31 (Spring 2004): 35–66.

dependent on it.[8] The delicate mix of cohesiveness and displacement experienced by American Catholics in the early part of the twentieth century has some echoes in our contemporary cultural context of interconnectedness and fragmentation (more on that in a moment). It is this fragmentation-yet-connection to which Chauvet refers when he opens *Symbol and Sacrament* with the proliferation of questions about Christian identity arising in the pastoral sphere in 1980s France. And he works to develop a pervasive fundamental theological norm that is not dependent on the claims to glaring presence of neoscholasticism.

Directions and Implications

The interplay of fragmentation and connection intensifies after Chauvet produces his main body of work in the cultural context of globalization. Thus we now turn to some possible directions in which the research here could be developed, first in view of the arguments it makes about the historical flow of mystical body theology, and then with respect to our contemporary context.

Historically Speaking

The foregoing analysis holds several implications for continued historical-theological investigation of what has oftentimes been seen as a monolith: mystical body theology in the twentieth century. If the argument here is correct—that Michel and Chauvet inhabit the same broad stream of French socio-liturgical thinking about the mystical body of Christ—then there is potential for much more investigation of this and other streams of mystical body theology.

If we understand mystical body of Christ only as an ecclesiological model or image, then its variations—which we have begun to show here are many—are not so important as its contradistinctions to other models or images. But if we scratch the surface of its historical forms, there may be better ways of understanding its role in twentieth-century theology and perhaps more resources for contemporary theology.

---

[8] Michel elaborates in *Christian Social Reconstruction: Some Fundamentals of the Quadragesimo Anno* (Milwaukee, WI: Bruce, 1937).

Delineating, with a rather broad sweep, three streams of mystical body theology as I have done here only begins that process. There are nuances that I have only been able to nod to along the way. For example, we noted the German-liturgical theology of Guardini as well as the differences between the mystical body theology of Mersch and Beauduin—less and more liturgically inflected, respectively, though both grounded in the liturgy and sacraments of the church. These examples demonstrate that more needs to be done to see mystical body theologies even more clearly.

"Direct Access"

In Charles Taylor's imposing *A Secular Age*, the Canadian thinker brings a variety of tools to his diagnosis of the contemporary. As he promises, Taylor tacks back and forth between a more analytical philosophical view and a historical one, often dealing with cultural contexts as well as philosophical ideas.[9] Nevertheless, what emerges from his study are a variety of aspects that compose a diagnosis of our contemporary and how it is that this particular contemporary came to pass. Two aspects of Taylor's analysis are of particular interest here: his description of a "direct-access society" and his treatment of "excarnation."

One of the characteristics of what Taylor calls "the modern social imaginary" is the establishment of a "direct-access society." This is a component of what it means to live in a secular age, wherein the conditions for belief have shifted from an unquestioned belief in God to belief as one option among many.[10] A growing flat sense of time—every moment is both simultaneous and relentlessly chronological—accompanies a corresponding flat society, a "radical horizontality."[11] Flat time stands in contrast to the celebration of the high feast, which pauses the workaday slog and, importantly, casts us forward and backward because "it is close to eternity, or the time of origins, or the events it prefigures."[12]

A secularized, that is, flat, sense of time pairs with a secularized, that is, unmediated, sense of the corporate. "The modern social imaginary

---

[9] Charles Taylor, *A Secular Age* (Cambridge, MA: Harvard University Press, 2007), 24.

[10] Ibid., 3.

[11] Ibid., 209.

[12] Ibid.

no longer sees the greater trans-local entities as grounded in something other, something higher, than common action in secular time." [13] "In the earlier form, hierarchy and . . . mediacy of access went together." [14] From this perspective, we can see that the Roman stream of mystical body theology tried to recover this altogether—a strong sense of mediation via a strong grounding in hierarchical structure. In most cases, the structure was in the lead. With Taylor's lens we can see that the French stream represents an attempt to recover mediation and, of course, some sense of the hierarchical, with liturgy and sacraments in the lead.

The shift, Taylor tells us, is from relational identities to categorical identities.[15] The ground still proves difficult, and there are a variety of other factors at play that lead us to think only in terms of direct access between myself and society, which eviscerates an imagination of the common good. There are plenty of positive elements to this shift, not the least of which being that serfs are no longer beholden to their lords to gain any kind of subjectivity within the broader power structures of society. Though what results is either nationalism, the virulent kind to which some in the German stream succumbed in the 1930s and 1940s, or a more atomized individual sense of access. On the religious plane, this becomes a "me and God" kind of direct access that eliminates mediation across the board.

Perhaps the beginnings of cultivating an alternative imagination resides in the French stream. As Taylor demonstrates, the idea of direct access is partly an imaginary.[16] It is supported by certain social practices (e.g., fewer formal patrons to which we need appeal for favors; calling a customer service line to reach a company directly), but others clearly reinforce a different idea (the maxim "it is not what you know, but who"; the differences in levels of access of celebrities vs. noncelebrities). Thus, while mystical body theology does not serve as a social practice, it has

---

[13] Ibid., 207.

[14] Ibid., 210.

[15] Ibid., 211.

[16] Ibid., 146. Taylor describes the term "social imaginary" as "the way we collectively imagine, even pre-theoretically, our social life in the contemporary Western world." Thus, there are social constructs and practices that are part of it, but there is also an overriding sense of "this is the way things are" that does not line up with every aspect of social life.

potential to work on the imaginary side of the equation—that is, the way we see the world. We have noted almost *ad nauseum* how for the French stream, mystical body theology was a fundamental christological vision of the world that embraces mediation in a nonstifling way.

For example, Michel's mystical body theology included a fundamental emphasis on the little mystical body of the family, which situated human existence in the context of mediating relations early on, tapping us into this reality.[17] Chauvet emphasizes that we always come to be and continue to be in a network of relations. The primordiality of the symbolic, which forms us in its womb and appears as gift preceding us, opens us up to reflect on a God who precedes us. This is both a protological and an eschatological point. We are constituted by God and move forward toward God in ultimate consummation. This is an insight that grows out of our very corporality. We are constituted by corporality and depend on it for growth and learning.[18] Our very physical bodies open up beyond themselves. They are not discrete entities. Chauvet uses the example of the navel—a trace that we have been sewn up in our own unique sack of skin; our bodies bear the marks of a primordial openness that is not autonomous, but they also admit of other openings (eyes, ears, mouth, the open palm) which make any coming-to-subjectivity of the human being possible.[19]

Mystical body theology in the French stream was successful in opening up both imaginations and experiences of a broad horizontal society that has a vertical thrust. The solution of the Roman stream—wherein the structure was the primary means of securing the vertical, moving from laity to priests to bishops to the pope and, ultimately, to God—proved

---

[17] See Virgil Michel, "The Family and the Mystical Body," *Orate Fratres* 11 (1937): 295–99. Much has changed, of course, in family dynamics since Michel's day. The phenomenon of "helicopter parents," who hover over every activity of their children, and, more recent, "snowplow parents," who remove every obstacle for their children, testifies to the enduring nature of parental mediation. Perhaps these tendencies represent the strong assertion of parents in light of the dynamics Taylor describes. On "helicopter parents," see Jessica Skolnikoff and Robert Engvall, *Young Athletes, Couch Potatoes, and Helicopter Parents: The Productivity of Play* (Lanham, MD: Rowman and Littlefield, 2014).

[18] Chauvet, *Symbol and Sacrament*, 446.

[19] Ibid., 147.

inadequate. But a workable approach cannot jettison these structural elements either, as Taylor demonstrates.

Bodies in Our Contemporary Context

Another aspect of the modern social imaginary that Taylor develops is what he calls "excarnation," in which "embodied feeling is no longer a medium in which we relate to what we recognize as rightly bearing an aura of the higher; either we do recognize something like this, and we see reason as our unique access to it; or we tend to reject this kind of higher altogether, reducing it through naturalistic explanation." [20] Taylor describes an overrationalization of our age (of Christianity rooted in sixteenth-century reform more specifically) to the epistemological detriment of embodied ways of knowing. It is against this backdrop that the burgeoning interest in bodies since Nietzsche must be understood.[21] But the swing back is inherent to Christianity itself, explains Taylor: "There is something in Christian civilization which resists excarnation." [22]

Chauvet developed and appropriated the French stream in the philosophical context of France in the 1970s and 1980s. His thinking on the body grows more complex in dialogue with Lacan, Merleau-Ponty, Heidegger, and Levinas, and his theological engagement with the body in the context of postmodern thought has been followed with a host of studies of all different stripes.[23]

---

[20] Taylor, *A Secular Age*, 288.

[21] Ibid., 613.

[22] Ibid., 615.

[23] To name only a few: Susan Ross, "'Then Honor God in Your Body' (1 Cor 6:20): Feminist and Sacramental Theology on the Body," *Horizons* 16, no. 1 (1989): 7–27; Vergote, "The Body as Understood in Contemporary Thought and Biblical Categories"; Louis-Marie Chauvet and François Kabasele Lumbala, eds., *Liturgy and the Body*, Concilium 1995, no. 3 (Maryknoll, NY: Orbis Books, 1995); Morrill, ed., *Bodies of Worship*; Anthony J. Godzieba, "Incarnation, Theory, and Catholic Bodies: What Should Post-Postmodern Catholic Theology Look Like?," *Louvain Studies* 28, no. 3 (Fall 2003): 217–31; Gareth Moore, *Body in Context: Sex and Catholicism*, Contemporary Christian Insights (New York: Continuum, 2005); Gerard Loughlin, ed., *Queer Theology: Rethinking the Western Body* (Malden, MA: Blackwell, 2007); Brunk, "Consumer Culture and the Body"; M. Shawn Copeland, *Enfleshing Freedom:*

Questions surrounding our understanding of embodiment are rife in our current globalized context. Forces drive us in both excarnating and reincarnating directions. Ours is a context deeply conflicted about the body. It is, on one hand, the limiting sack of skin that holds us in one particular place while we are virtually transported around the globe, the fleshy mass that sits idle as capital whizzes from Los Angeles to Dubai to Beijing and back again. On the other hand, bodies themselves are commodified in various ways, enlisted in those structures and put to very specific ends in various new forms of slavery that move miles with relative ease. Insidious corporate networks are easier to create and sustain with technological support. Simultaneously, we have technological avenues for entering into the experiences of persons around the globe—and therefore potential for a deep sense of corporality—and yet the temptation arises that those mediated entrées remain merely voyeuristic and disembodied. Yet, many thinkers have struggled to find some other way to ground important universals such as human rights. Some have turned to the body.[24]

Vincent Miller warns of resting too easily with embodiment as a panacea in our contemporary, globalized consumer context: "Constructing ourselves by choosing among and acting upon passive objects, we are particularly ill suited to understand ourselves as gift," because "the formation of our imaginations on this side of the veil of the commodity makes us appear autonomous, unrelated to anything."[25] Nevertheless, Miller argues, "our response to the challenge of global consumption must focus on cultivating awareness of [our] interconnections."[26] These dynamics that lead to fragmented persons, identities, and cultures cry out for a substantive account of the corporate nature of human life.

While different in analysis and emphasis, Taylor and Miller agree that we have a sense of bodiliness but that it does not take us to God. It

---

Body, Race, and Being (Minneapolis: Fortress Press, 2010); Eduardo J. Echeverria, *"In the Beginning . . . : A Theology of the Body* (Eugene, OR: Wipf and Stock, 2011).

[24] Bryan S. Turner, *Vulnerability and Human Rights* (University Park, PA: Penn State University Press, 2006).

[25] Vincent J. Miller, "The Body Globalized: Problems for a Sacramental Imagination in an Age of Global Commodity Chains," in *Religion, Economics and Culture in Conflict and Conversation*, 116–17.

[26] Ibid., 119.

is closed off. Taylor refers to a "buffered" rather than "porous" self.[27] A connection has been severed, an opening sealed. Taylor describes widespread privileging of the rational, so that what is bodily is not taken as a conduit for reality. Miller emphasizes our obsession with bodies in several respects, which nevertheless fails in itself to move us toward a sense of the sacramental.

Miller's analysis, in particular, derives from the effects of consumer practices among global commodities and warns us to avoid too much sanguinity concerning invocations of embodiment. In light of the work here, further exploration of mystical body theology in the French stream as a theological framework for bringing our interconnections to the surface is necessary. Theologically speaking, bodies are always more complex than their fleshiness. The glorified body of Christ is fleshy and yet mistaken as a ghost (see Matt 14:26; Luke 24:37-39). The tradition has long wrestled with how to articulate that there is body and more than body (i.e., soul) without dualism.[28] Mystical body of Christ fits into this same complex conversation. There are fleshy and bodily elements, as Timothy Kelly points out: "Since body firstly *means* body, there is always a certain physical dimension when the word is used."[29] Yet, the mystical body of Christ has been traditionally distinguished from the historical body of Christ and, despite some of the eucharistic physicalism cited by de Lubac, led to reflections on the interconnectedness among human bodies in time predicated on the liturgy.

While fleshiness seductively promises to be an entrée into that resistance to excarnation characteristic of Christianity, Miller demonstrates that it is not so simple. He points to John Tomlinson's definition of globalization as "complex connectivity," whereby the key characteristic of global culture is that we are related to one another and other things in multilayered

---

[27] See Taylor, *A Secular Age*, 27–42, 131–42.

[28] See Godzieba, "Bodies and Persons, Resurrected and Postmodern," in Haers and De Mey, *Theology and Conversation*, 211–25. Godzieba works out a nondualistic account of body and soul in light of phenomenology.

[29] Timothy Kelly, "Christ and the Church: *Duo in Carne Una*; A Study of the Union of Christ and the Members of His Mystical Body from the Vantage Point of Its Bodiliness" (PhD diss., University of Fribourg, 2010), 56. In support of his point, Kelly cites Pierre Benoit, "Corps, Tête et Plérome dans les épîtres de la Captivité," *Revue Biblique* 63 (1956): 111.

ways, ways of which we are often unaware.[30] In a different, but still significant way, this was precisely the point that Michel and others on this side of the Atlantic, such as Day, made about the mystical body—it was complex connectivity. Day describes gaining a first apprehension of the mystical body of Christ before her conversion when Sacco and Vanzetti were executed.[31] Michel, in a passage cited above, reflects on "the organic fellowship in which all men are actually, or by destiny, true members with Christ of His Mystical Body."[32] This is an element—supernatural solidarity—that is more strongly emphasized by Michel and underemphasized by Chauvet.[33] The supernatural solidarity of mystical body theology drives us to consider what is now fully a situation in which we are inserted into a web of relationships without our explicit choice and challenges us to think about the narrowness of the network of relationships that we do choose. The French stream was able to hold these two elements—corporality and sacramentality—together in a way that other streams of mystical body theology were not. This is promising. A theological account can only go so far in this context, but there is potential, nevertheless, for examining virtual (and other nonphysical connections) in the theological light of the mystical body of Christ.[34]

[30] John Tomlinson, *Globalization and Culture* (Chicago: University of Chicago Press, 1999), esp. 1–12. Miller, *Consuming Religion*, 108–9, 118–19.

[31] Day, *The Long Loneliness*, 147. Sacco and Vanzetti were Italian-American anarchists convicted of robbery-murder in Massachusetts despite shoddy evidence.

[32] Michel, "The Liturgy and Catholic Life," 119.

[33] While Chauvet does not develop the idea of organic fellowship explicitly, there are conceptual resources within Chauvet's model that would support fleshing out of this aspect of mystical body theology. For Chauvet, these appear when he discusses the church as sacrament and the "broken line" of Christian identity in a community. See *Symbol and Sacrament*, 180–81.

[34] For a creative theological engagement with virtual space that engages some thinkers in the French stream, see Katherine G. Schmidt, "Virtual Communion: Theology of the Internet and the Catholic Imagination" (PhD diss., University of Dayton, 2016). There have been several theological attempts to engage questions of embodiment, taking account of mystical body theology. Among them are Rebecca Clouse, "A Postmodern Look at the Mystical Body," *Mystics Quarterly* 20, no. 1 (March 1994): 3–9; Cooke, "Body and Mystical Body: The Church as *Communio*"; Kelly, "Christ and the Church: *Duo in Carne Una*"; Joseph Rivera, "*Corpus Mysticum* and Religious Experience: Henry, Lacoste, and Marion," *International Journal of Systematic Theology*

In 1998, Pope John Paul II acknowledged the growth of globalization, remarking on its potential to bring people together accompanied, however, with the threat of increasing marginalization. John Paul described our challenge, especially that of the United Nations, as ensuring "globalization in solidarity, a globalization without marginalization. This is a clear duty in justice, with serious moral implications in the organization of the economic, social, cultural and political life of nations."[35]

More recently, Pope Francis has called the world's attention to Lampedusa, a small island off the coast of Italy where a boat filled with African émigrés had wrecked, killing many. He demonstrated his solidarity with the dead by celebrating Mass with a chalice fashioned from the wood of a broken ship. Then, in his homily, he connected this seemingly accidental event with "the globalization of indifference [which] makes us all 'unnamed,' responsible, yet nameless and faceless." And then he called on the world to pay greater attention to our complex connections:

> How many of us, myself included, have lost our bearings; we are no longer attentive to the world in which we live; we don't care; we don't protect what God created for everyone, and we end up unable even to care for one another! And when humanity as a whole loses its bearings, it results in tragedies like the one we have witnessed.

14, no. 3 (July 2012): 327–49. Rivera's work is of particular interest because it studies Marion, Lacoste, and Henry on "the 'mystical body of Christ,'" which "has become a theological grammar for understanding both the limits and possibilities of religious experience in recent continental philosophy of religion" (327). His work demonstrates the more-than-ecclesiological heritage of mystical body theology in French circles. He does not, however, engage the question of embodiment directly. It bears mentioning that Rivera is incorrect in claiming that de Lubac wrote *Corpus Mysticum* "in part, as a response to the 1943 papal encyclical titled *Mystici Corporis Christi.*" As mentioned above, that work was written in the late 1930s, though a second edition did appear in 1949. Nevertheless, these studies largely do one of two things: they either define mystical body of Christ as simply an ecclesiology or move more in the direction of mystical experience. There is room, then, for a study of how the French stream provides resources for engaging questions concerning bodies.

[35] Pope John Paul II, "From the Justice of Each Comes Peace for All," Message for the Celebration of the World Day of Peace (1 January 1998), no. 3.

"Where is your brother?" His blood cries out to me, says the Lord. This is not a question directed to others; it is a question directed to me, to you, to each of us. These brothers and sisters of ours were trying to escape difficult situations to find some serenity and peace; they were looking for a better place for themselves and their families, but instead they found death. How often do such people fail to find understanding, fail to find acceptance, fail to find solidarity.[36]

Of course, mystical body theology is not a cultural practice that in itself would lead to furthering efforts at genuine solidarity. It does, however, provide a theological account of solidarity rooted in Christ that could be even further developed. If the German-Romantic stream of mystical body theology taught us the dangers of not taking the christological moment to be transformative enough, these are lessons well learned in our contemporary context. On the other side, trajectories in Catholic sensibility that aim to narrow the boundaries of the church, effectively blunting its capacity to serve as a gateway to that same solidarity, may be challenged by the Roman stream's failure to grip the hearts of people and to further just causes of the day. With a clear christological reference point, the theology of the mystical body of Christ, especially in the French stream, portends an eschatological unity realized in pockets, at times surprising and always at the "risk of the body." That deep sense of bodiliness at its best pairs an attention to mediation with a sense of the corporate that is bounded but not in a strict fashion, in other words, a deep attention to solidarity.

[36] Pope Francis, "Homily," Lampedusa, Italy (8 July 2013).

Bibliography

Archival Sources

Virgil Michel Papers, Saint John's Abbey Archives, Saint John's Abbey, Collegeville, MN (SJAA).

Patrick Cummins Papers, Conception Abbey Archives, Conception Abbey, Conception, MO (CAA).

Books, Articles, Manuscripts, and Magisterial Documents

Unless otherwise noted, all magisterial documents were accessed via http://www.vatican.va.

Adam, Karl. *The Christ of Faith: The Christology of the Church*. New York: Pantheon, 1957.

———. "Ekklesiologie im Werden? Kritische Bemerkungen zu M. D. Koster's Kritik an den ekklesiologischen Versuchen der Gegenwart." *Theologische Quartalschrift* 122 (1941): 145–66.

———. "The Mystery of Christ's Incarnation and of His Mystical Body." *Orate Fratres* 13, no. 9 (1939): 337–44, 392–99, 433–40.

———. *One and Holy*. New York: Sheed and Ward, 1951.

———. *The Spirit of Catholicism*. Translated by Justin McCann. Milestones in Catholic Theology. New York: Macmillan, 1948; German original, 1927.

Alberigo, Giuseppe, and Joseph A. Komonchak, eds. *The History of Vatican II*. 5 volumes. Maryknoll, NY: Orbis Books, 1995–2006.

Allmen, Jean-Jacques von, ed. *Veilleur Avant L'Aurore: Colloque Lambert Beauduin, Chevetogne, du 30 Août au 3 Septembre 1976*. Chevetogne, BE: Éditions de Chevetogne, 1978.

Ambrose, Glenn P. "Eucharist as a Means for 'Overcoming' Onto-Theology? The Sacramental Theology of Louis-Marie Chauvet." PhD diss., Graduate Theological Union, 2001.

———. "Psychoanalysis, Social Psychology, and the Sacramental Theology of Louis-Marie Chauvet." Paper presented at the annual meeting of the College Theology Society, Portland, OR, 3–6 June 2010.

———. *The Theology of Louis-Marie Chauvet: Overcoming Onto-Theology with the Sacramental Tradition.* Burlington, VT: Ashgate, 2012.

Anderson, R. Bentley. *Black, White, and Catholic: New Orleans Interracialism, 1947–1956.* Nashville, TN: Vanderbilt University Press, 2008.

Anger, Joseph. *The Doctrine of the Mystical Body of Christ According to the Principles of St. Thomas.* Translated by John J. Burke. New York: Benziger, 1931.

Appleby, Scott. *Church and Age Unite! The Modernist Impulse in American Catholicism.* Notre Dame Studies in American Catholicism. Notre Dame, IN: Notre Dame University Press, 1992.

Arraj, James. *Mind Aflame: The Theological Vision of One of the World's Great Theologians, Émile Mersch.* Chiloquin, OR: Inner Growth Books and Videos, 1994.

Athans, Mary Christine. *The Coughlin-Fahey Connection: Father Charles E. Coughlin, Father Denis Fahey, C.S.Sp., and Religious Anti-Semitism in the United States, 1938–1954.* New York: Peter Lang, 1991.

Aumann, Jordan. *Christian Spirituality in the Catholic Tradition.* San Francisco: Ignatius Press, 1985.

Barth, Karl. "A Theological Dialogue." *Theology Today* 19, no. 2 (1962): 171–77.

Bauerschmidt, Frederick Christian. "'The Body of Christ Is Made From Bread': Transubstantiation and the Grammar of Creation." *International Journal of Systematic Theology* 18, no. 1 (January 2016): 30–46.

Baum, Gregory. "The Laity and the Council." *New Blackfriars* 43, no. 500 (1962): 59–69.

Baxter, Michael J. "Reintroducing Virgil Michel: Towards a Counter-Tradition of Catholic Social Ethics in the United States." *International Catholic Review: Communio* 24 (Autumn 1997): 499–528.

Beauduin, Lambert. "Abbot Marmion and the Liturgy." *Orate Fratres* 22 (May 1948): 303–14.

———. "Jubilé du Monastère de l'Union (1925–1950)." *Irénikon* 23 (1950): 369–76.

———. *Liturgy, the Life of the Church.* Translated by Virgil Michel. Collegeville, MN: Liturgical Press, 1926.

————. *Liturgy, the Life of the Church.* Translated by Virgil Michel. Introduction by Alcuin Reid, OSB. 3rd ed. Hampshire, UK: Saint Michael's Abbey Press, 2002.

————, ed. *Mélanges liturgiques: Recueillis parmi les œuvres de Dom Lambert Beauduin à l' occasion de ses 80 ans (1873–1953).* Louvain, BE: Centre Liturgiques, 1954.

————. *Notre piété pendant l'avent.* Louvain, BE: Mont César, 1919.

————. "Sur le sens des mots 'présence sacramentelle.'" *Les Questions Liturgiques et Paroissiales* 27 (1946): 150–54.

Benedict of Nursia. *The Holy Rule of St. Benedict.* Translated by Rev. Boniface Verheyen, OSB. 1949. Accessed via http://www.ccel.org/ccel/benedict/rule.txt.

Benedict XVI, Pope. *Jesus of Nazareth: From the Baptism in the Jordan to the Transfiguration.* New York: Doubleday, 2007.

Blankenhorn, Bernhard. "The Instrumental Causality of the Sacraments: Thomas Aquinas and Louis-Marie Chauvet." *Nova et Vetera* 4, no. 2 (2006): 255–94.

Bluett, Joseph J. "The Mystical Body: A Bibliography, 1890–1940." *Theological Studies* 3 (1942): 260–89.

————. "'Mystical Body of Christ' and 'Catholic Church' Exactly Coextensive." *Ecclesiastical Review* 103, no. 4 (1940): 305–28.

————. "The Theological Significance of the Encyclical 'Mystici Corporis.'" *Proceedings of the Catholic Theological Society of America* 1 (1946): 46–60.

Boeve, Lieven, and Lambert Leijssen, eds. *Contemporary Sacramental Contours of a God Incarnate.* Studies in Liturgy 16. Proceedings of the International Leuven Encounters in Systematic Theology Conference. Louvain, BE: Peeters, 2001.

————. *Sacramental Presence in a Postmodern Context.* Louvain, BE: Peeters Publishing, 2001.

Bolduan, Kathleen Agnes. "The Life and Work of Dom Ermin Vitry, O.S.B." PhD diss., Washington University, 1976.

Bonaventure. *Itinerarium Mentis ad Deum.* In *Doctoris Seraphici S. Bonaventurae Episcopi Cardinalis Opera Omnia.* Vol. 5. Quaracchi: 1891. Available from: http://faculty.uml.edu/rinnis/45.304%20God%20and%20Philosophy/ITINERARIUM.pdf.

Bordeyne, Philippe, and Bruce T. Morrill, eds. *Sacraments: Revelation of the Humanity of God, Engaging the Fundamental Theology of Louis-Marie Chauvet.* Collegeville, MN: Liturgical Press, 2008.

Botte, Bernard. *From Silence to Participation: An Insider's View of Liturgical Renewal*. Translated by John Sullivan. Washington, DC: Pastoral Press, 1988.

Bousquet, François, et al., eds. *La responsabilité des théologiens: mélanges offerts à Joseph Doré*. Paris: Desclée, 2002.

Bouyer, Louis. *The Church of God: Body of Christ and Temple of the Spirit*. Translated by Charles Underhill Quinn. San Francisco: Ignatius Press, 2011. French original, 1970.

———. *Dom Lambert Beauduin: Un homme d'église*. Paris: Casterman Books, 1964.

———. "Où en est la théologie du corps mystique?" *Revue des Sciences Religieuses* 28 (1948): 313–33.

———. "Où en est le mouvement liturgique?" *La Maison Dieu* 25 (1951): 34–46.

Bracken, Joseph A. "Toward a New Philosophical Theology Based on Intersubjectivity." *Theological Studies* 59 (1998): 703–19.

Breitenfeld, Walter C. "Nazi Liturgy." *New Blackfriars* 27, no. 311 (1946): 44–50.

Brunk, Timothy. "Consumer Culture and the Body: Chauvet's Perspective." *Worship* 82, no. 4 (July 2008): 290–310.

———. *Liturgy and Life: The Unity of Sacraments and Ethics in the Theology of Louis-Marie Chauvet*. American University Studies, 7: Theology and Religion. New York: Peter Lang, 2007.

Burrell, David B. "Perspectives in Catholic Philosophy II." In *Teaching the Tradition: Catholic Themes in Academic Disciplines*, edited by John J. Piderit and Melanie M. Morey, 85–106. New York: Oxford Press, 2012.

Cabezón, José Ignacio, ed. *Scholasticism: Cross-Cultural and Comparative Perspectives*. Albany: State University of New York, 1998.

Callahan, Sidney. "We, the People—of God: The Church Needs a Constitution." *Commonweal* 124, no. 9 (1997): 6–7.

Campbell, Debra. "The Nunk Controversy: A Symbolic Moment in the Search for a Lay Spirituality." *U.S. Catholic Historian* 8, no. 1/2 (1989): 81–89.

Capelle, Bernard. "Crise du movement liturgique?" *Questions Liturgiques et Paroissiales* 32 (1951): 209–17.

Capelletti, Lorenzo. "Sixty Years after *Mystici Corporis*: The Distinction between Creator and Creature." *Thirty Days in the Church and in the World* 21, no. 6 (2003): 44–50.

Carey, Patrick, ed. *American Catholic Religious Thought: The Shaping of a Theological and Social Tradition*. Milwaukee, WI: Marquette University Press, 2004.

———. *Avery Cardinal Dulles: A Model Theologian, 1918–2008*. Mahwah, NJ: Paulist Press, 2010.

———. "Avery Dulles, St. Benedict's Center, and No Salvation Outside the Church, 1940–1953." *Catholic Historical Review* 93 (July 2007): 553–75.

Carstens, Christopher, and Douglas Martis. *Mystical Body, Mystical Voice: Encountering Christ in the Words of the Mass*. Chicago: Liturgy Training Publications, 2011.

Cavanaugh, William T. *Torture and Eucharist: Theology, Politics, and the Body of Christ*. Challenges in Contemporary Theology. Malden, MA: Blackwell Publishing, 1998.

Cerfaux, Lucien. *The Church in the Theology of St. Paul*. Translated by Geoffrey Webb and Adrian Walker. New York: Herder and Herder Publishing, 1959.

Cessario, Romanus. *A Short History of Thomism*. Washington, DC: The Catholic University of America Press, 2005.

Chauvet, Louis-Marie. *Du symbolique au symbole: Essai sur les sacrements*. Paris: Cerf, 1979.

———. "L'Église fait L'Eucharistie; L'Eucharistie fait L'Église: Essai de lecture symbolique." *Catéchèse* 71 (1978): 171–82.

———. "La fonction du prêtre dans le récit de l'institution à la lumière de la linguistique." *Revue de l'Institut Catholique de Paris* 56 (1995): 41–61.

———. "The Liturgy in Its Symbolic Space." *Concilium* (June 1995): 29–40.

———. "Nova et vetera: quelques leçons tirées de la tradition relative au sacrement de la réconciliation." In *Rituels: Mélanges offerts au Pierre-Marie Gy, OP*, edited by Pierre-Marie Gy, Paul de Clerck, and Eric Palazzo, 201–35. Paris: Cerf, 1990.

———. "Le peuple de Dieu et ses ministères." *Prêtres diocésains* 1280 (1990): 127–55.

———. "Ritualité et théologie." *Recherche de Science Religieuse* 78, no. 4 (1990): 535–64.

———. *The Sacraments: The Word of God at the Mercy of the Body*. Translated by Madeleine Beaumont. Collegeville, MN: Liturgical Press, 2001.

———. *Sacrements: Parole de dieu au risque du corps*. Paris: Les Éditions Ouvrières, 1993.

————. "Le sacrifice de la messe: Représentation et expiation." *Lumière et vie* 146 (1980): 69–85.

————. *Symbol and Sacrament: A Sacramental Reinterpretation of Christian Existence*. Translated by Patrick Madigan and Madeleine Beaumont. Collegeville, MN: Liturgical Press, 1995.

————. *Symbole et sacrement: Une relecture sacramentelle de l'existence chrétienne*. Paris: Cerf, 1987.

Chauvet, Louis-Marie, and François Kabasele Lumbala, eds. *Liturgy and the Body*. Concilium 1995, no. 3. Maryknoll, NY: Orbis, 1995.

Chenu, Marie-Dominique. *Aquinas and His Role in Theology*. Translated by Paul Philibert. Collegeville, MN: Liturgical Press, 2002.

————. "Catholic Action and the Mystical Body." In *Restoring All Things: A Guide to Catholic Action*, edited by John Fitzsimmons and Paul McGuire, 1–15. New York: Sheed and Ward, 1938.

————. *Faith and Theology*. Translated by Denis Hickey. New York: Macmillan, 1968; French original, 1964.

————. "Position de la théologie." *Revue des Sciences Philosophiques et Théologiques* 24 (1935): 232–57.

————. *The Theology of Work: An Exploration*. Translated by Lilian Soiron. Chicago: H. Regnery, 1963; French original, 1955.

Chiesa, Lorenzo. *Subjectivity and Otherness: A Philosophical Reading of Lacan*. Cambridge, MA: MIT Press, 2007.

Chinnici, Joseph P., and Angelyn Dries, eds. *Prayer and Practice in the American Catholic Community*. Maryknoll, NY: Orbis Books, 2000.

Chupungco, Anscar J., ed. *Handbook for Liturgical Studies: Fundamental Liturgy*. Collegeville, MN: Liturgical Press, 1998.

Clark, Meghan J. *The Vision of Catholic Social Thought: The Virtue of Solidarity and the Praxis of Human Rights*. Minneapolis: Fortress Press, 2014.

Clouse, Rebecca. "A Postmodern Look at the Mystical Body." *Mystics Quarterly* 20, no. 1 (March 1994): 3–9.

Congar, Yves. *Le Concile de Vatican II: Son église, peuple de Dieu, et corps du Christ*. Théologie Historique 71. Paris: Editions Beauchesne, 1984.

————. *L'Eglise: De Saint Augustine à l'époque moderne*. Paris: Cerf, 1970.

————. *My Journal of the Council*. Translated by Mary John Ronayne and Mary Cecily Boulding. Collegeville, MN: Liturgical Press, 2012.

————. *The Mystery of the Church*. Translated by A. V. Littledale. London: Geoffrey Chapman, 1965; French original, 1953.

————. "Theology in the Council." *The American Ecclesiastical Review* 155, no. 4 (October 1966): 217–30.

Congar, Yves, and Jean-Pierre Jossua, eds. *La liturgie après Vatican II: Bilans, études, prospective.* Unam Sanctum 66. Paris: Cerf, 1967.

Connell, Francis. Review of *The Mystical Body of Christ as the Basic Principle of Religious Life* by Friedrich Jürgensmeier. *Franciscan Studies* 6 (September 1946): 380–81.

Connelly, John. "Reformer and Racialist: Karl Adam's Paradoxical Legacy." *Commonweal* 136 (18 January 2008): 10–13.

Connolly, Michael. "The Glory of Mother Church." *The Irish Monthly* 72, no. 857 (1944): 458–65.

Conway, B. "The Communion of Saints." *Homiletic and Pastoral Review* 7 (1907): 592–600.

Copeland, M. Shawn. *Enfleshing Freedom: Body, Race, and Being.* Minneapolis: Fortress Press, 2010.

Cottier, Georges Cardinal. "The Perception of the Church as 'Reflected Light' That Unites the Fathers of the First Millennium and Vatican Council II." *Thirty Days in the Church and in the World* 29, no. 7/8 (2011): 36–40.

Cyprian of Carthage. *De dominica oratione.* Translated by Robert Ernest Wallis. In *Ante-Nicene Fathers.* Volume 5. Edited by Alexander Roberts, James Donaldson, and A. Cleveland Coxe. Buffalo, NY: Christian Literature Publishing Co., 1886.

Daniélou, Jean. "Les orientations présentes de la pensée religieuse." *Études* 249 (April 1946): 5–21.

Davis, F. Adrian. Review of *It Is Paul Who Writes*, by Ronald Knox and Ronald Cox. *Religious Education* 55, no. 4 (1960): 316.

Day, Dorothy. "Beyond Politics." *Catholic Worker* (November 1949): 1–2, 4.

————. "Explains CW Stand on Use of Force." *Catholic Worker* (September 1938): 1, 4, 7. Dorothy Day Library on the Web. http://www.catholicworker.org/dorothyday.

————. "Liturgy and Sociology." *Catholic Worker* (December 1935): 4. Dorothy Day Library on the Web. http://www.catholicworker.org/dorothyday.

————. *The Long Loneliness.* San Francisco: Harper, 1952.

————. "The Mystical Body of Christ." *Catholic Worker* (October 1934): 3.

————. "On Pilgrimage." *Catholic Worker* (November 1952): 1, 4. Dorothy Day Library on the Web. http://www.catholicworker.org/dorothyday.

Day, Helen Caldwell. *Color, Ebony.* New York: Sheed and Ward, 1951.

————. *Not without Tears.* New York: Sheed and Ward, 1954.

de Certeau, Michel. *The Mystic Fable: The Sixteenth and Seventeenth Centuries.* Chicago: University of Chicago Press, 1992. French original, 1982.

―――. *The Possession at Loudun.* Translated by Michael B. Smith. Chicago: University of Chicago Press, 2000.

de Lubac, Henri. *Catholicism: Christ and the Common Destiny of Man.* Translated by Elizabeth Englund. San Francisco: Ignatius Press, 1988.

―――. *Church: Paradox and Mystery.* Translated by James R. Dunne. New York: Ecclesia Press, 1969. French original, 1967.

―――. *Corpus Mysticum: The Eucharist and the Church in the Middle Ages.* Translated by Gemma Simmonds with Richard Price and Christopher Stephens. Notre Dame, IN: University of Notre Dame Press, 2006.

―――. *The Splendor of the Church.* Translated by Michael Mason. San Francisco: Ignatius Press, 1986.

de Paul, Vincent. *Common Rules* for the Congregation of the Mission (1658). Available from: http://famvin.org/wiki/Common_Rules.

Deck, Allan Figueroa, ed. *Frontiers of Hispanic Theology in the United States.* Maryknoll, NY: Orbis Books, 1992.

Deville, Raymond. "The Seventeenth-Century School of French Spirituality." *Vincentian Heritage Journal* 11, no. 1 (Spring 1990): 17–28.

Diekmann, Godfrey. "The Apostolate." *Orate Fratres* 15, no. 1 (1940): 43.

Doherty, Catherine de Hueck. *Essential Writings.* Selected with an introduction by David Meconi. Maryknoll, NY: Orbis, 2009.

Domenach, Jean-Marie, and Robert de Montvalon, eds. *The Catholic Avant-Garde: French Catholicism Since World War II.* New York: Holt, Rinehart, and Winston, 1967.

Donnelly, Doris, ed. *The Belgian Contribution to the Second Vatican Council.* International Research Conference at Mechelen, Leuven, and Louvain-la-Neuve, September 12–16, 2005. Dudley, MA: Peeters, 2008.

Donnelly, Malachi J. "Magnetic Power of Christ." Review of *The Mystical Body of Christ as the Basic Principle of Religious Life*, by Friedrich Jürgensmeier. *Review for Religious* 5, no. 4 (July 1946): 33–42.

Doyle, Dennis M. *Communion Ecclesiology: Vision and Versions.* Maryknoll, NY: Orbis Books, 2000.

―――. "Otto Semmelroth and the Advance of Church as Sacrament at Vatican II." *Theological Studies* 76, no. 1 (2015): 65–86.

―――. "Otto Semmelroth, SJ, and the Ecclesiology of the 'Church as Sacrament' at Vatican II." In *The Legacy of Vatican II*, edited by Massimo Faggioli and Andrea Vicini, 203–25. Mahwah, NJ: Paulist Press, 2015.

Duby, George. *Guerriers et paysans, vii-xiie siècle. Premier essor de l'économie européenne.* Paris: Gallimard, 1973.

Duff, Howard. "Virgil Michel's Approach to the American Liturgical Movement through His Writings in *Orate Fratres* (1926–1939)." MA thesis, Villanova University, 2016.

Dulles, Avery. "A Half Century of Ecclesiology." *Theological Studies* 50 (1989): 419–42.

———. *Models of the Church.* Exp. ed. New York: Doubleday, 1987.

Echeverria, Eduardo J. *"In the Beginning . . . :" A Theology of the Body.* Eugene, OR: Wipf and Stock, 2011.

Ellard, Gerald. *The Mystical Body and the American Bishops.* St. Louis: The Queen's Work, 1939.

Fagerberg, David W. "Divine Liturgy, Divine Love: Toward a New Understanding of Sacrifice in Christian Worship." *Letter and Spirit* 3 (2007): 95–111.

———. "Exegesis, Mystagogy, and Mystical Body." *Assembly* 35, no. 5 (2009): 77–80.

———. "Liturgy, Social Justice, and the Mystical Body of Christ." *Letter & Spirit* 5 (2009): 193–210.

Faggioli, Massimo. *True Reform: Liturgy and Ecclesiology in* Sacrosanctum Concilium. Collegeville, MN: Liturgical Press, 2012.

Fahey, Denis. *The Mystical Body of Christ and the Reorganization of Society.* Cork, IE: Forum Press, 1945.

Fenton, Joseph Clifford. "An Accusation Against School Theology." *American Ecclesiastical Review* 110, no. 3 (1944): 213–22.

———. "The Act of the Mystical Body." *Ecclesiastical Review* 100 (1939): 397–408.

———. "The Extension of Christ's Mystical Body." *American Ecclesiastical Review* 110, no. 2 (1944): 124–30.

———. "The Status of St. Robert Bellarmine's Teaching about the Membership of Occult Heretics in the Catholic Church." *American Ecclesiastical Review* 122 (March 1950): 207–21.

Finn, Seamus Paul. "Michel's Contribution to Linking Liturgical and Social Apostolates in the American Catholic Church: A 50-Year Perspective." PhD diss., Boston University, 1991.

The First Vatican Council. Divine Constitution on the Catholic Faith *Dei Filius.* 24 April 1870. Available from: http://www.ccel.org/ccel/schaff/creeds2.v.ii.i.html.

Fisher, James Terrence. *The Catholic Counterculture in America 1933–1962.* Chapel Hill: University of North Carolina Press, 1989.

Flynn, Gabriel, ed. *Yves Congar: Theologian of the Church.* Louvain, BE: Peeters, 2005.

Francis, Pope. "Homily." Lampedusa, IT. 8 July 2013.

Franklin, William R., and Robert Spaeth. *Virgil Michel: American Catholic.* Collegeville, MN: Liturgical Press, 1988.

Furfey, Paul Hanly. *Fire on the Earth.* New York: Macmillan Company, 1936.

Gabrielli, Timothy R. *Confirmation: How a Sacrament of God's Grace Became All about Us.* Collegeville, MN: Liturgical Press, 2013.

Gaillardetz, Richard R. *The Church in the Making:* Lumen Gentium, Christus Dominus, Orientalium Ecclesiarum. Rediscovering Vatican II. Mahwah, NJ: Paulist Press, 2006.

Garrigou-Lagrange, Reginald. "L'Église, corps mystique du Christ." *La Vie Spirituelle* 18 (1928): 6–23.

———. *Reality: A Synthesis of Thomistic Thought.* Translated by Patrick Cummins. St. Louis: B. Herder, 1950.

———. *The Three Ages of the Interior Life.* Translated by M. Timothea Doyle. Volume 1. St. Louis: B. Herder, 1947.

Garry, W. J. Review of *The Mystical Body of Christ as the Basic Principle of Religious Life*, by Friedrich Jürgensmeier. *America* 62, no. 3 (28 October 1939): 80.

Girard, René. *Violence and the Sacred.* Translated by Patrick Gregory. Baltimore: Johns Hopkins University Press, 1979.

Gibeau, Dawn. "Fr. Virgil, St. John's Monks Spread Idea that Liturgy Creates Community." *National Catholic Reporter* 30, no. 13 (10 December 1993): 13.

Gleason, Philip, ed. *Contemporary Catholicism in the United States.* Notre Dame, IN: University of Notre Dame, 1969.

Godzieba, Anthony J. "*Agnus Dei*: Sin, Sacrament, and Subjectivity in the Liturgical Imagination." *Louvain Studies* 34, no. 2–3 (2010): 249–74.

———. "Bodies and Persons, Resurrected and Postmodern: Towards a Relational Eschatology." In *Theology and Conversation: Towards a Relational Theology*, edited by Jacques Haers and Peter De Mey, 211–25. Louvain, BE: University Press, 2003.

———. "Caravaggio, Theologian: Baroque Piety and Poiesis in a Forgotten Chapter of the History of Catholic Theology." In *Theology and Lived Christianity*, edited by David M. Hammond, 206–30. The Annual Publication of the College Theology Society. Volume 45. Maryknoll, NY: Orbis Books, 2000.

———. "Incarnation, Theory, and Catholic Bodies: What Should Post-Postmodern Catholic Theology Look Like?" *Louvain Studies* 28, no. 3 (Fall 2003): 217–31.

———. "Prolegomena to a Catholic Theology of God Between Heidegger and Postmodernity." *Heythrop Journal* 40 (1999): 319–39.

Godzieba, Anthony J., Lieven Boeve, and Michele Saracino. "Resurrection—Interruption—Transformation: Incarnation as a Hermeneutical Strategy, A Symposium." *Theological Studies* 67, no. 4 (2006): 777–815.

Goizueta, Roberto. "The Symbolic Realism of U.S. Latino/a Popular Catholicism." *Theological Studies* 65, no. 2 (June 2004): 255–74.

Goodier, Alban. "The Mystical Body." *The Month* 159 (1932): 289–97.

Grabmann, Martin. "The Influence of Medieval Philosophy on the Intellectual Life of Today." Translated by Virgil Michel. *The New Scholasticism* 3, no. 1 (January 1929): 24–56.

———. *Thomas Aquinas: His Personality and His Thought.* Translated by Virgil Michel. Collegeville, MN: Liturgical Press, 1928.

Grabowski, Stanislaus J. "St. Augustine and the Doctrine of the Mystical Body of Christ." *Theological Studies* 7, no. 1 (1946): 72–125.

Granfield, Patrick. "The Church as *Societas Perfecta* in the Schemata of Vatican I." *Church History* 48, no. 4 (1979): 431–46.

Groppe, Elizabeth Teresa. *Yves Congar's Theology of the Holy Spirit.* The American Academy of Religion Academy Series. Edited by Kimberly Rae Connor. New York: Oxford University Press, 2004.

Grumett, David. *De Lubac: A Guide for the Perplexed.* New York: T&T Clark, 2007.

Guardini, Romano. *The Church and the Catholic.* Translated by Ada Lane. New York: Sheed and Ward, 1940.

———. *The Church of the Lord: On the Nature and Mission of the Church.* Translated by Stella Lange. Chicago: Regnery, 1966.

———. *The Essential Guardini: An Anthology of the Writings of Romano Guardini.* Edited by Heinz R. Kuehn. Chicago: Liturgy Training Publications, 1997.

———. *The Spirit of the Liturgy.* Translated by Ada Lane. Milestones in Catholic Theology. New York: Crossroad Publishing, 1998.

Guarino, Thomas G. *Foundations of Systematic Theology.* New York: T&T Clark, 2005.

Gy, Pierre-Marie. *The Reception of Vatican II: Liturgical Reforms in the Life of the Church*. The Père Marquette Lecture in Theology. Foreword by John D. Laurance. Milwaukee, WI: Marquette University Press, 2003.

Hahnenberg, Edward. "The Mystical Body of Christ and Communion Ecclesiology: Historical Parallels." *Irish Theological Quarterly* 70, no. 1 (March 2005): 3–30.

Hall, Jeremy. *The Full Stature of Christ: The Ecclesiology of Virgil Michel*. Collegeville, MN: Liturgical Press, 1976.

Hammond, David M., ed. *Theology and Lived Christianity*. Mystic, CT: Twenty-Third Publications, 2000.

Harmon, Katharine E. *There Were Also Many Women There: Lay Women in the Liturgical Movement in the United States, 1926–59*. Collegeville, MN: Liturgical Press, 2012.

Hatch, Derek C., and Timothy R. Gabrielli, eds. *Weaving the American Catholic Tapestry: Essays in Honor of William L. Portier*. Eugene, OR: Wipf & Stock, 2017.

Hebden, Scott. "Liturgy and Social Justice: Recovering the Prophetic Vision of Virgil Michel." *Chicago Studies* 46, no. 2 (Summer 2007): 238–48.

Heidegger, Martin. "The Onto-Theo-Logical Constitution of Metaphysics." In *Identity and Difference*, 42–76. Translated by Joan Stambaugh. New York: Harper and Row, 1969.

———. *The Piety of Thinking, Essays by Martin Heidegger*. Translated by James G. Hart and John C. Maraldo. Bloomington: Indiana University Press, 1976.

Hemming, Lawrence Paul. "Henri de Lubac: Reading *Corpus Mysticum*." *New Blackfriars* 90, no. 1029 (September 2009): 519–34.

Hennesey, James. "Leo XIII: Intellectualizing the Combat with Modernity." *U.S. Catholic Historian* 7, no. 4 (Fall 1988): 393–400.

Henry, A. M., ed. *The Historical and Mystical Christ*. Theology Library. Volume 5. Chicago: Fides, 1958.

Hill, Roland. "Obituary: Johanna Breitenfeld." *The Independent*. 14 October 1992. Available from: http://www.independent.co.uk/news/people/obituary-johanna-breitenfeld-1557356.html.

Himes, Kenneth R. "Eucharist and Justice: Assessing the Legacy of Virgil Michel." *Worship* 62 (1988): 201–24.

Himes, Michael J. *Ongoing Incarnation: Johann Adam Möhler and the Beginnings of Modern Ecclesiology*. New York: Crossroad Publishing, 1997.

Horrell, David G. *Solidarity and Difference: A Contemporary Reading of Paul's Ethics*. London: T&T Clark, 2005.

Hurley, Denis E. "Council Reminiscences." Symposium at Heythrop College, Kensington, London, 12 October 2002. *The Downside Review* 422 (January 2003): 53–56.

Jodock, Darrell. ed. *Catholicism Contending with Modernity: Roman Catholic Modernism and Anti-Modernism in Historical Context*. Cambridge, UK: Cambridge University Press, 2000.

John Paul II, Pope. "From the Justice of Each Comes Peace for All." Message for the Celebration of the World Day of Peace. 1 January 1998.

———. *Sollicitudo Rei Socialis*, Encyclical Letter for the Twentieth Anniversary of *Populorum Progressio*. 30 December 1987.

Johnson, Luke Timothy, and William S. Kurz. *The Future of Catholic Biblical Scholarship: A Constructive Conversation*. Grand Rapids, MI: Eerdmans, 2002.

Jones, Cheslyn, Geoffrey Wainwright, and Edward Yarnold, eds. *The Study of Spirituality*. New York: Oxford University Press, 1986.

Josephinum Journal of Theology 18, no. 1 (2011).

Joyce, George H. "Mystical Body of the Church." In *The Catholic Encyclopedia: An International Work of Reference on the Constitution, Doctrine, Discipline, and History of the Catholic Church*, edited by Charles G. Herbermann et al., volume 10, 663. New York: Robert Appleton Company, 1911.

Jürgensmeier, Friedrich. *The Mystical Body of Christ as the Basic Principle of Religious Life*. Translated by H. Gardner Curtis. Milwaukee, WI: Bruce Press, 1939.

Kelleher, Margaret M. "Liturgy and Social Transformation: Exploring the Relationship." *U.S. Catholic Historian* 16, no. 4 (1998): 58–70.

Kelly, Anthony. "'Body of Christ: Amen!' The Expanding Incarnation." *Theological Studies* 71 (2010): 792–816.

Kelly, Timothy. "Christ and the Church: *Duo in Carne Una*; A Study of the Union of Christ and the Members of His Mystical Body from the Vantage Point of Its Bodiliness." PhD diss., University of Fribourg, 2010.

Kerkvoorde, Augustus. "La théologie du Corps Mystique au dix-neuvième siècle." *Nouvelle Revue Théologique* 67 (1945): 417–30.

Kerlin, Michael. "Reginald Garrigou-Lagrange: Defending the Faith from *Pascendi dominici gregis* to *Humani Generis*." *U.S. Catholic Historian* 25, no. 1 (Winter 2007): 97–113.

Klejment, Anne. "The Spirituality of Dorothy Day's Pacifism." *U.S. Catholic Historian* 27, no. 2 (June 2009): 1–24.

Komonchak, Joseph. "Theology and Culture at Mid-Century: The Case of Henri de Lubac." *Theological Studies* 51, no. 4 (1990): 579–602.

Krieg, Robert A. *Catholic Theologians in Nazi Germany.* New York: Continuum, 2004.

———. *Karl Adam: Catholicism in German Culture.* Foreword by Walter Kasper. Notre Dame, IN: University of Notre Dame Press, 1992.

———. "Karl Adam, National Socialism, and Christian Tradition." *Theological Studies* 60 (1999): 432–56.

LaFarge, John. *The Catholic View Point on Race Relations.* Garden City, NY: Hanover House, 1960.

———. *Interracial Justice: A Study of the Catholic Doctrine of Race Relations.* New York: America Press, 1937.

———. *The Race Question and the Negro.* New York: Longmans, 1943.

Lakeland, Paul. *Church: Living Communion.* Engaging Theology: Catholic Perspectives. Collegeville, MN: Liturgical Press, 2009.

Lamberts, Jozef. "The Abbey of Mont-César in Louvain: One Hundred Years Young." *Worship* 73, no. 5 (September 1999): 425–42.

Lechner, Frank J., and John Boli. *The Globalization Reader.* 2nd ed. Malden, MA: Blackwell, 2004.

Lee, Michelle. *Paul, the Stoics, and the Body of Christ.* Society for New Testament Studies Monograph Series. Cambridge, UK: Cambridge University Press, 2006.

Leeming, Bernard. "Doctrine of the Mystical Body and Its Connection with Oecumenical Work." *Eastern Churches Quarterly* 7 (October 1948): 519–37.

Leo XIII, Pope. *Aeterni Patris*: On the Restoration of Christian Philosophy. 4 August 1879.

Lescher, Bruce H., and Elizabeth Liebert, eds. *Exploring Christian Spirituality: Essays in Honor of Sandra M. Schneiders.* Mahwah, NJ: Paulist Press, 2006.

———. *Satis Cognitum*: On the Unity of the Church. 29 June 1896.

Lialine, D. C. "Une étape en ecclésiologie: Reflexions sur l'encyclique 'Mystici Corporis.'" *Irénikon* 19 (1946): 129–52, 283–317; 20 (1947): 34–54.

Livingston, James C., et al. *Modern Christian Thought: The Twentieth Century.* 2 Volumes. 2nd ed. Minneapolis: Fortress Press, 2006.

Loonbeek, Raymond, and Jacques Mortiau. *Un pionnier: Dom Lambert Beauduin (1873–1960): Liturgie et unité des chrétiens.* University of Louvain Works of History and Philology. Volume 1. Louvain-la-Neuve, BE: Éditions de Chevetogne, 2001.

Lord, Daniel A. *Our Part in the Mystical Body.* St. Louis: The Queen's Work, 1935.

Lortz, Joseph. *History of the Church.* Milwaukee, WI: Bruce, 1938.

Loughlin, Gerard, ed. *Queer Theology: Rethinking the Western Body*. Malden, MA: Blackwell, 2007.

Maas-Ewerd, Theodor. *Die Krise der liturgischen Bewegung in Deutschland und Österreich: Zu den Auseinandersetzungen um die "liturgische Frage" in den Jahren 1939 bis 1944*. Regensburg, DE: Pustet, 1981.

MacCarthy, Sean. "Teaching the Mystical Body: A Suggestion." *The Furrow* 4, no. 5 (1953): 269–70.

Macy, Gary. *The Theologies of the Eucharist in the Early Scholastic Period*. Oxford, UK: Clarendon Press, 1984.

Malanowski, Gregory E. "The Christocentrism of Émile Mersch and Its Implications for a Theology of Church." STD diss., The Catholic University of America, 1988.

———. "Émile Mersch, SJ (1890–1940): Un Christocentrisme unifié." *Nouvelle Revue Théologique* 112 (1990): 44–66.

Marchetti-Selvaggiani, F. Cardinal. "Letter to Archbishop Richard J. Cushing. 8 August 1949." *The American Ecclesiastical Review* 127 (1952): 307–15.

Marx, Paul. *Virgil Michel and the Liturgical Movement*. Collegeville, MN: Liturgical Press, 1957.

Mauss, Marcel. "Essai sur le don." In *Sociologie et anthropologie*, 143–279. Paris: Presses Universitaires France, 1950.

McBrien, Richard P. *The Church: The Evolution of Catholicism*. New York: Harper Collins, 2008.

———. "The Church (*Lumen Gentium*)." In *Contemporary Catholic Theology: A Reader*, edited by Michael A. Hayes and Liam Gearon, 279–93. New York: Continuum, 1998.

McGinn, Bernard, John Meyendorf, and Jean Leclerc, eds. *Christian Spirituality: Origins to the Twelfth Century*. New York: Crossroad Publishers, 1987.

McGreevy, John T. *Catholicism and American Freedom: A History*. New York: Norton, 2003.

———. *Parish Boundaries: The Catholic Encounter with Race in the Twentieth-Century Urban North*. University of Chicago Press, 1998.

McKenna, Stephen M. "The Mystical Body in the Political and Social Sphere." *Ecclesiastical Review* 103, no. 3 (September 1940): 209–18.

McNamara, Kevin. "The Ecclesiological Movement in Germany in the Twentieth Century." *Irish Ecclesiastical Record* 102 (November 1964): 345–58.

McSorley, Joseph. "The Mystical Body of Christ." *Catholic World* 131 (1905): 307–14.

Merleau-Ponty, Maurice. *Phenomenology of Perception.* Translated by Colin Smith. New York: Humanities Press, 1962.

———. *The Visible and the Invisible.* Edited by Claude Lefort. Translated by Alphonso Lingis. Northwestern University Studies in Phenomenology and Existential Philosophy. Evanston, IL: Northwestern University Press, 1968.

Mersch, Émile. *Le corps mystique du Christ: Études de la théologie historique.* 2 volumes. Louvain, BE: Museum Lessianum, 1933.

———. *Le corps mystique du Christ: Études de la théologie historique.* 2 volumes. 2nd ed. Paris: Desclée de Brouwer, 1946.

———. *The Theology of the Mystical Body.* Translated by Cyril Vollert. St. Louis: B. Herder Publishing, 1951.

———. *The Whole Christ: The Historical Development of the Doctrine of the Mystical Body in Scripture and Tradition.* Translated by John R. Kelly. Milwaukee, WI: Bruce, 1938.

Merton, Thomas. *The Ascent to Truth: A Study of St. John of the Cross.* New York: Harcourt and Brace Books, 1951.

Michel, Virgil. *Christian Social Reconstruction: Some Fundamentals of the Quadragesimo Anno.* Milwaukee, WI: Bruce, 1937.

———. "The Family and the Mystical Body." *Orate Fratres* 11, no. 7 (1937): 295–99.

———. "Foreword." *Orate Fratres* 1, no. 1 (1926): 1–4.

———. Foreword to *A Personalist Manifesto,* by Emmanuel Mounier. Translated by the monks of Saint John's Abbey. New York: Longmans, Green Co., 1938.

———. "I Am the Vine, You Are the Branches." *Orate Fratres* 5 (1931): 190–92, 242–44, 286–88, 337.

———. "The Intellectual Confusion of To-day and the '*Philosophia Perennis.*'" *The Fortnightly Review* 33, no. 10 (1926): 211–12.

———. "The Liturgical Movement and the Future." *America* 54, no. 1 (1935): 6–7.

———. "The Liturgy and Catholic Life." Unpublished manuscript (1936). Virgil Michel Papers. SJAA. Series Z, Box 33, Folder 3A.

———. *The Liturgy of the Church: According to the Roman Rite.* New York: Macmillan Company, 1937.

———. "The Mansions of Thomistic Philosophy." Unpublished manuscript. Virgil Michel Papers. SJAA. Series Z, Box 33, Folder 8.

———. *My Sacrifice and Yours.* Collegeville, MN: Liturgical Press, 1926.

———. "The Mystical Body." *Commonweal* 29 (1938): 18.

———. "The Mystical Body." *Orate Fratres* 10 (1936): 419–21.

———. "The Mystical Body of Christ in the Modern World." *Orate Fratres* 10 (1936): 236.

———. "Mysticism and Normal Christianity: The Place of Liturgy in Mysticism." *Orate Fratres* 13 (1939): 545–48.

———. "Natural and Supernatural Society." *Orate Fratres* 10 (1936): 243–47, 293–96, 338–42, 394–98, 434–38.

———. "An Organic Superpersonality?" *The Philosophical Review* 36, no. 2 (March 1927): 178–80.

———. "Political Principles of St. Thomas." Unpublished manuscript. Virgil Michel Papers. SJAA. Series Z, Box 33, Folder 8.6.

———. "Ownership and the Human Person." *The Review of Politics* 1, no. 2 (March 1939): 155–78.

———. "The Parish, the Cell of Christian Life." *Orate Fratres* 11 (1937): 433–40.

———. "The Philosophical and Theological Bases of the Liturgical Movement." Unpublished manuscript. Virgil Michel Papers. SJAA. Series Z, Box 33, Folder 5.

———. *Philosophy of Human Conduct*. Minneapolis: Burgess Publishing Company, 1936.

———. "Political Catholicism." *Orate Fratres* 13 (1938): 79–81.

———. "Reflections on a Scholastic Synthesis." *The New Scholasticism* 2, no. 1 (January 1928): 1–17.

———. "Religious Experience: Liturgy Depersonalizes Piety?" *Orate Fratres* 13, no. 11 (1 October 1939): 493–96.

———. Review of *The Church Catholic and the Spirit of the Liturgy*, by Romano Guardini. *Orate Fratres* 10 (1936): 238.

———. Review of *The Mystical Body of Christ*, by Fulton Sheen. *Orate Fratres* 10 (April 1936), 281–85.

———. *The Social Question: Essays on Capitalism and Christianity by Fr. Virgil Michel, O.S.B.* Edited by Robert L. Spaeth. Collegeville, MN: Saint John's University, 1987.

———. "The True Christian Spirit." *The Ecclesiastical Review* 82 (February 1930): 128–42.

———. "Why Scholastic Philosophy Lives." *The Philosophical Review* 36, no. 2 (March 1927): 166–73.

———. "With Our Readers." *Orate Fratres* 3 (April 1929): 186–87.

Michel, Virgil, and Martin B. Hellriegel. *The Liturgical Movement*. Collegeville, MN: Saint John's Abbey, 1930.

Michel, Virgil, in collaboration with the monks of Saint John's Abbey, Collegeville, MN, and the Sisters of the Order of St. Dominic, Marywood, Grand Rapids, MI. *Our Life in Christ.* The Christian Religion Series for College. Collegeville, MN: Liturgical Press, 1939.

Michel, Virgil, with the assistance of the Sisters of St. Dominic, Grand Rapids, MI. *The Christian in the World.* Christ-Life Series in Religion. Second Series. Volume 4. Collegeville, MN: Saint John's Abbey, 1937.

Miller, Vincent J. "An Abyss at the Heart of Mediation: Louis-Marie Chauvet's Fundamental Theology of Sacramentality." *Horizons* 24, no. 2 (1997): 230–47.

———. *Consuming Religion: Christian Faith and Practice in a Consumer Culture.* New York: Continuum, 2004.

———. "Where Is the Church? Globalization and Catholicity." *Theological Studies* 69, no. 2 (June 2008): 412–32.

Möhler, Johann Adam. *Unity in the Church or the Principle of Catholicism, Presented in the Spirit of the Church Fathers of the First Three Centuries.* Edited and translated with an introduction by Peter C. Erb. Washington, DC: The Catholic University of America Press, 1996.

Moloney, Raymond. "Henri de Lubac on Church and Eucharist." *Irish Theological Quarterly* 70, no. 4 (December 2005): 331–42.

Moore, Brenna. "How to Awaken the Dead: Michel de Certeau, Henri de Lubac, and the Instabilities between the Past and the Present." *Spiritus* 12 (Fall 2012): 172–79.

Moore, Gareth. *Body in Context: Sex and Catholicism.* Contemporary Christian Insights. New York: Continuum, 2005.

Moran, Annette. "The Church and the Fiction Writer: The Fiction of Flannery O'Connor and the *Corpus Christi Mysticum* Ecclesiology." PhD diss., Graduate Theological Union, 1994.

Morrill, Bruce T., ed. *Bodies of Worship: Explorations in Theory and Practice.* Collegeville, MN: Liturgical Press, 1999.

Myers, Edward. *The Mystical Body of Christ.* London: Burns and Oates, 1930.

Napiwodzki, Piotr. "Eine Ekklesiologie im Werden: Mannes Dominikus Koster und sein Beitrag zum theologischen Verständnis der Kirch." PhD diss., University of Fribourg, 2005.

Nédoncelle, Maurice, et al., eds. *L'Ecclésiologie au XIXe siècle.* Unam Sanctam no. 34. Paris: Cerf, 1960.

Newman, John Henry. *Roman Catholic Writings on Doctrinal Development.* Translated with commentary by James Gaffney. Kansas City, MO: Sheed and Ward, 1997.

Noble (Dolejšová), Ivana. "Apophatic Aspects of Theological Conversation." In *Theology and Conversation: Towards a Relational Theology*, edited by Jacques Haers and Peter De Mey, 163–76. Louvain, BE: University Press, 2003.

———. "From the Sacramentality of the Church to the Sacramentality of the World: An Exploration of the Theology of Alexander Schmemann and Louis-Marie Chauvet." In *Charting Churches in a Changing Europe: Charta Oecumenica and the Process of Ecumenical Encounter*, edited by Tim and Ivana Noble, Martien E. Brinkman, and Jochen Hilberath, 165–200. Currents of Encounter Series. New York: Rodopi, 2006.

———. "The Symbolic Nature of Christian Existence According to Ricoeur and Chauvet." *Communio Viatorum* 43, no. 1 (2001): 39–59.

Novick, Peter. *That Noble Dream: The "Objectivity Question" and the American Historical Profession*. Cambridge, UK: Cambridge University Press, 1988.

O'Brien, Kenneth Paul, and Lynn Hudson Parsons, eds. *The Home-Front War: World War II and American Society*. Contributions in American History 161. Westport, CT: Greenwood, 1995.

O'Connell, Marvin R. *Critics on Trial: An Introduction to the Catholic Modernist Crisis*. Washington, DC: The Catholic University of America Press, 1995.

O'Connell, Maureen, and Laurie Cassidy, eds. *Religion, Economics, and Culture in Conflict and Conversation*. The Annual Publication of the College Theology Society. Volume 56. Maryknoll, NY: Orbis Books, 2011.

O'Connor, William R. "The Mystical Body of Christ: Reality or Metaphor?" *The Irish Ecclesiastical Record* 46 (1935): 136–53.

Osborne, Kenan. *A Theology of the Church for the Third Millennium: A Franciscan Approach*. Leiden, NL: Brill, 2009.

Ott, Ludwig. *Fundamentals of Catholic Dogma*. Translated by Patrick Lynch. Cork, IE: Mercier Press, 1955.

Pecklers, Keith F. *The Unread Vision: The Liturgical Movement in the United States of America, 1926–1955*. Collegeville, MN: Liturgical Press, 1998.

Peddicord, Richard. *The Sacred Monster of Thomism: An Introduction to the Life and Legacy of Reginald Garrigou-Lagrange, O.P.* South Bend, IN: St. Augustine's Press, 2005.

Pelz, Karl. *Der Christ als Christus: Der Weg meines Forschens*. Berlin: Pelz, 1939. Printed from manuscript.

Pepper, George B. *The Boston Heresy Case in View of the Secularization of Religion: A Case Study in the Sociology of Religion*. Lewiston, NY: E. Mellen Press, 1988.

Phan, Peter C., ed. *The Gift of the Church: A Textbook on Ecclesiology in Honor of Patrick Granfield, O.S.B.* Collegeville, MN: Liturgical Press, 2000.

Philips, Gérard. *L'Église et son mystère au IIe Concile du Vatican: Histoire, texte, et commentaire de la constitution* "Lumen gentium." Volume 1. Paris: Desclée, 1967.

Pius X, Pope. *Pascendi Dominici Gregis: On the Doctrines of the Modernists.* 9 August 1907.

Pius XII, Pope. *Humani Generis:* Concerning Some False Opinions Threatening to Undermine the Foundations of Catholic Doctrine. 12 August 1950.

———. *Mediator Dei:* On the Sacred Liturgy. 20 November 1947.

———. *Mystici Corporis Christi:* On the Church as the Mystical Body of Christ. 29 June 1943.

Pomedli, Michael M. "Ojibwa Influences on Virgil Michel." *Worship* 70, no. 6 (1996): 531–42.

Portier, William L. "*Ancilla Invita:* Heidegger, the Theologians, and God." *Sciences Religieuses* 14, no. 2 (Spring 1985): 161-80.

———. *Divided Friends: Portraits of the Roman Catholic Modernist Crisis in the United States.* Washington, DC: The Catholic University of America Press, 2013.

———. "'Good Friday in December': World War II in the Editorials of Preservation of the Faith Magazine, 1939-1945." *U.S. Catholic Historian* 27, no. 2 (2009): 25-44.

———. "Paul Hanley Furfey: Catholic Extremist and Supernatural Sociologist, 1935-1941." *Josephinum Journal of Theology* 16, no. 1 (Winter/Spring 2009): 24-37.

Prentiss, Craig. *Debating God's Economy: Social Justice in America on the Eve of Vatican II.* University Park, PA: Penn State University Press, 2008.

Preston, Geoffrey. *Faces of the Church: Meditations on a Mystery and Its Images.* Text prepared by Aidan Nichols. With a foreword by Walter Kasper. Grand Rapids, MI: Eerdmans, 1997.

Prétot, Patrick. "Louis-Marie Chauvet à l'Insitut Supérieur de Liturgie." *Transversalités* 111 (July–September 2009): 177-83.

Prusak, Bernard P. *The Church Unfinished: Ecclesiology Through the Centuries.* Mahwah, NJ: Paulist Press, 2004.

Quitslund, Sonya A. *Beauduin: A Prophet Vindicated.* New York: Newman Press, 1973.

Ratzinger, Joseph. *Church, Ecumenism, and Politics: New Endeavors in Ec-clesiology.* Translated by Michael J. Miller, et al. San Francisco: Ignatius Press, 2008. German original, 1987.

————. *Principles of Catholic Theology: Building Stones for a Fundamental Theology.* Translated by Mary Frances McCarthy. San Francisco: Ignatius Press, 1987. German original, 1982.

Rausch, Thomas. *Towards a Truly Catholic Church: An Ecclesiology for the Third Millennium.* Collegeville, MN: Liturgical Press, 2005.

Reher, Margaret M. "Cardinal Dougherty and the IHMs: The Church as the 'Juridic/Mystical' Body of Christ." *U.S. Catholic Historian* 14, no. 4 (1996): 53–62.

Reid, Alcuin. *The Organic Development of the Liturgy: The Principles of Liturgical Reform and Their Relation to the Twentieth-Century Liturgical Movement Prior to the Second Vatican Council.* Farnborough, UK: St. Michael's Abbey Press, 2004.

Reinhold, H. A. "Denver and Maria Laach." *Commonweal* 45 (1946): 86–88.

Rice, Lincoln R. "Confronting the Heresy of 'The Mythical Body of Christ': The Life of Dr. Arthur Falls." *American Catholic Studies* 123, no. 2 (2012): 59–77.

Rikhof, Herwi. *The Concept of Church: A Methodological Inquiry into the Use of Metaphors in Ecclesiology.* London: Sheed and Ward, 1981.

Rivera, Joseph. "*Corpus Mysticum* and Religious Experience: Henry, Lacoste, and Marion." *International Journal of Systematic Theology* 14, no. 3 (July 2012): 327–49.

Roach, John, ed. *The Future of the Catholic Church in America.* Papers Presented at the Symposium Honoring Virgil Michel, OSB, from July 11–14, 1988, at Saint John's Abbey in Collegeville, MN. Collegeville, MN: Liturgical Press, 1991.

Ross, Susan. "'Then Honor God in Your Body' (1 Cor 6:20): Feminist and Sacramental Theology on the Body." *Horizons* 16, no. 1 (1989): 7–27.

Ruokanen, Miikka. *The Catholic Doctrine of Non-Christian Religions.* Leiden, NL: Brill, 1992.

Russett, Bruce. "We the People of God: How Democratic Should the Church Be?" *Commonweal* 130, no. 15 (2003): 27–30.

Saint John's Abbey, compiler. *The Mystical Body and Social Justice.* The Social Problem: Lectures Given during the Central Verein Institute for Social Study. Book 4. Collegeville, MN: Saint John's Abbey, 1936–1938.

Sandbrook, Dominic. *Eugene McCarthy: The Rise and Fall of Postwar American Liberalism*. New York: Alfred A. Knopf, 2004.

Schloesser, Stephen. *Jazz Age Catholicism: Mystic Modernism in Postwar Paris, 1919–1933*. Toronto: University of Toronto Press, 2005.

Schmidt, Katherine G. "Virtual Communion: Theology of the Internet and the Catholic Imagination." PhD diss., University of Dayton, 2016.

Schneiders, Sandra M. "Spirituality in the Academy." *Theological Studies* 50, no. 4 (1989): 676–97.

Scully, J. Eileen. "The Theology of the Mystical Body of Christ in French Language Theology 1930–1950: A Review and Assessment." *Irish Theological Quarterly* 58, no. 1 (March 1992): 58–74.

The Second Vatican Council. *Ad Gentes*: Decree on the Mission Activity of the Church. 7 December 1965.

———. *Apostolicam Actuositatem*: Decree on the Apostolate of Laity. 18 November 1965.

———. *Christus Dominus*: Decree on the Pastoral Office of Bishops. 28 October 1965.

———. *Lumen Gentium*: Dogmatic Constitution on the Church. 21 November 1964.

———. *Perfectae Caritatis*: Decree on Renewal of Religious Life. 28 October 1965.

———. *Sacrosanctum Concilium*: Constitution on the Sacred Liturgy. 4 December 1963.

Segal, Alan. *Paul the Convert: The Apostolate and Apostasy of Saul the Pharisee*. New Haven, CT: Yale University Press, 1992.

Sheen, Fulton. "Catholic Action and the Mystical Body." *Homiletic and Pastoral Review* 35 (1935): 866–73.

Skolnikoff, Jessica, and Robert Engvall. *Young Athletes, Couch Potatoes, and Helicopter Parents: The Productivity of Play*. Lanham, MD: Rowman and Littlefield, 2014.

Spicer, Kevin P., ed. *Antisemitism, Christian Ambivalence, and the Holocaust*. Papers from a Workshop at the Center for Advanced Holocaust Studies of the United States Holocaust Memorial Museum in Washington, DC, Summer 2004. Bloomington: Indiana University Press, 2007.

———. *Hitler's Priests: Catholic Clergy and National Socialism*. DeKalb: Northern Illinois University Press, 2008.

Stamps, Mary E. *To Do Justice and Right upon the Earth: Papers from the Virgil Michel Symposium on Liturgy and Social Justice*. Collegeville, MN: Liturgical Press, 1993.

Sturzo, Luigi. *Spiritual Problems of Our Times*. New York: Longmans, Green, and Company, 1945.

Taylor, Charles. *A Secular Age*. Cambridge, MA: Harvard University Press, 2007.

Thomas Aquinas. *Summa Theologiae*. Available from: http://www.corpus thomisticum.org/sth0000.html.

Thompson, William M. *Bérulle and the French School: Selected Writings*. Mahwah, NJ: Paulist Press, 1989.

Thorn, William J., Phillip M. Runkel, and Susan Mountin, eds. *Dorothy Day and the Catholic Worker Movement: Centenary Essays*. Marquette Studies in Theology 32. Milwaukee, WI: Marquette University Press, 2001.

Tomlinson, John. *Globalization and Culture*. Chicago: University of Chicago Press, 1999.

Torrell, Jean-Pierre. *Saint Thomas Aquinas*. Volume 1: *The Person and His Work*. Rev. ed. Translated by Robert Royal. Washington, DC: The Catholic University of America Press, 2005.

Tracy, David. "The Uneasy Alliance Reconceived: Catholic Theological Method, Modernity, and Postmodernity." *Theological Studies* 50, no. 3 (September 1989): 548–70.

Tromp, Sebastian. *Corpus Christi, Quod Est Ecclesia*. Volume 1: *Introductio Generalis*. Rome: Gregorian University, 1937.

———. *Corpus Christi, Quod Est Ecclesia*. Volume 1: *Introductio Generalis*. Rev. and exp. ed. Rome: Gregorian University, 1946.

———. *Corpus Christi, Quod Est Ecclesia*. Translated by Ann Condit. New York: Vantage Press, 1960.

Turner, Bryan S. *Vulnerability and Human Rights*. University Park, PA: Penn State University Press, 2006.

Tyrrell, George. "The Relation of Theology to Devotion." *The Month* (November 1899): 461–73.

Vereb, Jerome-Michael. *"Because He Was a German!" Cardinal Bea and the Origins of Roman Catholic Engagement in the Ecumenical Movement*. Grand Rapids, MI: Eerdmans, 2006.

Vergote, Antoine. "The Body as Understood in Contemporary Thought and Biblical Categories." *Philosophy Today* 35 (1991): 93–105.

———. "Lacan's Project of Retrieving Freud's Theory of the Subject." In *Phenomenology and Lacanian Psychoanalysis*, edited by Richard Rojcewicz, 29–51. The Eighth Annual Symposium of the Simon Silverman Phenomenology Center. Pittsburg, PA: Duquesne University, 1992.

Vitry, Ermin. "The Spiritual Doctrine of Abbot Marmion." *Orate Fratres* 15, no. 1 (December 1940): 7–11.

Voegelin, Eric. "The Growth of the Race Idea." *The Review of Politics* 2, no. 3 (1940): 283–317.

von Teuffenbach, Alexandra. *Aus Liebe und Treue zur Kirche: Eine etwas andere Geschichte des Zweiten Vatikanums.* Berlin: Morus Publishing, 2004.

Webb, Eugene. *The Self Between: From Freud to the New Social Psychology of France.* Seattle: University of Washington, 1993.

Weisheipl, James A. "Scholasticism." In *The Encyclopedia of Religion*, edited by Mircea Eliade, 118. Volume 13. New York: Macmillan, 1987.

Wikenhauser, Alfred. *Pauline Mysticism: Christ in the Mystical Teaching of St. Paul.* Translated by Joseph Cunningham. 2nd ed. New York: Herder and Herder, 1960.

Wood, Susan K. "Continuity and Development in Roman Catholic Ecclesiology." *Ecclesiology* 7 (2011): 147–72.

———. *Spiritual Exegesis and the Church in the Theology of Henri de Lubac.* Grand Rapids, MI: Eerdmans, 1998.

Woods, Michael J. *Cultivating Soil and Soul: Twentieth-Century Catholic Agrarians Embrace the Liturgical Movement.* Collegeville, MN: Liturgical Press, 2010.

Woollen, C. J. "Christ the Light of the World." *The Clergy Review* 15 (1938): 309–14.

Yocum Mize, Sandra. "'A Catholic Way of Doing Every Important Thing': U.S. Catholic Women and Theological Study in the Mid-Twentieth Century." *U.S. Catholic Historian* 13, no. 2 (1995): 49–69.

Yocum Mize, Sandra, and William L. Portier, eds. *American Catholic Traditions: Resources for Renewal.* The Annual Publication of the College Theology Society. Volume 42. Maryknoll, NY: Orbis Books, 1996.

Index

Adam, Karl
  on church as "organic unity," 24
  comparing the mystical body
    theology of Mersch and, 37
  de Lubac's *Corpus Mysticum* as
    implicit critique of, 140–41
  Guardini's mystical body theology
    compared to, 28–29
  influence of the Tübingen heritage
    upon, 23
  Nazism and *Volk* association in the
    mystical body theology of, 23,
    25–28, 37, 47, 168n.53
  The Spirit of Catholicism on
    solidarity of the mystical body,
    23–24, 27–28
  on the supernatural union of the
    mystical body of Christ, 24,
    25–26, 48, 85
Aeterni Patris (1879), 18, 30, 33n.112,
  59, 137
Alfrink, Bernard, 96
alter Christus (another Christ), 42,
  83, 90
Ambrose, Glenn, 168, 169, 170–71
Ambrose, St., 152
American Ecclesiastical Review, 104,
  114
Anderson, R. Bentley, 111
Anger, Abbé Joseph, 90
anti-Semitism
  Coughlin's mystical body theology
    supporting his, 27n.89

and racism of Adam's mystical
  body theology, 23, 25–28, 37,
  47
Arianism, 10–11
asceticism, 35, 43, 74, 80, 88
Augustine, St., 27, 119, 152, 177

baptism, 24, 91n.3, 93, 118, 122, 176
Baum, Gregory, 104
Bea, Augustin, 93
Beauduin, Lambert
  on Christ as sole mediator of God,
    45–47
  collaboration with Botte by,
    133–34
  on Eucharist as center of liturgical
    celebration, 39–40, 47
  influence on Michel by, 64–65,
    68–70, 135
  influence on the modern liturgical
    movement by, 38, 64–65,
    68–70, 131–35
  as inspiration for founding of the
    ISL, 154
  Irénikon journal established by, 44,
    104
  joining Mont César, 41
  on mystical body of Christ as life
    after incarnation, 42–43, 46
  mystical body theology of, 7,
    37–47, 48
  social emphasis of, 64, 69, 70, 148
  work as labor chaplain by, 38, 80